Four Years Remembered

Leicester During The Great War

Four Years Remembered

Leicester During The Great War

Ben
Beazley

First published in Great Britain by
The Breedon Books Publishing Company Limited
Breedon House, 44 Friar Gate, Derby, DE1 1DA.
1999

This paperback edition published in Great Britain in 2014
by DB Publishing, an imprint of JMD Media Ltd

for Jack and Joseph

ISBN 978-1-78091-063-5

Printed and bound in the UK by Copytech (UK) Ltd Peterborough

Contents

Acknowledgments

This book could not have been written without the help given to me by a considerable number of people. I would therefore like to take the opportunity to thank the following for their time and efforts so freely given which have made the final product possible.

Carl Harrison, the County Archivist at the Record Office for Leicestershire, Leicester and Rutland, along with his staff, especially Dianne James, Sherry Nesbitt and Clive Chandler, who have spent so much of their time tracking down elusive documents for me. Emma Bond, the Curator of the British Red Cross Museum and Archives, for her efforts in the researching of archives to provide material relating to the activities of Flora Scott. Alan Jeffreys and his colleagues at the Imperial War Museum, who have so patiently dealt with my queries regarding military matters. Thomas H. B. Allen of Pick Everard, Architects, for allowing me to reproduce documents relating to the 5th Northern General Hospital. Jane Collins, Principal of the Sir Jonathan North Community College, for allowing me to reproduce material held by the College relating to Jonathan North. Malcolm Tovey for the loan of photographs and for his invaluable knowledge of fire brigade matters. The *Leicester Mercury* for the access so freely given to their invaluable sources of information and photographic library and to Steve England for his assistance in helping me to source those photographs. Finally my wife Judy, without whose patience and encouragement this work would never have been completed.

To all these people, and any other who I may have inadvertently missed, I extend my sincerest thanks.

Ben Beazley
Leicester
Summer 1999

Introduction

THE events of August 1914 responsible for precipitating the First World War – the 'Great War' – were the hinge upon which modern history irrevocably pushed open a door which could never again be closed. During the following four years, irreversible changes were to take place in the lives of every person in the civilised world. The social structure throughout Europe, which had rested since time immemorial on the premise of 'a place for everyone and everyone in their place' was overturned by the inconceivable happenings of those years. Events which would result in the deaths of millions of ordinary people throughout the known world. Fathers and sons, husbands and lovers, there was hardly a street in any town or village in Europe where not just a death, but an entire memorial to victims of the conflict was recorded. Previous wars had impacted upon those non-combatants unfortunate enough to be directly in the path of advancing armies; in this war every adult and child was to be touched by the conflict. For the first time, technological developments were driven by the desperate need of nations as opposed to the curiosity of individuals. After November 1918, irrespective of who were the victors and who the vanquished, the world to which reason returned was a very different place to the one from which it had departed four years earlier.

At the outbreak of war Leicester was a prosperous Midlands county town. During the previous half century it had progressed from being an unhealthy and unremarkable borough of some 68,000 residents in 1861, to a busy industrial centre with a population of 227,000 in 1911[1]. The basic ingredient for this success was the town's departure, during the second part of the 19th century, from its almost total reliance upon the hosiery and stocking making trades (which were heavily centred around cottage industry), into the world of boot and shoe production, along with an accompanying boom in the light engineering required to service it. By 1911 the *Leicester and District Trades Directory* records a total of 414 firms large and small, such as heel makers, lace producers, boot and shoe knife manufacturers, all of whom were directly dependent upon the main boot and shoe industry.

A prime example of this prosperity was the shoe firm of Freeman Hardy and Willis – boasting over 470 retail outlets with local shops in Granby Street, Cheapside, and The Haymarket – whose managing director, Jonathan North was to become a central political figure in Leicester's war effort during the next four years. One of the largest manufacturers in the world, the American-based British United Shoe Machinery Company, who in 1899 had acquired the local firm of Pearson and Bennion, was now also a significant employer in the town.

On an individual basis the oldest of the town's inhabitants would be well able to recall events during those years of the last century which had accompanied this burgeoning prosperity: the purchase of Danet's Hall on the death of its owner, Dr Noble, in 1861, followed during later years by the acquisition of the Westcotes Estate, resulting in the building of new houses on the west side of the town soon to be known as the 'West End'; the Reverend Vaughan's Working Men's College, offering evening classes for those wishing to better themselves, which was opened in 1862; and the subsequent terrible smallpox epidemic of 1863-64[2].

Among their most clear recollections would be the completion in the summer of 1868 of the Clock Tower in the centre of the town which for the first time attempted to regulate the flow of horses, carts,

1. *Leicester Past & Present*, Jack Simmons.
2. *Leicester Past & Present*, Jack Simmons.

carriages and pedestrians around and through the town centre.

The middle-aged working man and woman – the mothers and fathers of those young men soon to join the Colours, in order to fight and die for King and Country – would as children have taken their first rides on the new horse-drawn trams, the most fortunate of them being aboard the inaugural run from the Clock Tower to Belgrave on Christmas Eve 1874. Although education did not become compulsory until 1880, many would have been among the first pupils to attend the newly-created 'Board Schools' at King Richard's Road or Syston Street in 1874. In many instances, their growing to adulthood in a town prone annually to the diseases brought about by unhygienic living, with several families sharing one privy and a common water source drawn from the sewage-polluted river, could be attributed to the improvement in living conditions resulting from the flood prevention scheme which widened and deepened the River Soar and rebuilt the West Bridge. Completed in 1891 after 15 years, the scheme successfully removed the problem of regular flooding in the town with its attendant overflowing of drains and sewage which brought the inevitable outbreaks of typhoid and summer diarrhoea.

The magnificent 'New Town Hall', with its Central Police Station, and Magistrates Courts, erected on the site of the 'Old Horse Fair', was completed at a cost of £53,000 in August 1876. Six years later the occupants of the town, old and young alike, were treated to the pomp and circumstance of the royal visit attendant upon the opening of Abbey Park by Prince Edward, Prince of Wales (later Edward VII), and his wife, Alexandra of Denmark, Princess of Wales.

It was in this steadily developing and progressive environment that the young men and women of Leicester, who were eventually to witness at first hand the consequences of the forthcoming war, grew up. In any society there will always be a gulf between the haves and have-nots, the highly affluent and the extremely poor. In this respect, Leicester at the turn of the century, was little different to any other town. Some citizens were wealthy and lived in large houses in newly developed areas such as London Road, in what were then the outskirts of the borough. Many were poor, living in the older parts of the town in small and often overcrowded housing – in extreme cases having to subsist upon outdoor relief granted by the Poor Law Guardians, or actually living in the workhouse.

In his annual report on the state of public health for 1913, published just seven weeks before the outbreak of war, the borough medical officer of health, Dr C. Killick Millard commented: '…there is much old cottage property in need of overhauling and putting into repair, which can only be done by an expenditure that owners, [landlords], naturally hesitate to make except under compulsion. The Health Department has inspected 10,427 houses under the Housing and Town Planning Act, the number of dwellings considered to be in a state so dangerous or injurious to health as to be unfit for human habitation was 316. The number of closing orders issued was 157. In 54 cases defects were remedied without making closing orders.'

The vast majority of the people fell somewhere between the two – working families, living usually in rented accommodation, with a husband in some form of employment and a wife at home bringing up their children. As a balance to Dr Millard's doleful assertions, the quarterly report on housing submitted to the Town Council one week later on 26 June, optimistically pointed out that since the end of March 1914 a total of 339 building plans had been passed in the town by the Local Authority, included in which were plans for 134 new houses, 13 new factories and warehouses and seven new streets.

The day of the working wife had not yet arrived, but its imminence was much closer than anyone realised. The coming war was to force employers and unions alike to accept a workforce which included a liberal dilution of female labour. The welfare state was still a thing of the future and in an era when the only way for the working man to acquire the means to live and support a family was through regular work, old age and sickness were things to be dreaded. Time and again newspaper reports and inquests referred to labourers and tradesmen in their middle to late 70s who died in varying circumstances in the workplace.

It would be wrong to infer that during those early years of the new century there was always full employment and that master and man worked alongside each other in uninterrupted harmony. As in any industrialised community there were good and not-so-good times. Generally the work forces of the majority of the countries which were to become embroiled in the war were better educated and informed than ever before. Throughout Europe literacy among the working classes, while not universal, was higher than at any other time in history. In Britain, daily and weekly newspapers were readily available to everyone. In Leicester alone, in addition to the nationals, the man on the street had a choice of reading a variety of local papers such as the *Leicester Daily Mercury*, and the *Leicester Daily Post* for a ha'penny, or the *Leicester Journal*, published every Friday for one penny. For the first time, the population as a whole had access simultaneously to news of events throughout the country. Trades unions were formed by the workers. Employers instituted federations to represent the factory owners and manufacturers. With increased awareness, expectations grew and organised trade disputes and protests began to manifest themselves. A trade depression in 1904-05 prompted a protest march to London by 400 Leicester men in June 1905. They were organised by two local labour leaders, Jabez Chaplain and Amos Sherriff, who, nine years later held influential positions on the Leicester Corporation. One of the factors in the huge equation of circumstances that resulted in the outbreak of the Great War was an apprehension by governments throughout Europe of the latent power which the trade union movement held. There was a feeling that war would curtail such a threat. Conversely the Labour Movements felt that they, by a concerted withdrawal of labour, could prevent any such war occurring. In the event both were proved to be wrong.

Some aspects of life, then as now, were common to all levels of society. Rich and poor alike were reliant on the illumination provided by gas jets both in their homes and in the streets after dark. The regular visitation of epidemics such as typhoid, smallpox and a particularly virulent 'summer diarrhoea' took a toll on all and sundry, high and low. After diverse experiments of varying success it was not until 1890 that an effective means of dealing with the town's sewage was arrived at with the opening of the pumping station at Beaumont Leys. Prior to this a pail closet system, initiated in 1872, had alleviated the inadequate sewage network by providing for the emptying during the night of toilet buckets on to rail wagons for removal and disposal. This system actually continued until 1895. In contrast, 1912, the year that piped water began to arrive from the new Derwent Reservoir, was the first year when no summer diarrhoea was recorded in Leicester.

While motor cars and motor cycles were rapidly becoming more readily available to those who could afford them, the road system throughout the country was not as yet anywhere near sufficiently adequate to cope with this new phenomenon. Locally, as late as March 1915 members of the Town Council were reminded: 'The section of Fosse Road, on the way to Newarke must be improved. Its surface is in a very uneven condition and dangerously narrow in places. To pass agricultural vehicles, motorists have to rely upon the courtesy of the wagon driver to drive along the grass verge, and the passing by of two motor vehicles is attended with grave difficulty…The Leicester to Fleckney road needs to be improved, the road needs to be fenced and the five gates removed'.

In August 1914, apart from the electric tramways system operated by the Corporation, the prime source of transport for the average citizen was still the horse. Although the Watch Committee notes for 1 February 1916 agree that 'the Coalville Bus and Motor Company, who propose to include Enderby in their district, be allowed to proceed by way of Southgate Street, the Newarke, the Boulevard, and Upperton Road Bridge, and be allowed to stand their vehicles on the Boulevard near to the canal bridge for the purpose of picking up passengers', it was not until the Birmingham-based Midland Red bus company extended its interests to include Leicester in 1922, that the tramcar had any real rival.

Undertaking a journey of any distance usually involved catching a train from the Midland Railway Station which connected together London, Leicester, Derby and Nottingham, or alternatively taking the Great Northern line from Belgrave Road if travelling eastwards to Peterborough. The Great Central Railway also had extensive goods yards and warehouses which it had opened in 1899 at its station in Great Central Street. The existence of this network of railway lines running through Leicester, combined with the town's geographical location in the heart of the country, was a crucial factor in the development of the town's economy.

Not unnaturally, this upward curve in the town's fortunes over a period of time attracted other diverse business interests. By the turn of the century, there were some 18 iron foundries, including firms such as Gimson and Co in Vulcan Road, William Richards & Son at their Phoenix Works in Martin Street, and Russell's in Bath Lane, all supplying to engineering firms the materials required for the production of the machinery upon which the boot and shoe manufacturers were reliant. Companies producing for the first time high quality precision instruments established themselves in the borough. By the end of the first decade of the new century, Gent and Company, at their Faraday Works on St Saviour's Road East were listed as 'manufacturing electricians, patentees and makers of electric impulse clocks, water level indicators, watchmen's clocks, secret intercommunication telephones, etcetera'. In nearby Stoughton Street South, the company of Taylor, Taylor and Hobson, trading as Lenses Leicester, were producing high quality optical goods soon to be used in the war effort. The Gillette Safety Razor Company (USA), trading as Nostrop, Leicester, were another producer based in the North Evington suburb at 332 St Saviour's Road East.

Corah's hosiery factory, backing on to the canal and Abbey Park at St Margaret's Works, employed in excess of 1,000 people in the early years of the 20th century.

Another major employer to have settled in the town was the Imperial Typewriter Company. Established in 1908 in Wharf Street, as it expanded the firm moved in 1911 to the premises in North Evington from where it sent typewriters to all corners of the world until its closure in 1974.[1]

The weather during the summer of 1914 was particularly good. Local people, their day's work completed, returned to their home or lodgings to spend their leisure time, then as now, in the pursuits of the day. After-work entertainment usually revolved around passing the evening in one of the many local pubs and ale houses, or a trip to the cinema, where for less than a shilling, the best seat in the house could be obtained to watch what were then 'silent movies'. The Tudor Cinema, on Vaughan Street, for instance, required its patrons to pay tuppence, fourpence and sixpence for the privilege. For a weekend treat, an evening's entertainment at the Theatre Royal, or the Opera House, was a must – or for patrons with a slightly more rowdy taste there was Oswald Stoll's, Palace of Varieties, in Belgrave Gate. Those seeking a little more sophistication could visit the newly-opened De Montfort Hall on the edge of Victoria Park, to listen to orchestral music and concerts of band music.

In an era when, other than the performing of necessary chores, time spent in the home was restricted to the reading of books and newspapers, sewing, knitting and other handicrafts, or singing around the piano – supposing that one could afford such a luxury – entertainment was extremely limited. The use of the radio had, since its invention by the Italian Guglielmo Marconi just under 20 years earlier, begun to be developed for communication purposes between individuals such as ship-to-shore transmissions, but mass broad-casting as a means of information and entertainment was still a thing of the future. The BBC did not start broadcasting to the nation until 1922.

On the domestic front, for those lucky enough to have a garden, as opposed to a tiny back yard with a shared privy, time could be spent tending flowers and vegetables, or for the enthusiast an allotment could, by diligent care and attention, be persuaded to augment the weekly housekeeping by supplying vegetables and produce.

Western Park provided for the residents of the Hinckley Road, 'West End', somewhere to take an evening stroll through its newly laid-out grassy slopes. Laid down at the turn of the century and comprising some 78 acres of ground, this was to be the Corporation's last venture in opening up ground for public use and recreation before the war interrupted the programme of civic amenities. For those inhabitants of Arthur Wakerley's suburb at North Evington, a leisurely stroll from the bottom gates at East Park Road, over the tree-lined Willow Brook and up the steep slopes of Spinney Hill Park, brought them to a panoramic view from the top, away to the eastern side of town over St Stephen's Church and the Crown Hills. The strategically-placed drinking fountain at the junction of the upper and central pathways, with comfortable benches provided refreshment and rest for the tired and the thirsty. The centrally-situated bandstand on the top path, overlooked by the tall houses in Mere Road, afforded a peaceful Sunday afternoon's entertainment for music lovers.

1. Although Imperial is probably the largest and best known typewriter manufacturer of the time, there were in fact three other Leicester firms producing typewriters during the early years of the century. – Monarch Typewriter, 6 Pocklington's Walk; Arthur Moore & Co, 53 London Road; and the Oliver Typewriter Co, 34 London Road.

Spinney Hill Park had the added attraction that during the winter, when the annual snows arrived (the seasons seem to have followed a more traditional pattern at this time and the expectation of a winter snowfall at some time between November and March was seldom disappointed), its steep slopes afforded an excellent venue for tobogganing and sliding. Care had to be taken, however, to avoid the large trees that dot the park and in most years accidents inevitably resulted from sledges crashing headlong into one of them.

To the south side of the town the flat expanse of Victoria Park, given over solely to public recreation since the removal of the racecourse to Oadby in 1880, provided a facility for the residents of Clarendon Park to exercise and enjoy a few hours of relaxation.

A short tramcar ride from any of the town's suburbs, the jewel in the Corporation's crown was, of course, Abbey Park. Acquired in the middle years of the 19th century and opened to the public in 1882, the 57 acres of Abbey Marsh, lying between the River Soar and the Leicester Canal, were a triumph of planning and landscaping for the Corporation. It was here on the firm green grass swards that young men, soon to be drowning in shell holes full of mud, walked with their wives and sweethearts during the long warm afternoons and evenings of the summer of 1914. The main path winding around the inner perimeter, interspersed with side paths, wandered along by the river and through beautifully laid-out flower beds, eventually returning the visitor to their original starting point.

Contained within the park were the ruins of the old abbey, two fine bandstands along with a bowling green, a boating lake and an adjacent pavilion where refreshments could be readily obtained. In short, it was an idyllic spot from which to escape the daily realities of factory and shop life.

Those who could afford a summer holiday usually left by rail for the East Coast during the August Bank Holiday period. Establishing a tradition that was to continue through the inter-war years and after, Leicester people arrived in their thousands at such favourite resorts as Skegness and Mablethorpe. Those who, by choice or necessity, remained at home had the opportunity to pack a picnic for the family and take the organised omnibus trips out to Bradgate Park, where they were allowed to wander freely over the estate – a more highly prized consideration for the town dwellers of that time than may be appreciated by later generations. Until 1928 the estate was owned by the Grey family – the descendants of Lady Jane Grey. It was then purchased by Charles Bennion, the chairman of the British United Shoe Machine Company, who gifted it to the local authority for use by the public.

In the summer sunshine of Bank Holiday Tuesday, 4 August 1914, all of this was to change, both for those who went away and for those who remained at home.

Early Days

AT LUNCHTIME on Sunday, 2 August 1914, in drenching rain, accompanied by thunder and lightning, the men of the 5th Battalion of the Leicestershire Regiment, having travelled from their headquarters at Loughborough, arrived for their Bank Holiday training camp at the East Coast seaside resort of Bridlington. Escaping the worst of the inclement conditions, their sister battalion, the 4th, based in the Magazine Barracks at Leicester, marched into the camp at 4pm the same afternoon. Within a short space of time the two battalions were under canvas adjacent to the Lincolns and in sight of the sea. Their stay was to be short-lived.

During that Sunday, while the officers and men of the Territorial Force battalions settled in for a long weekend of training in pleasant surroundings and fresh sea air, events elsewhere in the world were rapidly overtaking them. On that same day, Kaiser Wilhelm II, Emperor of Germany and King of Prussia, was demanding from Belgium a right of passage for German troops through its territory to facilitate the invasion of France in accordance with the Schlieffen Plan.[1]

During the early hours of the following morning, Monday, 3 August, as the alarm bells started to ring throughout Europe, camp was struck and all the various units ordered to return to their respective home towns. The 4th Battalion was fortunate. Having pulled down their tents at 5.30am, they had completed their return journey and marched behind the Regimental band back into barracks at the Magazine by half past eight in the evening. Due to the chaotic situation at Bridlington, the 5th Battalion did not make it home to Loughborough until 2.30am on Tuesday morning. They, however, were luckier than many of the hastily-recalled units. Despite being one of the last to be marched out of the camp, the 5th were almost immediately

entrained. As their long journey home commenced, they passed many others who had broken camp much earlier in the day, still sitting with their equipment on the platform or worse, waiting in railway carriages in the sidings.

The Leicester branch of the Royal Horse Artillery had a similar experience. Having left Leicester for Salisbury Plain on Sunday, they passed through the storms which were deluging the country and arrived at Oswestry to rendezvous with their horses as planned. From there they made their way to Fargo Camp by mid-afternoon. On arrival at 3.30pm they were somewhat puzzled to discover that all the lines were deserted. The answer was quickly to hand – the regular cavalry and artillery had been withdrawn during the night and the guns towed off by motor lorries. The newest arrivals were hastily turned around and sent home.

At the Newarkes, the Magazine was in a state of intense activity. Armed sentries were posted at all the entrances as an indication of a state of readiness. Once the last of the recalled sections – the men of the 2nd North Midland Field Ambulance and those of the 5th Northern General Hospital who had been away at Netley – were accounted for, the barrack gates were closed. The CO at the Magazine, Colonel Harrison, addressed the soldiers as to the current situation – namely that the nation was now on a war footing and that they would soon be required for active service. They were then allowed to return to their homes for the night before parading on Western Park at 9am the following morning.

In the ensuing days the town and its environs seethed with activity as preparations for action and the posting of troops progressed.

On Tuesday, 4 August, notices were posted throughout the borough for the general mobilisation of the Regular Army and Special Army

1. Count Alfred von Schlieffen (1833-1913), Chief of German General Staff. Architect in December 1905 of the German invasion plan of France.

Reserve along with the embodiment of the Territorial Force. Embodiment was at this time a new concept. Basically it meant that members of the Territorial Force were from that point engaged on active service at home. Exactly where that service was to be was not always clear, however. The Leicestershire men were told that they would probably go to Aldershot. To regularise the situation locally, Colonel Harrison paraded the 4th Battalion on the Magazine parade ground and asked for volunteers who were prepared to serve overseas to take one pace forward. Almost to a man the entire battalion stepped forward. For the time being, the precept laid down by the Duke of Wellington that any soldier serving overseas must be a volunteer still held good.

Thereafter, daily, up to 1,000 men at a time of the 4th Battalion were to be seen drilling and performing musketry practice on Western Park on the outskirts of the town. Crowds gathered outside the barrack gates in Oxford Street to watch the comings and goings of the Army Service Corps bringing in stores and the team of soldiers busily repainting in drab the newly commandeered vehicles parked along the barrack paths. Police took possession of the keys to numerous schools within the town in anticipation of them being used as temporary barracks. The Royal Horse Artillery were billeted in Hazel Street School, training during the day on the Filbert Street recreation ground.

The *Leicester Daily Mercury* for Wednesday, 5 August reported that 'the 4th Battalion is now up to strength with 1,006 men. Since yesterday when recruiting began, 70 men have volunteered. Swearing in was commenced this morning.'

Amongst those immediately called to the Colours were the army reservists. Seventy-five postal workers, 70 motor men and conductors from the Tramways Department, 20 men from the Electricity Department, 14 police officers, a large number of railwaymen and uncounted factory workers were recalled to the various corps in which they had originally served. During Thursday and Friday, 6-7 August, 600 men of the National Reserve reported to the office at the Magazine which had been specially opened to receive them. At the close of Friday, 7 August, the Leicestershire and Rutland Detachment of the National Reserve was up to strength at 3,100 rank and file.

The Leicestershire Imperial Yeomanry, having been mobilised, reported to their headquarters at the yard of the Blue Boar in Southgate Street during the morning of Wednesday, 5 August.

At the end of the first week after mobilisation, troops began moving out. Military police replaced the regimental sentries guarding the entrances to the Magazine. And an increasing number of volunteers, still dressed in civilian clothing pending the arrival of uniforms and having filled the places of the men leaving for France, could be seen drilling on the barrack square.

On Monday, 10 August the Lincolnshire and Leicestershire Brigade Army Service Corps left the town, to be quickly followed by the 2nd North Midland Field Ambulance.

Throughout the morning of Wednesday, 12 August, people gathered in Oxford Street to watch the passage of the horse-drawn wagons loaded with ammunition and stores heralding the departure of the 4th Battalion later in the day. The exodus from the town of its own local men was treated as a major event. Recorded for posterity by local photographers, pictures of the occasion were later available for purchase from either the offices of the *Leicester Daily Post* or Messrs Rowe & Son in Belvoir Street. In the presence of the Duchess of Rutland (whose son, the Marquis of Granby, was a lieutenant in the battalion), the Mayor of Leicester, John Frears, and several past colonels of the regiment, the Regimental Colours were trooped to the Magazine from St Martin's Church by 'B' Company under the command of Lieutenant Newill. After a short religious ceremony conducted by the Bishop of Peterborough, and having being addressed in turn by Colonel Harrison and the Mayor, they were ready to depart. Led from the Newarkes by a contingent of Boy Scouts, the battalion marched through the crowded streets of the town, along Belvoir Street and up Granby Street to the Midland Railway Station. When they departed from there at 2.45pm that afternoon, the battalion was not to return to Leicester for the next four years.

The following morning the excited inhabitants were given the further impressive spectacle of the departure of the Yeomanry and the Artillery. At 10.30am, the Leicester Squadron of Yeomanry (Prince Albert's Own), rode off in formation from the Boulevard led by their CO, Lieutenant Colonel Evans-Freke. The Royal Horse Artillery under Major W. B. Du Prè left Filbert Street to follow the cavalry out at 11.30am. Large crowds, many given time off from their work, thronged the perimeter of the Filbert Street recreation ground from nine o'clock onwards. Wives and children of the departing men were forced to say their farewells through the park railings surrounding the ground as none were allowed into the assembly area. Once on the move, the close timetable of the procession was disrupted for a short while, when a horse drawing an ammunition wagon slipped and fell in Welford Road. However, by soon after midday both sections had passed through the Clock Tower and marched off to war.

During that period of the First World War, when the War Office was totally reliant upon men volunteering for active service, much acrimonious comment was levelled at Leicester to the effect that the district lagged behind other towns in relation to recruiting. The published figures cannot be argued against and other towns certainly did achieve a higher recruiting rate. Figures for 1915 show that in nearby Nottingham, over 18 per cent of the available population volunteered; in Sheffield the figure was 6.7 per cent. For the same period Leicester managed only 2.6 per cent.

Distanced by time from the events of the day, it is now difficult to ascribe to this vexed question any really accurate answer. First, what is essentially a highly-subjective accusation – an arbitrary look at figures cannot be viewed as anything other – needs to be put into the context of the time and then examined objectively.

Great Britain, along with France, Belgium and Russia, was plunged headlong into a war with Germany, the magnitude of which was unprecedented. Historically, reliant solely upon a small standing army, Great Britain was from the outset at a distinct numerical disadvantage both among the allies and the enemy.

Each of the other combatants had in place a tried and tested system which enabled them in time of war to draw upon a 'reservist army'. The young men of France were required to serve in the regular army for a period of three years followed by a placement in the reserve forces or the territorial army up to the age of 48. To the east, Russia maintained an immense peacetime army of 1.423 million men, which on initial mobilisation would swell to 3.5 million and after total mobilisation achieve 6.5 million. On the enemy side, Austro-Hungary's standing army could, on mobilisation, be increased from 450,000 to 3 million, while Germany, with its complicated system of conscription and reservists, locked men into the reserve until the age of 48 and could, on a war footing, put 3.8 million troops directly into the field with an ultimate potential of a massive 8.5 million.

Great Britain, on the other hand, with no form of conscription and a volunteer army, backed up by a limited reserve (men who enlisted usually served a seven-year engagement, followed by a period of five years on the reserve list) was from the outset unable to contribute anything approaching a comparable number of men needed to effectively fight in a major European war.

After the Liberals came into government in 1906, in the aftermath of the Boer War, it was obvious that an overhaul of the British Army was an urgent priority. The task fell in 1908 to Richard Burdon Haldane KC (later Lord Haldane of Cloan), a 52-year-old Scot with a background in law. As Secretary of State for War, by 1908 Haldane had replaced the existing archaic structure of a Volunteer Reserve and the militia with a Territorial Force of volunteer soldiers, a Special Reserve intended on mobilisation to top up the Regular Army, and a National Reserve to provide replacements within the Territorial Force. Under this arrangement, on the eve of war in 1914, the typical configuration of a British regiment was: 1st and 2nd Battalions – Regular Army; 3rd Battalion – Special Reserve; 4th, 5th, etc., Battalions – Territorial Force. (At this time a battalion strength was usually made up of 1,009 men divided into eight companies.)

There was however still a basic flaw. Each of the other combatants operated a system of conscription which enabled them, to impose upon their entire male populations a requirement to serve for a specified time, based on the age of the individual, as a reservist. Thus each was able to maintain a huge pool of men on a permanent basis. Although for many years, people such as Field Marshal Lord Roberts and Winston Churchill had advocated the need in Britain for conscription, the opposition of the working people was such that no British government had dared to implement it – now they were to pay dearly for their omissions.

The net result of Haldane's efforts was that the British Army divided its attentions between guarding the outposts of the Empire (as a general rule, the two regular battalions of a regiment, would take alternate tours of duty, one at home the other abroad) and providing an Expeditionary Force, based in Britain, for the purposes of home defence, strengthening garrison troops overseas or supporting a Continental ally.

Thus, despite their best efforts, when in August 1914 the call came for mobilisation, the British Army available for service on the European Continent consisted of six divisions plus one cavalry division – a total of 160,000 troops. Having left sufficient men for home defence in case of invasion, the British Expeditionary Force which eventually crossed the Channel numbered some 120,000 men.

So the first piece of logic settles into place. On the declaration of war we have a government desperately in need of men who were prepared to volunteer to leave their homes and families in order to serve in an army overseas. Whilst young single men seeking adventure might reasonably be expected to readily accept such a proposition, others who were married with responsibilities could not be criticised for standing back, taking a deep breath and assessing the situation. For those pausing for thought, one very obvious fact was that many of the reservists leaving the town to return to the army were married men who had to leave behind wives and families to fend for themselves in an era when no bread winner meant no bread.

Without doubt, initially there was a euphoria attendant upon the news that 'War against the Kaiser' had been proclaimed. Not just in Leicester and other such market towns throughout the country, but in Paris, Vienna and Berlin. The populace of each had been nurtured for years on a diet of undefeatable nationalism. The great British Empire had its trading fleets and colonies throughout the world. British soldiers and reservists were there who would take with them to this conflict first-hand experiences from such encounters as the Zulu Wars, and the South African War against 'Old Man Krüger's' Boer commandos. France was steeped, since her ignominious defeat in the Franco-Prussian War of 1870-71, in the concept of *Èlan,* and the recovery of her territories in Alsace-Lorraine at the point of a bayonet. Germany was where militarism ruled – its Kaiser and Prussian aristocracy obsessed by the need to be taken serious-ly as a major power.

In reality, while France and Germany were inextricably locked into the opening moves of the war being played out in Belgium and Northern France, the elected members of the British government were split into two factions. The hawks on one side, with proponents of war such as the Foreign Secretary, Sir Edward Grey, and the First Lord of the Admiralty, Winston Churchill, were opposed by the anti-war group, led by Lord Morley and supported by the Attorney General, Sir John Simon, and the Colonial Secretary, Lewis Harcourt, on the other. Parliament itself was by no means united in its attitude towards the question of whether or not Great Britain should be lead into what was perceived by many to be an essentially foreign affair.

At this point a second cloud appears on the horizon. Unfortunately for Leicester, probably the most outspoken opponent of the war was one of the two elected Members of Parliament for the borough – James Ramsay MacDonald. MacDonald, unlike the many others in Parliament who, once the die was cast, threw themselves into winning the war, continued to harass and harangue the Government at every opportunity during the next four years. Indeed, his first anti-war diatribe locally was during the first week of war. On Saturday, 8 August 1914, while mobilisation was in full swing, MacDonald, addressing a Labour group at the Trade Hall in Leicester, made the first of his many speeches outside of the Commons decrying the involvement of Great Britain in the war. The response from local political opposition was swift. At an hastily-convened public meeting in the Market Place the next day, Councillor Hincks and other members of the Corporation, in a demonstration of cross-party solidarity, roundly rejected MacDonald's views before a large crowd of outraged townspeople. Even among his own local Labour followers, such as Alderman George Banton, MacDonald was never given the support which later critics of the town attributed to it. In common with the majority of the Government, once the commitment to war had been made, those among the Town Council who had reservations about Britain's involvement, put their reservations aside and gave themselves whole-heartedly to the job of winning.

Inevitably, speeches made by Ramsay MacDonald from platforms in his consistency were going to have some effect upon the judgement of the men and women listening to him.

Whether MacDonald's political stance did or did not appreciably affect recruiting figures cannot effectively be judged. It certainly could not have helped. What is assured is that the condemnation levelled at him had a dramatic affect upon the attitude of outsiders towards the electorate who were responsible for his presence in Parliament. The name of Leicester became a byword in many circles for pacifism, to the extent that many Leicester volunteers on their arrival at the Front, were vilified by other men in the trenches when it was discovered whence they came.

In one respect Leicester was a victim of its own success. The industrial diversification made during the previous 50 years, combined with a central location served by good rail links, placed the town in an unassailable position when, within weeks of the outbreak of hostilities, the race to supply the emerging war machine began. By the end of the second week in August, the reservists had departed the town bound for their regiments and France. Almost without exception, each left behind a job whether as a tramcar driver, factory hand or any other of the myriad occupations which were suddenly depleted. Following a momentary blip on the employment screen due to employers and manufacturers panicking over the implications of the war, employment took off to unprecedented levels. Contracts for boots, clothing, equipment and stores were tendered for and snatched up – there was not just full employment, but previously unheard of overtime to be had for the asking. Had instead of this, the town become depressed, then many more men might have chosen to volunteer; instead they took what is, with hindsight, the natural option and stayed to service the growing war machine.

This situation was not peculiar to Leicester. However, the implications in respect of the effect on men volunteering for the army and navy cannot be avoided. It must also be put into context nationally. From early 1915 through to the very end of the war, the civil government was constantly in conflict with the military over the equation of supply and demand. The military minds of Kitchener and Haig perceived every man in the nation to be a potential soldier. To the politician such as David Lloyd George, a balance had to found between fighting soldier and the civilian servicing the essential war machine on the Home Front. Over a period of time, two huge circles were to emerge. In the first, soldiers became casualties; casualties required replacing; replacements could only come from the male civilian population. In the second, an army was needed to win the war; that army could not function without manpower, or supplies and equipment; manpower was required to service the industries producing the supplies and equipment. The common denominator in both cases was that the nation had a finite supply of manpower.

The only way in which the Government could express its frustration and attempt to squeeze a quart out of a half-pint pot was to publish subjective recruiting statistics, which levelled an accusing finger at whoever was at the lower end of the scale and to demand more!

One immutable fact remains. During the Great War, between August 1914 and November 1918, some 9,284 men from the borough and county of Leicester died fighting for their country.[1]

During the first six weeks of the war, the recruiting office at the Magazine was inundated as men in Leicester, as elsewhere, flocked to join the Colours. Up to 15 September, 7,045 men from the town and county had volunteered: 3,545 for the Regular Army; 2,400 to Kitchener's New Army; 1,100 to the Territorial Force. As from 7 August, the famous poster of a heavily-moustached Lord Kitchener, pointing accusingly out at the beholder with the immortal exhortation, 'Your Country Needs You!' appeared throughout the land. The initial response was tremendous, both locally and nationally. Young men, promised a short adventure in uniform abroad and assured that they would 'be home for Christmas', answered the call in droves.

As early as the end of the first week of September, due to the high level of response to the Territorial Force, men were, after acceptance into the battalion, sent back home on a weekly allowance of 3s 6d to continue with their employment until called back to join the regiment.

Despite the fact that general opinion at home and abroad – both political and military – held that the forthcoming conflict was to be a short, sharp exercise in strategic manoeuvres conducted according to grand infallible plans, contingency measures aimed at providing for the families of men who had

1. Roll of Honour: Leicestershire Record Office.

enlisted or been recalled were set in motion. Within days of the general mobilisation, committees were being established at both local and national levels to ensure the well-being of these dependents.

A War Relief Fund under the direction of Councillor Hincks was established at 2 New Street (the landlord, Mr Preston, having loaned the premises rent-free until Christmas) for the relief of those residents in the borough who were directly or indirectly in need as a result of the war. For the purposes of this particular fund the town was divided up into 16 divisions. Each family that applied for relief was to be treated as a unit, the expectation being that the majority of claimants would be the wives of men who had joined the Colours. In an unexpected moment of social awareness, a decision was taken that payments should be delivered discretely to the claimants' homes by voluntary workers in order to preserve the dignity of the individual family. This courtesy was accompanied by the pragmatic stricture that assessment was to be based upon immediate need as opposed to prior income or social standing.

On 12 August, Ramsay MacDonald took time out from his duties at the House of Commons to return to his constituency and discuss with the Town Council the administration of the newly-founded Prince of Wales Fund, of which he was a committee member.

Established by the Government to alleviate distress among the families of regular soldiers, sailors and territorials arising from their absence at war, the fund was to be administered locally by duly-appointed committees. Throughout the country, these were to be established under the chairmanship of either the local Mayor or leader of the council. Clear guidelines were given as to the constitution of each panel. Representatives of the Education, Poor Law, and Distress Committees, along with spokesmen for the trades unions and philanthropic societies, were to be included. In Leicester, whether by oversight or design, the Poor Law Guardians were initially excluded from membership. The Guardians, one of the most powerful of the groups within the local authority, always jealous of their relationship with the Corporation, were swift to point out the omission, which was hastily remedied. The fund, which was to tie in with the local Distress Committee, would be financed partly by central government and partly by local subscriptions. From

this point onwards, until the end of the war, regular appeals were made through factories and other workplaces for employees to make donations from their pay packets. Details of the current national level of the Prince of Wales Fund, which by Tuesday, 1 September already stood at an incredible £2 million, were published on a regular basis by the local newspapers.

Under the presidency of the Duke of Rutland, funded partly by the Prince of Wales Fund and partly by local charity, the Leicester and Leicestershire Patriotic Fund opened an office at 37 Millstone Lane. The purpose of the fund, like others, was to assist the wives and dependants of men who had joined the Colours.

Not unexpectedly, the number of applicants for relief was considerable. The abstraction from the community of a significant number of men, often the sole wage earners in a family, was bound to create severe problems. In a time of minimal public assistance, many women, left alone with small children and no immediate source of income, were faced with extreme hardship.

On the morning of Saturday, 22 August a crowd of between 1,000 and 1,200 young women, many carrying babies and accompanied by small children, presented themselves at the Magazine Drill Hall in the Newarkes, in order to register and receive the few shillings which the Patriotic Fund was able to offer to them.

Unfortunately for those concerned, the August day was a particularly hot one. Arriving before eight o'clock in the morning, in order to be assured of a place when the office opened two hours later at ten, many of the women standing in the hot sun fainted through exhaustion and had to be revived by the two Voluntary Aid Detachment nurses on duty. Boy Scouts armed with water containers passed along the lines of women, handing out drinks. With only eight clerks on duty to deal with all the applications, the majority of the women had to endure the arduous conditions for almost the entire day, not daring to leave their places in the queue to obtain food or for other needs. For many of the petitioners, clutching throughout the long wait the required marriage certificates, it was a futile exercise. Disappointment awaited many of the women when they eventually stood before the desk and attempted to register. Those in receipt from the army or navy of a separation allowance, or any other allowance, were precluded from receiving the Patriotic Fund's weekly payments of 5s for a married woman plus 1s for each child.

Dependents and kin were not the only ones to become victims of circumstance. Caught up in a backlash against all things German, many small and vulnerable traders suddenly found themselves destitute. One such example was Neil Watson, an itinerant pedlar. Watson, a 47-year-old Scotsman who was an engineer by trade, had lost a leg in an industrial accident. Unable to find employment due to his disability, Watson was forced to take to the road, travelling up and down the country selling postcards. Unfortunately these were of German manufacture and within a few weeks of the opening of hostilities, unable to dispose of his wares, he was starving and penniless. On 11 September 1914 he was brought before the magistrates at Leicester for causing 3s 6d worth of malicious damage to the window of an empty house in Loughborough Road. Watson explained that on arrival in Leicester he was unable to obtain Poor Relief, or any other help because he was not a resident of the town. He had spent two nights in the workhouse on Swain Street, classed as a vagrant. Under the rules governing the workhouse he was then obliged to leave there and not return for a period of one month. In desperation he had broken the window in an attempt to obtain a bed for the night in the police cells. A sympathetic bench remanded him for reports to see if they could arrange any form of assistance for him.

Local government employers who were among those best able to bear the burden, made genuine attempts to alleviate the suffering. All single men employed by the Great Central Railway who volunteered were to be treated as being on leave on full pay. Their superannuation was to be paid by the company and advancements of pay scales during their absence were to be acknowledged as if they were working until their return. Similar arrangements were made for those employees of the Corporation Tramways and Electricity Departments who were subject to immediate recall as reservists.

Exceptionally generous employment commit-ments, made under the delusion that the absentees would be back in the workplace within a matter of months, were to haunt many large scale employers such as the Corporation for the next four years. As the realisation that the war was to be a long drawn-out affair gradually dawned upon them, the shrewd businessmen and town fathers, accustomed to controlling local finances with an iron hand, watched in dismay as over the coming months and years budgets, directly linked to wages and the cost of materials, spiralled uncontrollably upwards.

Much discussion took place in those early weeks over the status of firemen and police constables who went to join the Colours. An early problem encountered was that a considerable number of these men were ex-servicemen who were still on the reserve list. Recalled to their regiments, many found themselves being penalised for leaving without the consent of the Watch Committee. Half-pay for the wives of men such as Fireman James 'who has gone to the Colours without first seeking permission' was withheld by the Watch Committee. It was resolved that Constables 255 James Shepherd and 33 William Dickinson should each be subject to discipline upon their return from the war for rejoining the reserve without prior consent of the head constable.

Once the matter of men in the fire brigade and police force had been resolved to the satisfaction of the Watch Committee, the further question of pay and allowances was approached. In line with the other Corporation employees it was deemed that the police officers and firemen were to be considered to be away on a secondment until the end of hostilities. On their return each would be reinstated in his old job. Later, when it became apparent that the men would not be returning for a period of some years, a proviso was made that police constables would have to be sworn in anew prior to returning to duty.

By 11 August an extempore scale of allowances was agreed. The wives of married firemen and constables would receive half of the man's weekly pay – in August 1914 a fireman received between 28s and 31s per week, a constable between 29s and 33s and a sergeant, 39s to 42s. The widowed mothers of single men such as James Gotheridge and George Banton were allowed 7s 6d a week.

Seven months later, in March 1915, this was to be amended to the more formal arrangement whereby married men would have their separation allowance (paid by the army) made up to their police pay. Single men would receive one-third of their pay in addition to any army allowances to which they were entitled. The Police (Emergency Provisions) Act 1915 ratified the pension rights of police officers and prevented retirement of those retained on the

Home Front, for reasons other than for ill health, for the duration of the war. Following suit, the fire brigade also restricted retirement. In March 1915, Second Officer Kinder was prevailed upon to postpone his retirement for 12 months due to the exigencies of war. He subsequently left the brigade at the end of March 1916 having completed 29½ years' service. As late as June 1917, Third Officer Smith and Fireman Hames were refused permission to retire on pension after 28 years, due to continuing hostilities.

Once the initial flood of reservists had been absorbed into the army, the pressure increased on all employers to release further men as recruits to all branches of the armed services. In October 1914 the Watch Committee passed a resolution that 'no obstacle be placed in the way of the Leicester Borough Police joining the Colours and that they be not asked to resign and that they be reinstated on their return from the war'. The Watch Committee were soon to regret this well-meaning, if sweeping statement. Twelve months later, in October 1915, perturbed at the continuing drain on manpower within Leicester police and fire brigade, a further resolution was passed in relation to the police 'that no further applications for permission to join the army or navy from members of the force be considered'. In an attempt to back the issue both ways, this resolution was tempered by a clause allowing a further six officers to be released, provided that they were single men.

As the war was drawn out from weeks into months and months into years, the demand for men at the Front became more and more urgent. Gradually, as it became apparent that essential services were becoming depleted to a dangerous level, the War Office issued policy directives giving clear guidelines on recruiting from essential services nationally.

Eventually the dependents of men in both services received varying levels of payments comprising part of the man's salary added to the separation allowance made by the army or navy to his wife or other dependents. In a period not celebrated for the charity of employers to their servants, it is clear that there was a dogged determination to be seen to be supporting the war effort in every way possible.

Owners of motor cars and motor cycles in the town and county were asked to contact Mr R. Sutton Clifford, a Loughborough solicitor who was establishing on behalf of the Leicester and Leicestershire Automobile Club a mobile network dedicated to the defence of the Home Front. By 21 August 1914, Clifford had supplied to the Home Office a list of names of those local motorists prepared to put their vehicles and motor cycles at the disposal of the Government. Over 100 names were given to the County Director of Voluntary Aid Detachments, Arthur Faire, of those motorists available for convoy work ferrying wounded men from the railway station to the various hospitals. Sutton also envisaged a strong force of motorcyclists complete with travelling repair shops, along with ambulance and wireless telegraphy equipment, immediately at the disposal of the country.

The establishment of Voluntary Aid Detachments for clearing hospital duties in the borough and county was put in hand. St John Ambulance men were called upon to volunteer for the Expeditionary Force as Royal Army Medical Corps personnel. Dr Pemberton Peake, a local surgeon who was soon to leave for the Front as a lieutenant colonel in command of the North Midland Clearing Hospital, held first-aid classes for women at the Trinity Hospital. Further classes for men, were run at the Working Men's College, which was later to become the Vaughan College.

Throughout the country, the Boy Scout movement was mobilised to guard telegraph lines and telephone cables, railway bridges and culverts. On 20 October 1914, for instance, a grant of £10 was made to local Scouts by the Watch Committee for their services in guarding Knighton tunnel.

During the first few hectic days following the declaration of war, a group of local dentists – Frank Lankester of Lankester and Crockett in De Montfort Street, along with Alfred Rowlett, John Craig and Campbell Baxter, who each had practices on London Road, and Messrs Rose and Cooper of 17 Halford Street – offered their professional services to assist the recruiting campaign. They offered to put into good order the teeth of any men of the 4th Leicestershire Battalion or other local branch of the army who were leaving for the Front. In an era when dental hygiene for the majority of the population was virtually non-existent, this was no mean undertaking, as the greater part of those presenting themselves for examination would need to have some degree of work carried out. Figures quickly revealed that between three and five per cent of prospective recruits were being rejected because of the bad condition of their teeth. It was estimated that this offer of remedial dental work would ensure that the offices at the Magazine would secure an additional 200 men during the next 12 months.

This offer was also to be of immense value in keeping fit men at the battle front. In Gallipoli alone during the disastrous summer and winter campaign of 1915 a large number of men already weakened by diarrhoea and dysentery, suffered dreadfully from a combination of bad teeth and a low quality diet. Many are reported as losing several teeth biting into the hard-baked biscuits with which they were fed.

Shopkeepers were under siege by a populace determined to beat any shortages however brief the duration was to be. By Friday of the first week of war, grocers such as Simpkin and James, with stores in the Market Place and Horsefair Street, had sufficient orders to take them into the following week. Co-operative stores adopted a policy of refusing to fill out orders which they considered to be excessive. Home and Colonial Stores undertook a pledge not to increase their prices while stocks held out. On the Saturday after the declaration of war, Liptons grocers placed an advertisement in the *Leicester Daily Post* assuring their customers that there would be no increase in the prices of tea, coffee, cocoa, condensed milk, biscuits, jam, or marmalade. (An unfortunate excess of patriotism on the part of Liptons later resulted in the firm being sued by Lyons Tea for alleging that Lyons board of directors was made up of Germans.)

In a rather expensive demonstration of patriotism, on Saturday, 29 August, Gollands of 47 High Street, gave away free of charge 1,000 bags of sugar and 4,000 quarter-pounds of treacle and mint toffee. Their attendant declaration read that it was 'to show our confidence that the British Fleet will keep our Trade Routes open, thus ensuring the free passage of sugar to this country'.

While many prices held steady (a pound of tea was still 1s 4d, a loaf of bread 6d, and sugar 3d a bag), retailers felt the pressure from a very early stage. Heavy orders for flour were being placed with local bakers. Small shopkeepers, experiencing a run on stocks, had to close their doors and some items were soon priced out of the reach of the poorer inhabitants.

Officers of the Army Remounts Division –

accompanied by veterinary surgeons and police constables to persuade the more recalcitrant owners – swiftly requisitioned all available horses in the town and county. This resulted in the unusual sight of delivery boys in flat caps and aprons, travelling on tramcars, accompanied by heavy baskets of groceries, meat and other provisions.

By Monday, 10 August, local industrialists had started to react to the implications of a rapidly diminishing male workforce and the attendant problems of supply and demand. Messrs Corah and Sons, who with a workforce of 2,300 were one of the borough's largest employers, placed all their staff, with the exception of those already engaged on government work, on half time while they negotiated for further contracts. The majority of local boot and shoe factors were soon to follow suit. (This depression was very short lived, within a few weeks, War Office contracts would turn the town into a hive of activity.) One of the few employment areas to escape this temporary problem was the building industry. With immediate effect, several hundred men from the building and associated trades were urgently needed to work on the transformation of the old County Lunatic Asylum into the new 5th Northern General Hospital before the onset of winter hampered construction work.

Voluntary aid workers were now also having their work cut out. The first of the Belgian refugees, fleeing from the invading German armies, started to arrive in the town and county during mid-September. Working in collaboration with the Belgian Legation and the Central War Refugees Committee at Aldwych, in London, the Leicester branch of the Women's Catholic League, operating from Waterloo House at the corner of Hastings Road, under the presidency of Lady Agnes de Trafford, set about finding homes for these unfortunates. The flow of refugees into the town soon became a matter necessitating the involvement of the local authority.

At the end of September 1914 the Borough of Leicester Belgian Refugees Committee was formed to administer to the needs of those being cared for by the town. (At this time there were a total of 344 living in the town and county; at the end of the war the figure for the town itself was around 300.) The president of the committee was the town's newly-appointed Mayor, Jonathan North, with the County Director of Education, William Allport Brockington, as co-ordinator. The members of this committee, giving their time and energies without payment, as did the legion of other committees formed in the next four years, took their responsibilities seriously. As in other parts of the country, the plight of the Belgians arriving in Leicester was desperate. With little or no money and only the clothes on their backs, they were totally dependent upon the charity of the communities into which they were introduced. Local residents were visited and persuaded to give living space in their homes to the displaced families, few of whom could speak any English. Landlords were prevailed upon to loan out properties at minimal rents. In cases, where no rent was charged, rates were reduced to ten per cent of the full charge and water rates dispensed with. Gas was supplied at cost and use of the Corporation baths was free. A clothing depot for the refugees was opened by Miss Barlow and her ladies at the Mayor's Rooms in the Museum Buildings in New Walk. Originally this clothing was gifted, but as needs became more pressing, funds had to be made available from central resources. Local doctors and pharmacists made no charges for their services.

In order to establish some form of common social ground, the Leicester Club made some of those considered suitable, honorary members. In an essential move to integrate the Belgians into the town's society, children were admitted into the schools, and evening classes teaching English were held for the adults. Men who were either unfit, or debarred by age from military service, were found work in the factories of the town. During those early days the highest number of Belgians in the borough at any one time was estimated to be around 750.

The ready acceptance of this upheaval, by a community expecting the whole affair to be resolved within a matter of months, is again a reflection of the intense fervour of nationalism which at that point was sweeping the country and Europe in general.

As soon as hostilities were declared, it became a matter of necessity to identify and control enemy nationals resident in Britain. The Aliens Restrictions Act 1914, initially applying only to Germans, was brought into force within days. (It was quickly amended to include Austrians and Hungarians of which there were 20 in the town.) Nationally, all German citizens were required to register immediately with the police in the area in which they resided. Every householder letting accommodation to a German had to report the fact to the local police. No German was allowed to travel a distance of more than five miles from their place of residence without a police permit and had to return within 24 hours. Germans were prohibited from possessing any firearm or ammunition, any explosive substance, petroleum spirit, benzol, or any inflammable liquid in excess of three gallons. They were also prohibited from possessing a motor car or motor cycle. The Act was given a slightly John Buchan flavour by making it a further offence for a German to possess any homing pigeons, signalling apparatus, cypher or code, or any other means of conducting secret correspondence. Several Germans were arrested in the town and about 50 were held in custody by the military at the Corn Exchange while their status was resolved. Of these, six, who were still classed in their homeland as reservists, were regarded by the authorities as prisoners-of-war and removed under armed escort to the district military headquarters at York. A further dozen were similarly arrested and despatched to York in mid-September. One week later all were released, having sworn an oath not to take up arms against Great Britain.

When Field Marshal Sir John French set off across the Channel with the British Expeditionary Force, he took with him virtually the entire available British Army. Lord Kitchener, as Secretary of State for War, was appalled. His specific instructions to French were that at all costs he must conserve manpower and keep British losses to a minimum. In the short term, until a second army had been recruited and trained, there were no replacements.

On 10 August 1914 an advertisement appeared in the *Leicester Daily Post* for men to volunteer for the 'New Army', or 'Kitchener's Army' as it was soon to become known.[1]

Some 100,000 men were desperately needed. The terms were quite clear: this was not a standard recruiting appeal, it was an appeal for the creation of a second army. Territorial Force regiments that were up to strength would not be allowed to engage further recruits until the 100,000 target for the New Army had been met. The only exception to this rule was the replacement of any man who had

---

1. Kitchener was most scathing in his opinions of the soldiers of the Territorial Force, holding them to be mere amateurs who could not be entrusted with the fighting of a war. Consequently he determined to establish a second army. His prejudice was proven by events to be ill founded.

transferred from the Territorial Force to Kitchener's Army. (In early November recruiting for Kitchener's New Army was moved from the Magazine to a separate office at 31 Humberstone Gate.)

Recruiting of an Officers Corps began at the Magazine. By 17 August, 400 rank and file had been recruited locally for the New Army and were under training at Glen Parva Depot. It was anticipated that within another two weeks the number would have reached 960 – sufficient to establish a full battalion. (An unsuccessful attempt was made to form a Leicester and Leicestershire Athletes' and Comrades' Battalion. With the volume of men already joining other units, the effort drew little support and had to be abandoned.)

Once the initial wave of jubilation had passed, the drive to enlist every able-bodied man began in earnest. In October advertisements appeared in local and national newspapers for ex-NCOs of all ranks, of any branch of the services to join the New Army. As an added incentive, these men would continue to receive any existing pension in addition to whatever payment they received on re-enlisting, plus immediate promotion to NCO rank, with, if over 45 years of age, no liability for overseas service.

The pressures at the recruiting office in the Magazine, under the management of Captain Goddard, were exacerbated by the added burden upon the staff of providing men for other than the local regiment. Recruiting was not just for the front-line regiments but also for other integral units. Local men were canvassed to form two new companies of the Army Service Corps – one for the Mechanical Transport, one for the Horse-Drawn Transport – by the end of the second week of October, 100 of the 163 men required, had volunteered.

The hastily-formed Leicester and Leicestershire Recruiting Committee, under the chairmanship of Sir Arthur Hazelrigg and meeting at the premises of Warner Sheppard and Wade, in Halford Street, began to formulate strategy. Fifty thousand recruiting booklets were printed and distributed throughout the town, 9,750 Union Flag posters were prepared in readiness to announce the venues of recruiting meetings, a recruiting office was opened at the corner of New Street and Peacock Lane. Patriotic meetings were held in every possible venue from church halls to school rooms all over the town. On the afternoon of Saturday, 10 October a huge military parade was held.

A Soldier of the KING.

AFTER the War every man who has served will command his Country's gratitude. He will be looked up to and *respected* because he answered his country's call.

The Regiments at the Front are covering themselves with Glory.

Field-Marshal Sir John French wrote in an Order of the day,

"It is an Honour to belong to such an Army."

Every fit man from 19 to 38 is eligible for this great honour. Friends can join in a body and serve together in the same regiment.

Rapid Promotion

There is rapid promotion for intelligence and zeal. Hundreds who enlisted as private soldiers have already become officers because of their merits and courage, and thousands have reached non-commissioned rank.

Enlist To-day.

At any Post Office you can obtain the address of the nearest Recruiting Office. Enter your name to-day on the Nation's Roll of Honour and do your part.

GOD SAVE THE KING

Resplendent with banners exhorting every available man to join Lord Kitchener's New Army, headed by the Leicester Imperial Band and some 600 recruits to the New Army and the Territorial Force, the procession left Victoria Park at 2.30pm to the cheers of the huge crowds that had gathered along the route passing through the town centre and down Welford Road to the Tigers' football ground. Following behind the banners, accompanied by sections of the Church Lads' Brigade, 300 Boy Scouts and their respective bugle bands, Belgian refugees and 100 members of the newly-formed Leicester Citizens Corp, came the full pipe and drum band of the Argyll and Sutherland Highlanders. The band's travelling expenses had been paid for by Theodore Walker, a member of the Recruiting Committee.

At the packed rugby ground, spectators were treated to a concert of music played by the band of the Highlanders and the regimental band of the 4th

Leicestershire Regiment followed by a rugby match between Tom Crumbie's XV and a team of soldiers from the 4th Leicesters. All the proceeds – non-members paid 1s for a grandstand seat, 6d in the stands and 3d to view the spectacle from the banks – went to the war effort and charity. The day was rounded off with recruiting speeches during the evening and a further military tattoo at the football ground.

Groups sprang up all over the place, aimed at preparing for the army the youths who were presently too young to volunteer.[1]

There were associations such as the YMCA Volunteer Corps, whose objective was to ensure that 'young men, 19 years of age or over, who for various reasons cannot go into the army can be got into readiness for an emergency', and a Junior Cadet Corps under the auspices of the Leicester Rugby Football Club. A Junior League of Patriots was inaugurated on 2 October at the Newarke Secondary School – unemployed boys aged between 14 and 17 were to be trained by the Boy Scouts in drilling and marching, and by others in life saving skills and ambulance work. The Parks Committee agreed to the use of public parks for their training and the Corn Exchange was offered for use in wet weather.

As a result of the heightened activity at Glen Parva Depot, the village of South Wigston had taken on the aspect of a garrison town. The narrow streets were crowded with uniformed soldiers mingling with the inhabitants. Drafts of men from all over the region were arriving and leaving daily. On Saturday, 5 September some 1,500 soldiers left in the morning, to be replaced by a similar number before nightfall. Exactly one month after mobilisation, 5,000 recruits had passed through the depot.

With accommodation at Glen Parva originally intended for 500 men, the CO, Colonel Burne, found himself tested to the utmost in coping with the massive influx. When the men of the 3rd Battalion of the Leicestershire Regiment left for active service, they took with them all his permanent staff, leaving him devoid of trained professional soldiers. Charles Cattell, an ex-army sergeant, currently serving with Leicester police as a constable, was recalled, given the rank of sergeant-major and put to organising matters.

In an attempt to house and feed recruits, 12 marquees were erected on the parade square. This was still inadequate. Each man was allotted a ration of one and a quarter pounds of bread and one pound of meat a day. To many, coming from the poor industrial towns of the Midlands, this was probably better fare than they had ever experienced in their lives. Feeding was conducted in relays of 200 men at a time, which was all that the dining hall and kitchens could cope with.

Many of the men, unable to find sleeping space in the overcrowded camp, were forced to sleep rough in the nearby fields or walk the streets. The result was that the villagers of South Wigston often fed the men from their own supplies, and gave them beds in their homes. Local churches and the Salvation Army opened their doors for men in need of somewhere to pass the night.

Back in Leicester itself, at the Magazine on Saturday, 5 September, a contingent of 250 recruits left to join the 4th Battalion of the Leicestershire Regiment as replacements for those who had been declared unfit for active service. While waiting to entrain on the platform of the Midland Railway Station along with 60 or 70 men of the Officers Training Corps, they were to witness to an unusual sight. A locomotive passed through the station carrying men of the Legion of Frontiersmen. Raised during the Boer War by one Colonel Driscoll and known as 'Driscoll's Scouts', this was a highly-élite fighting unit. In order to qualify for membership, a man must have seen active service in some part of the world, be able to ride a horse and be a crack shot with both rifle and pistol. Dressed in their uniform of khaki trousers, blue cowboy shirt and wide-brimmed colonial hat, they were later described by a local correspondent as 'a magnificent body of men, each standing almost six feet tall, mature in years and physique'. Anxious to serve with the British Expeditionary Force in France, Driscoll and his men were en route to London to offer their services.

1.Recruits to the New Army were required to be between 19 and 38 years of age (ex-soldiers accepted up to 45), not less that five feet three inches tall, with a minimum chest measurement of 34½ inches..

Seen from Oxford Street, The Magazine, home of the Leicestershire Regiment, was an impressive structure. In later years, following the demolition of the barracks, the impressive tower was given over to house the Regimental Museum

This side view of the Magazine, taken from the Newarkes gives a view of the Drill Hall. The gates into the barracks are behind the young boy in the centre of the picture. (Until the road layout was altered in 1905 all traffic passed under the archway.) Initially thronged with eager recruits it was soon to witness a more sombre gathering, when on Saturday, 22 August 1914 over one thousand local women stood for hours in the hot sun in order to register with the Patriotic Fund for supplementary allowances.

In the hot summer days of August 1914, men flocked to the Magazine in order to sign on. Whilst the volunteers seen here have all put on their best Sunday suits for the occasion, the soldier taking the applications details has stripped down to his shirt and braces.

It was not unusual for the flood of volunteers to exceed the supplies of uniform and equipment. Seen here in September 1914 this group of recruits are drilled on the Magazine Parade Ground in civilian clothes.

The slopes of Western Park served ideally for the training of raw recruits in the art of soldiering. The regular soldier in uniform on the right of the picture carries a small drum with which to beat out time.

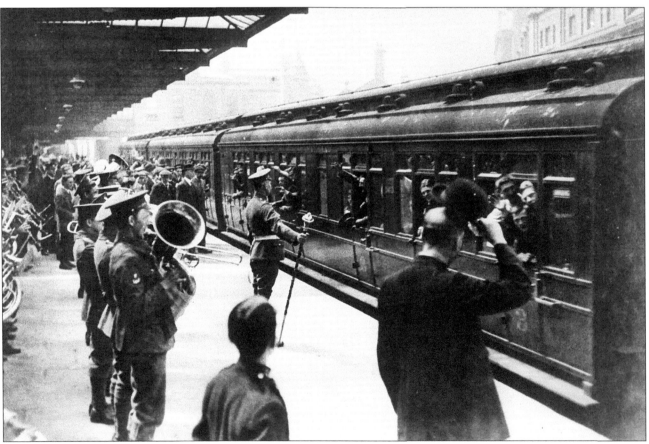

Departing from the Midland Railway Station to the strains of a military band, the party atmosphere indicates a date early in the war – probably early summer 1916.

Often accompanied by a veterinary surgeon and a Constable, men of the Army Remounts Division were given the difficult task of requisitioning horses to send to France with the BEF. The horses seen here, prior to being shipped away were 'loaned' by a Leicester mineral water company.

One of the borough's biggest manufacturers employing 2,300 people in August 1914, and worried about the implications of a major war, the firm of N. Corah & Sons initially placed the workforce at their six-acre St Margaret's site on half-time. A decision quickly rescinded, they were soon in full production and at the end of the war when this photograph was taken, employed 2,500 people – predominantly women.

The First Winter

THROUGHOUT the autumn of 1914, the pattern of the forthcoming conflict was becoming more clearly defined. The early promise of 'home before the leaves fall' was already proving to be a fallacy.

Germany's 'Schlieffen Plan' to encompass France in a great cartwheel of troop movements had ground to a halt which was to last for the next four years. France's 'Plan 17' to counter any aggression with a philosophy of 'attack at all costs, á l'outrance!' had been proved an impossible dream. With the fall of Antwerp early in October, any effective Belgian resistance was destroyed. The British Expeditionary Force under Sir John French, forced to retreat at Mons, had fallen back to fight the First Battle of the Marne.

At sea even that impregnable bastion of British Empire, the Royal Navy, had been shown in September to be fallible, when three armoured cruisers on patrol in the North Sea were sunk by a solitary German submarine.[1]

This was followed, only weeks later, with the loss off Coronel of Sir Christopher Cradock's flag ship *Good Hope* and the armoured cruiser *Monmouth* in an engagement with the German East Asia Squadron under Vice-Admiral Graf Maximilian von Spee.

There were, of course, also successes to lighten the picture. In early November the German enclave of Tsingtao in the Chinese coastal province of Kiaochow had fallen to a Japanese force which was accompanied by two battalions of the South Wales Borderers and the 36th Sikhs. The German sea raider, *Emden,* was run aground off the Cocos Islands in the Indian Ocean by Captain Glosson in *HMAS Sydney*. (Curiously, both the captain of the *Emden*, Karl von Müller, and the pilot of the only German aircraft at Tsingtao, Oberleutnant Günther Plüschow, were later to be held as prisoners-of-war at Donington Camp near Loughborough.) A minor revolt by pro-German Boers under de Wet in South Africa had been squashed.

The realities of the situation were becoming all too apparent. On both sides, the carnage which was to be the hallmark of this conflict had begun and men were dying in their thousands. By Christmas 1914, what had begun with the fluid movement of armies chasing each other across the map of Europe had deteriorated through the early battles at Mons and Ypres into a stalemate. The combatants were gridlocked into a network of trenches 500 miles (800 kilometres) long, stretching from Switzerland to the North Sea.

At home, national and local newspapers kept the populace abreast of happenings with a blow-by-blow account of the fortunes of war on a daily basis. As is to be expected, much of the reporting, based upon War Office Press releases, and buoyant despatches, reproduced verbatim from the pen of Field Marshal Sir John French, was of a highly patriotic nature. The *Leicester Daily Mercury*, priced at a ha'penny a copy and still published in broadsheet format, kept its readership informed as to the current state of the siege of Tsingtao, the doings of local Leicester men in Northern France and tales of the latest iniquities of the Kaiser and his entourage. (It is one of the more bizarre aspects of the situation at this point that news items, often of a quite trivial nature, continued to flow freely between the two camps.)

---

1. On 22 September 1914, the armoured cruisers, *HMS Hogue, Cressy* and *Aboukir*, while on patrol in the North Sea, were sunk by torpedoes launched from the U-9 under the command of Leutnant Otto Weddigen. Loss of life was extremely heavy, out of a total complement of approximately 2,200; 1,397 men and 62 officers were lost. The embarrassment of the Admiralty was heightened by the fact that the cruisers were patrolling together, allowing U-9 to complete the action in less than an hour.

On 6 October, the *Leicester Daily Mercury* offered its readers [the] 'War Map issued by the *Leicester Post* price 3d.' The promised map depicted the war zones in five different colours and was bordered by photographs of, 'HM the King, President Poincarré, HM King of the Belgians, Lord Kitchener, Admiral Sir John Jellicoe, Field Marshal French, General Joffre, Grand Duke Nicholas, and General Lèman (*'the hero of Liège'*).' To people who had in many cases only a vague idea of where Northern France was, and to whom the faces of foreign leaders were a total mystery, this was no doubt thruppence well spent.

As the weeks passed, while national papers presented to the best of their ability an holistic view of the war, local journals by the very nature of their being, presented (however unintentionally), another dimension to the news. On a daily basis, photographs of men who were casualties (usually about four or six portrait shots of individuals supplied from family albums) appeared on the inside pages of the *Mercury*, along with rank and regiment (or in the case of naval personnel, the man's ship), and brief details of his fate. Killed in action, died of wounds, missing at sea following a naval engagement. Ironically these shared space – often on the same page – with studies of family groups, giving the name and the street in which they lived, listing a husband and perhaps two three, or on occasions four sons who were serving with the Colours. Once a week, up to half a page was given over to lists of casualties admitted to the local 5th Northern General Hospital. Divided meticulously into seriously wounded and less serious cases, it then sub-divided into regiments, battalions and other units, giving a concise appraisal of the numbers of men arriving in the town on the convoy trains of casualties. The message was clear: men were desperately needed for the war – but there was a terrible price to be paid for volunteering.

Whilst it was realised that there may be temporary setbacks, the full implications of the war had not yet become completely apparent to the general public. The patriotic fervour still prevalent at this juncture provided a tremendous impetus to the recruiting of men and women for the war effort. A crucial factor in the conduct of the entire war was 'voluntarism' – the hope and expectation that men and women would give freely of themselves in the service of King and Country. The assumption was that those who remained at home, rich and poor alike, would give generously from their own personal pockets in support of the myriad calls upon them to finance everything from comforts for the men at the Front to equipping hospitals for the wounded. From buying bonds intended to stabilise the economy to paying for aeroplanes bearing the name of the town or city which donated them. Even after conscription was implemented at the beginning of 1916, the spirit of voluntarism pushed on. Volunteers were sought for National Service (an inherently doomed scheme to create a national civilian workforce), donations of all kinds were still demanded, attempts were even made to voluntarily ration food supplies prior to formal rationing becoming unavoidable towards the end of the war.

Throughout this early period, recruiting continued apace. Captain Heath, the recruiting officer for the 17th Recruiting Area (Leicestershire), based at Glen Parva Depot, supplied to the Recruiting Committee at the end of the first week of November the following figures in relation to the number of men from the town and county who had joined up during the first 12 weeks since mobilisation.

	Regulars	Special Reserve
Leicestershire Regt	3,392	812
Other Corps	119	60
Household Cavalry	3	***
Dragoon Guards	3	1
Hussars	146	30
Lancers	35	1
Royal Horse Artillery	45	5
Royal Field Artillery	39	12
Royal Engineers	30	10
Coldstream Guards	33	1
Army Service Corps	71	7
Royal Army Medical Corps	46	8
Veterinary Corps	2	***
Flying Corps	2	***
Total	3,966	947

Always considered to be something of an élite (presumably because the prerequisite of being a horseman narrowed the candidature considerably), the Yeomanry now also began to solicit membership with the following advertisement which appeared on 19 October:

'It is proposed to raise a Reserve Leicestershire Yeomanry Regiment. The young men who work for weekly wages have responded, and are responding to the Nation's call as gallantly as our men at the Front have maintained British Honour and Tradition. Now we want the young men who are better circumstanced to avail themselves of the opportunity to do their duty to their Country – meetings to be held at the Town Hall, Leicester; the Assembly Rooms Market Harborough and the Town Hall, Lutterworth.'

Throughout the early autumn the hastily assembled units of troops departed for the Front. On Wednesday, 4 November, officers and men of the North Midland Divisional Clearing Hospital gathered at the Leicester Cripples' Guild in Colton Street, where a farewell address was made by the Lady Mayoress, Mrs Frears. The unit was presented by Mr Stanley Pochin, a local ironmonger, with an eight-gallon boiler to take with them, and each man was given warm clothing against the impending winter – a flannel shirt, woollen socks, pair of gloves, a body belt, muffler and balaclava. The following morning, the eight officers and 77 men of the Hospital Unit, following an address by Lieutenant-Colonel Pemberton Peake and led by the inevitable Boy Scouts' bugle band, entrained at the Midland Railway Station.

On Saturday, 14 November, the 4th and 5th Battalions of the Leicestershire Regiment left Luton for France. They followed on the heels of the 60 men of the Army Service Corps who had left Leicester bound for Luton and thence France during the third week of October.

Those same trains, which departed to the martial music of brass bands and the cheering crowds, were now beginning to make the return journey from the South Coast with a different cargo. Convoy trains were now arriving regularly, laden with sick and wounded men to be cared for at the newly-opened 5th Northern General Hospital. On Sunday, 15 November, 100 casualties arrived from a small section of the Front known to them as 'Wipers' – to history, it was the First Battle of Ypres. Ten days before Christmas the first victims of winter in the trenches arrived at the Midland Station – 160 men, mainly frostbite cases.

The offices of the Leicester War Relief Committee at 2 New Street, were already besieged by wives and dependents, seeking to obtain their just rights from a bureaucracy that was under pressures never previously envisaged and consequently never catered for. The staff at the office railed against the incompetence and shortcomings of those in charge at the War Office. In one week alone during October, more than 200 dependents had visited the office, 480 cases processed: 240 relating to military dependents, 240 concerning problems of unemployment, £183 15s 6d in cash paid out to claimants. Complaints over the incorrect payment of allowances abounded (a woman with four children was entitled to 22s a week.) Monies to be paid to individuals at Post Offices instead of by money orders had gone astray, money orders were made out for the incorrect amounts, or to the wrong recipients. The chaos of cause and effect.

Others involved themselves in the organisation of more support groups. Some 1,500 men over the age of 35 joined the newly-formed Leicester Citizens' Training League. Parading four nights a week at the Magazine Drill Hall, or on the County Cricket Ground, its inaugural meeting was to be the first public engagement for the newly-appointed Mayor, Jonathan North. Under the command of Captain R. M. Pritchard, the League was to be a loose forerunner of a Home Guard. Details of duties and activities, such as route marches, Swedish drill, rifle training and Sunday parades, were published in the local papers, in order, presumably, that members of the League could be apprised of their responsibilities. While this declaration of its activities, doubtless served as a morale booster for the general public, it also displayed a somewhat naïve absence of any sense of security. The Junior Cadet Corps, now organised by Tom Crumbie into the Leicester Junior Training Corps, under the command of Evan Barlow, a local solicitor[1], numbered by the middle of December around 1,800 youths. Thomas Henry Crumbie was, throughout the next four years, to involve himself tirelessly in all manner of schemes designed to ensure that the town's efforts to support the war did not flag. A diabetic, who was also a teetotaller, Crumbie owned a stationer's and printing business at 24 Halford Street. In later years he is probably best remembered locally through his long association with the Leicester Tigers Rugby Football Club of which he was the secretary from 1895 until 1928. (Rugby games virtually ceased for the duration of the war, other than two matches against the Barbarians in January and March 1915, all the games played being for recruiting purposes or

1. Evan Barlow, who lived in St John's Road was a solicitor and official receiver in bankruptcy, with offices at 1 Berridge Street.

the war effort.) Crumbie ensured that the club's facilities were put to good use, the ground being utilised for the training of various quasi-military organisations that proliferated and the club house being given over to serve as the headquarters for two artillery units and a Pioneers Corps battalion. During the inter-war years Tom Crumbie's health deteriorated and he died on 13 March 1928, one month after his 60th birthday.

The borough of Leicester at this time returned two elected members to Parliament. One, a Liberal, was Gordon Hewart KC, who at the end of the war was to be knighted and returned as Solicitor General; the other was James Ramsay MacDonald, later to become the nation's first Labour Prime Minister.

MacDonald was born into relatively poor circumstances on 12 October 1866 at Lossiemouth in Scotland. At the age of 18 he moved to London and became involved in the philosophy of the newly-emerging Labour Movement. Having joined the Independent Labour Party in 1894, MacDonald became a founder member of the Labour Party in 1900, standing unsuccessfully as a candidate for Leicester in the 'Khaki Election' of that year. In the election of 1906, however, then aged 40, Ramsay MacDonald was elected to the House of Commons as a member for Leicester. By 1911 he was the Labour Party chairman and thus a man of some political standing. He resigned from that position in 1914 when his party failed to support his view that Britain should not be involved in the war.

This view was, by association, to leave the town of Leicester open to much criticism throughout the war and would cost MacDonald his seat in the 1918 election.

Whilst the majority of those at Westminster who opposed the war came to a tacit agreement that 'if we are in – then we must win', Ramsay MacDonald did not. On Sunday evening, 18 October, less than 11 weeks into the war, he held one of the first of his local major political meetings at the Corn Exchange in Leicester. The doors of the hall were opened at 6pm. and it was in an atmosphere fraught with tension, that the chairman, Councillor J. W. Murby, introduced MacDonald to a packed crowd, several hundred of whom, unable to gain admission, spilled out into the Market Place. Not all those within the Corn Exchange were sympathetic to the views being put forward and the speaker was seriously heckled

from the outset, with cries of 'Traitor' and the loud singing of *God Save The King* and other patriotic songs. Despite the chairman's pleas for order, several people had to be ejected throughout what not unexpectedly turned out to be an evening of limited success for the organisers. By the time that the 'anti-war' meeting was under way, a counter, 'patriotic meeting', organised by Percy Hagon and Charles Pearce along with others, was being held simultaneously outside the Corn Exchange in the Market Place. Later estimates put the total crowd at between 10,000 and 15,000 people. Herbert Allen, the Chief Constable of Leicester, forewarned of the meeting, had stationed his deputy, Superintendent Cornelius Carson, with 100 men in the Market Place. Had they not been present it is fairly certain that some form of serious disorder would have arisen. As it was, his meeting over, Ramsay Mac-Donald was to be one of history's early examples of a politician beating a hasty and ignominious retreat under police escort to an awaiting motor car.

Surprisingly perhaps, one of the groups which essentially put their activities on hold until the outcome of the war was decided was the Suffragette movement. Under the leadership of the indomitable Emmeline Pankhurst, the Suffragettes had during the months prior to war breaking out orchestrated a campaign of disorder throughout the country. Leicestershire had not escaped their fervid attentions during the hot summer months of 1914.

On 2 June a rather amateurish attempt had been made to burn down Nevill Holt, a mansion house situated near to the village of Medbourne, between Market Harborough and Uppingham, the home of the shipping magnate, Sir Bache Cunard. The house was temporarily unoccupied while awaiting a new tenant – Mr Nevill Peak. During the day of the fire, a Tuesday, workmen carrying out renovations, along with the gamekeeper, spotted two women walking around, examining the exterior of the house. Before they could be challenged, the women left, making off in the direction of Medbourne. Unbeknown to the prospective arsonists, there were two gardeners living-in at the premises as caretakers. Late that night, while checking around (possibly alerted by the earlier sighting of the two mysterious women), the gardeners discovered an open window and the main staircase of the house in flames. The fire was quickly extinguished and a search of the grounds revealed a quantity of Suffragette literature strewn about along with accelerant liquids which were found in the private church of the mansion. The indications were that the gardeners had disturbed the women in an attempt to extend their activities to burning down the church as well as the house.

Given the seriousness of the offence, it is quite astounding how easily the Suffragettes managed to melt away. Initially they had been sighted in broad daylight and in distinctly suspicious circumstances by the gamekeeper (not a breed of men known for their timidity), and a group of workmen, but allowed to leave without any apparent challenge. When the gardeners discovered the blaze in the main house, the evidence indicates that the women were still at the premises, within yards of the men, in the process of setting light to the church. But yet again they managed to disappear into the darkness. In a rural area where a lone motor vehicle late at night would have been guaranteed to have drawn attention, their escape, presumably on foot or by pedal cycle, must have been a risky affair and to have put any distance between themselves and the scene of the crime, a lengthy process.

On Saturday, 13 June, a group of Suffragettes opened a stall in Leicester Market Place on behalf of the Women's Social and Political Union, near to the Old White Swan public house. Their purpose was to sell cakes and confectionery in order to gain funds for their organisation. Deeply suspicious of their activities and mindful of the recent Nevill Holt fire which was being openly attributed to the Suffragette movement, around lunchtime a large crowd gathered. After a deal of abuse and heckling by the throng, firelighters and produce began to be thrown at the women by the more extreme elements, followed by attacks upon them in which their clothes were torn and they were physically abused. At this point, a group of sympathetic market traders stepped in to assist the women and a general fist fight broke out. The mêlée was quickly broken up and the crowd dispersed by the timely arrival of Superintendent Carson accompanied by a contingent of police. As was often the case with low level public disorder at the time, there is no mention of any arrests resulting from this fracas. It is highly likely that in the absence of the public order legis - lation (other than a common law sanction against breaches of the peace), which was to be passed later in the inter-war years, the police were satisfied to restore good order and leave it at that. (Later in the war, the Defence of the Realm Act was amended to deal with public meetings which could cause undue nuisance.) The fact that Carson was on the scene so quickly with a substantial body of constables would indicate that the trouble was well anticipated and they were waiting in the wings on stand-by in the nearby New Town Hall Police Station.

Four weeks later, almost to the day, during the early hours of Sunday, 12 July, Blaby Railway Station was burned down. At half past midnight, having seen the last Leicester train safely through, the station master, Mr House, locked up and went off home. The driver of the 1.50a.m Birmingham-London fast goods train was the first to spot the fire. He alerted the duty signalman, who with great presence of mind put the stops up for the 2am express parcel train which was next along the line. Having stopped the parcel train, he directed the driver to uncouple his engine, which had 3,000 gallons of water in its boilers, and take it to Blaby Station where he instructed him to play the water on the fire by means of the engine's force pump which was used to draw water from the boilers, in the hope of controlling the conflagration until the arrival of the local fire brigade.

Meanwhile, two young local men, named Hallam and Clark, cycling home after a night out in Oadby, also saw the flames coming from the station and on checking, found the lamp room to be aflame. They dashed to the nearby home of the station master, and with the aid of the village constable, PC Button, the four men set about tackling the blaze. They were quickly joined by House's son and other local railwaymen who lived nearby including ganger Thorpe and his son, F. White the Narborough station master and H. Steers the Glen Parva station master.

Unable to make any headway, they contented themselves with saving as much as possible of the station's valuables. Before being driven back by the fire they succeeded in rescuing many of the railway documents in the offices, such as accounts and books of tickets along with £100-worth of silk which was awaiting delivery. The fire, which caused £500 worth of damage, destroyed the wooden platform, the booking office the waiting room and partially destroyed several other of the station buildings before the combined efforts of the Wigston and Leicester fire brigades brought the conflagration under control.

Investigation in daylight the next morning revealed that access to the station had been gained from a nearby footpath through a hole in the hedge. Suffragette literature and two pairs of ladies' gloves soaked in accelerant were found at the scene. Women's footprints were found on the embankment and some anglers who had been fishing in the local canal reported having seen two women in mackintoshes walking along the canal bank at about 3am. Once again the identity of those responsible was to remain a mystery. Despite their best efforts, the County Police in the form of Superintendent Bowley and Detective Inspector Taylor, failed in this case, as at Nevill Holt to satisfactorily resolve the matter.[1]

It is therefore quite interesting that the 56-year-old Emmeline Pankhurst, at the height of what can only be regarded as a controversial political campaign, decided to put on hold the activities of her organisation and throw in her lot with the 'if we are in – then we must win' element. With a shrewd eye to the future and more politically aware than Ramsay MacDonald, history has shown this to have been a most pragmatic decision on her part. Having made an unforgettable assertion on behalf of women's suffrage, she now had the unique opportunity to withdraw from the incendiary and disorder campaign and to present her cause as one mature enough to sublimate its interests before those of the nation.[2] On the night of Friday, 30 October, barely a fortnight after Ramsay MacDonald's débâcle at the Corn Exchange, Emmeline Pankhurst spoke to an assembly at the De Montfort Hall on the subject of 'the Queen's Work for Women Fund', liberally basted with criticism of MacDonald and his unpopular activities. With seats at 2s 6d, 1s and 6d, a collection was also taken, the proceeds of which were to be donated to the war effort. If on this occasion the ubiquitous Superintendent Carson was again on stand-by with his men, they were not required and the evening passed off without event, Mrs Pankhurst scoring a victory in the town which her prior activities had denied her.

Accompanying this frenetic activity, the normal everyday life and business of the townspeople continued as it had prior to 4 August. The long-awaited scheme to widen the High Street moved towards final fruition with the purchase for £300 by the Corporation from the Leicester Co-operative Society, of a strip of land covering 18½ square yards, which completed the necessary purchases on the north side of the development. Plans to extend the tramways routes along Evington Road to St Phillip's Church, Overton Road to Gipsy Lane and Welford Road as far as Clarendon Park, were progressed in order to accommodate the growing population of the town and 'to keep men in work'.

On Thursday evening, 12 November, Dorice Hilda Smith, a 19-year-old hosiery worker living at 112 Harrison Road, was killed when she stepped in front of a motor van at the junction of Belgrave Road and Buller Road. Four days later, Harriet Piggot, a 53-year-old barmaid from the Avenue public house in Cavendish Road, died in the Infirmary from the injuries she received when she fell under the wheels of a horse and trolley in Halford Street. Meanwhile, Mary Ann Gray, described to the magistrates as '59, married', was sentenced, despite her plea that she was seeking work, to seven days' imprisonment with hard labour for begging in West Street.

An unfortunate accident at the Midland Station in February resulted in the untimely death of Tom Kingdom, a goods porter who fell under a train while working. Busy unloading horse feed from a wagon in the sidings, Kingdom was clipped by a passing locomotive and fell on to the track under the wheels of the rolling stock.

Despite the sudden depletion in their strength, Leicester police still found time to deal with the day-to-day misdemeanours always present in society. William John Turner, a farmer, and William Howgill, a dairyman, were both fined two shillings and sixpence for allowing their cows to stray in Walnut Street and Aylestone Road. John Robert Walpole was fined 40s when he appeared before the magistrates charged with dangerous driving – in that he drove through the Haymarket at speeds of between 12 and 15 miles an hour. When stopped by Constable Earl, his explanation for this violation was that he 'had got a new machine and didn't understand it'. In a similar vein, Sidney Weston Knight, an outfitter of 81 London Road, was fined

---

1. In 1919 Supt. Levi Bowley and Det. Supt. Herbert Chiltern Taylor were involved as the senior local officers in the Green Bicycle Murder. In July 1921 Bowley became Deputy Chief Constable of the county police force.

2. Not all the women's groups followed Emmeline Pankhurst. Groups such as Sylvia Pankhurst's militant Women's Suffrage Federation continued in opposition.

£5 by the bench for what they considered to be a particularly bad case. William Middleton, a fruiterer, gave evidence that on 20 October, he was driving a horse and trolley out of Woodland Road into Uppingham Road when Knight 'driving a motor cycle and sidecar, at a terrible pace, collided with him, knocking down his horse and breaking the shafts of his trolley'.

The constabulary were also now to become involved in a new aspect of enforcement when three deserters from the Lincolnshire Regiment, on the run from Grimsby, were found hiding in a fish truck and detained to await military escort.

The jobs vacant columns of the local newspapers carried advertisements for men seeking employment as temporary gasfitters at ninepence an hour, to apply to the Gas Offices. At least one of these vacancies was the result of an industrial accident. In late August, George Howe, a 60-year-old labourer for the department, had been killed while working in a trench in Ross Walk when a 28lbs iron plug was blown out of a pipe which was under compression.

Ironically in view of the desperate recruiting situation, another advertisement sought to persuade farmhands between the ages of 16 and 21, or 30 and 45 to take an assisted passage for £2 to Australia, where work would be found for them on arrival.

Aside from the war, the main talking point in the town was the trial and subsequent execution of Arnold Warren for the murder of his baby son earlier in the year on Western Park. At 38, Warren, an engineer by trade, was a compulsive gambler with a failed marriage and heavy financial problems. His history of unsuccessful gambling, accompanied by a measure of domestic violence, resulted in his wife leaving him in May 1914, taking with her their two-year-old son, James Warren. On Friday, 10 July, James was left as usual with his grandmother, Elizabeth Warren, at 48 Gaul Street while his mother went to work. About 5.30pm the same day, a girl named Edith Skidmore, who lived in Vorley Street, collected the child to return him home. Shortly afterwards, Skidmore was stopped on a nearby recreation ground by Arnold Warren, who asked her to return to his mother's house with a note while he looked after the boy. On her return, both had disappeared. Later in the evening, shortly before eight o'clock, Stanley Hackney, a shoe hand, crossing the fields near to Western Park found Warren slumped on the ground unconscious with a bottle of laudanum in his hand, and an open razor nearby. Beneath him lay the body of James Warren with his throat cut. At his trial at Leicester Assizes before Mr Justice Avery, Warren told the court that on the day of the murder he was depressed, having lost heavily on a horse called Early Hope at Haydock Park. His plea of not guilty was dismissed by the jury and he was hanged at Leicester Prison at 8am on Thursday, 12 November 1914.[1]

In October 1914, with the long winter nights drawing in, the *Leicester Daily Mercury* and the *Leicester Post* turned their attention to the fact that Christmas was only a matter of weeks away and something needed to be done to ensure that the men in the trenches were not forgotten. A scheme was hit upon to launch an appeal asking every newspaper reader to donate one shilling towards the purchase of presents and comforts for local men from the town and county, irrespective of what unit they were serving in. An initial target of £1,000 was set. By the nature of the venture and the numbers involved, combined with the time constraints, this would not be an easy task. Advertisements were run in both papers explaining the object of the exercise and asking for donations. Recruiting officers were asked to help with lists of volunteers and reservists. Finally, all readers of the papers living within the borough and county, with relatives away in either the army or the navy, were asked to supply details to those collating the appeal.

A Grand Vocal Concert on Sunday evening, 8 November, at the De Montfort Hall gave the fund raising an added impetus.

Once again, those remaining behind gave generously. By early November sufficient money had been received to enable the first batch of gifts to be packaged. Working from the warehouse of the Worcestershire Furnishing Company in Princess Road, a group of Boy Scouts put together 2,300 parcels, each tied with red, white and blue string. Each gift contained a Christmas card signed by the Lord Lieutenant of the County, the Duke of Rutland, the High Sheriff and the Mayors of Leicester and Loughborough. Next came a quarter-pound box of chocolates, two pairs of leather

1. The uniform officer who arrested Warren, Constable Harry (Snowy) Ashburner, was after the war, to rise to the rank of Superintendent, eventually retiring as head of the City Police CID.

bootlaces and a note pad and 25 envelopes in a stiff writing case. Enclosed with the goods was a note explaining that a further two ounces of smoking mixture and 30 cigarettes would be forwarded later by the bonded warehouse.

As December wore on, a variety of items of clothing, food and other comforts were either bought or begged. Many items such as the five dozen pairs of woollen gloves donated by John Spencer & Sons of Wellington Street were given to the fund by local manufacturers. (Gloves for infantrymen were to be of standard army pattern, cavalry and artillery men received thick, five-finger gloves, while engineers required fingerless mittens.) Local ladies were kept busy knitting blue woollen mufflers, 11 inches wide and two yards long. As a substitute for matches, an old fashioned tinder lighter – the spark from which was sufficient to set a wick burning in winter conditions of wind and rain – was put into each package.

At the end of ten weeks the appeal was closed, having collected £2,000 – exactly double its original target.

In keeping with the spirit of Christmas, the undertaking was not without its lighter moments. On Wednesday, 9 December, the younger members of the populace were given an unforeseen treat. Workmen were carefully loading 1,000 packets of chocolate, for despatch to the Front, on to an handcart in the narrow confines of Albion Street when a runaway horse, careering around the corner, collided with the truck, upturning it and scattering its contents across the thoroughfare. Word spread quickly and faster than the men could recover their merchandise, local children, who at the best of times saw little of such delicacies, were busy liberating the unexpected windfall.

The eventual number of Christmas parcels distributed by the One Shilling Fund amounted to over 15,000. In addition to the Christmas greetings card and chocolates enclosed in the package, an enormous amount of other practical material found its way over the Channel in each container. Bootlaces, 6,000 pairs of gloves, 2,800 pairs of mittens, 600 mufflers, 550 pipe lighters, 6,000 stationery sets, 9,000 packets of tobacco, 45,000 cigarettes, 3,060 pocket knives, were sent to men serving at the Front and in the Royal Navy. Over 100 food hampers were sent out to the dependents of local men who had been killed in action. Food and

cards were distributed to Belgian refugees spending the first of many winters, homesick and impoverished, in temporary accommodation. Christmas fare was sent on behalf of the Leicester citizens to the staff and inmates, nurses and doctors of the local hospitals.

In view of the object of the appeal being to ensure that every local man serving in any unit of the army or navy should receive a gift, a fairly accurate appraisal of the contribution of the town and county to the war in terms of manpower can be made here by examining the distribution of presents from the One Shilling Fund. The following list indicates exactly how many Leicester men were serving in the various branches of the armed services that first Christmas.

Royal Navy	45
1st Battalion Leicestershire Regt.	1,100
2nd Battalion Leicestershire Regt.	1,500
4th Battalion Leicestershire Regt	1,100
4th Battalion Leicestershire Regt. (Reserve)	1,100
5th Battalion Leicestershire Regt.	1,100
5th Battalion Leicestershire Regt. (Reserve)	1,100
6th Battalion Leicestershire Regt.	1,100
7th Battalion Leicestershire Regt.	1,100
8th Battalion Leicestershire Regt.	1,100
9th Battalion Leicestershire Regt.	1,100
10th Battalion Leicestershire Regt.	500
Leicestershire Yeomanry	450
Leicestershire Royal Artillery	280
Local men serving in other Regiments	703
North Midland Mounted Brigade Transport and Supply Col	158
2nd North Midland Field Ambulance	480
North Midlands Divisional Clearing Hospital	40
Wounded in Hospitals, Nurses and Doctors	1,000
Hampers to dependents of men killed in action	100
Total	15,156

Although it was not a white one – the first heavy snowfalls of the winter were to come in the middle of March– the first Christmas of the Great War was celebrated by those at home, much as in prior years. The days became shorter and crisper as winter deepened, and during early December high winds caused considerable damage in the town. Festive decorations appeared in houses, and shop windows were decked out in seasonal splendour.

H. Samuel in Gallowtree Gate stocked their

window with patriotic brushes at 1s each, military hairbrushes 4s 6d, and a selection of wrist watches to suit most pockets – nickel 9s 11d, silver 12s 6d and rolled gold for 25s. (A forthcoming line which would sell well were their military wristwatches with luminous dials, 'as worn on night patrols'.)

Table d'hôte luncheon at the Stag and Pheasant Hotel in Humberstone Gate cost the discerning diner 2s. A supply of Marcella cigars could be obtained at 3d each or 1s for five. The producer's of Lloyd's 'Bondman', dark Virginia tobacco (usually 4½d an ounce), offered at the bargain price of 1s 6d per half-pound plus postage, to send their wares 'duty free to any soldier at the Front on the Continent, or to any sailor on any of His Majesty's vessels of war in the Home Fleet, including the North Sea.' (The postage amounted to 1s to France or 4d to the navy.) A new suit from Stewart's, 'The King Tailors', at 8 Silver Street, was priced at 13s 3d along with the option of a winter overcoat for 30s to wear with it.

The Leicester Co-operative Society offered plum puddings at 1s each (2s for a large one), or Christmas cakes from between 1s and 5s.

In keeping with the spirit of goodwill to all men, provision was made for those less fortunate in the borough. While the numbers on Poor Relief had reduced slightly as a result of many able-bodied men electing for the rigours of trench warfare in preference to those of the workhouse, there still remained in the borough a large number of families in dire straits. With little help available to those who for whatever reason were unable to support themselves, the spectre of the workhouse was ever a reality.

At the end of November 1914, the number of people in receipt of Out Relief from the Poor Law Guardians during the year averaged 2,907. This actually compared favourably with the figure of 3,072 for the previous year. The highest previous total in recent years had been the 5,228 recipients in 1906.

Those receiving Indoor Relief during the year of 1914 (including lunatics), totalled 3,016, which was 123 less than 1913.

The number of vagrants passing, however temporarily, through the workhouse doors during the year totalled 4,049. Although, in keeping with the other Poor Law figures, this was down by 764 on the previous year, it still reveals a staggering average of 77 homeless and destitute people a week seeking refuge at Swain Street. The figure, incidentally, shows the number of applications by vagrants to stay at the refuge, not the number of separate individuals. At this time a person classed as a vagrant was allowed to seek refuge at the workhouse for a period of no longer than two consecutive nights, after which they then had to vacate, but could return to repeat the process after a period of one month.

During the last week of December 1914, the Poor Law Guardians counted 790 inmates at the workhouse in Swain Street, which was a reduction of 80 on the same week for the previous year.

At noon on Christmas Day, the Leicester Free Christmas Dinner Fund (the president of which was Sir Edward Wood), distributed to the poor of the borough 1,270 free dinners which had been cooked at numerous bakeries throughout the town. On the previous Monday, the Leicester 'Blind and Crippled' had each been given by the Fund a parcel containing one and a half pounds of bacon, a quarter-pound of tea, two pounds of sugar and a cake.

On 25 December the workhouse was 'decorated as merrily as possible with patriotic emblems'. At 12.30pm, the Mayor and Poor Law Guardians visited the establishment when Alderman North addressed the inmates in the dining hall, wishing them all 'the compliments of the season'. Considering their straitened circumstances, it is hardly surprising that no account of the inmates' response to this blandishment still exists. Dinner, presided over by the keeper and his wife, Mr and Mrs Lovell, consisted of roast beef or roast pork and baked potatoes, followed by plum pudding. The men were presented with an ounce of tobacco and an orange, the women with tea, sugar and sweets. Children were given oranges and sweets. After a late tea of bread, butter and plum cake, the evening is recorded as being spent 'by the inmates singing to each other'.

Depressing as it may be, this account of the events of the day is immeasurably better than the only alternative available to the desperately poor of the time – namely to starve or freeze to death on the open streets of the town or in isolated country lanes. Determined not to further increase the overburdened system of relief, vagrants and those not local to the area were actively discouraged. Such a person was Joseph Brown, a 50-year-old itinerant labourer lodging in Waverley Place. Found guilty by the magistrates of being drunk in the town on

Boxing Day, Brown was released from custody after the holiday on his promise that he would leave the borough and not return.

As the old and most eventful year of the century to date came to a close, not for the first occasion of recent times, the townsfolk found themselves subjected to unsolicited pressure. Since late summer there had been a suggestion that an element of drunkenness was on the increase in Leicester and other towns. The Chief Constable, Herbert Allen, when asked by the licensing magistrates to comment, reported that, with a total of 630 prosecutions in the borough during the 12-month period, 1914 was certainly the highest year in the last two decades (since 1893), for public drunkenness. The question is why?

With a population of around 228,000, the town was served, according to the Chief Constable's report for 1914, by a total of 711 premises licensed for the sale of intoxicating liquor: *viz* 256 fully licensed premises, 104 beer houses, 300 beer 'off-licences' and 51 other licences. This was not disproportionate for an urban community of the time. A probable answer lies in the social upheaval of the latter part of the year. In August, answering the call to the Colours, there was a huge influx of army reservists and recruits into the town and to the depot nearby at Glen Parva. Significantly, August held the highest figure for the year with 65 convictions. Men stationed in a town – any town – in readiness for war are prime candidates for releasing tensions and boredom by frequenting local hostelries and places of entertainment. A degree of drunkenness is an inevitable consequence. Certainly with men entering and leaving the town in large numbers, this situation would endure up to the turn of the year and long after.

A wider and more sinister inference was drawn directly from the War Office and targeted an unexpected and particularly vulnerable group. The War Office maintained that while husbands were away fighting, wives in receipt of separation and other army allowances were squandering the money on drink.[1] To make such a conjecture in the total absence of any empirical data is, to say the least, wild speculation. Even without the benefit of history, any reasonably informed observer of the time must have been aware that, with a few ever-present exceptions,

this was just not true. The women being maligned were, for the most part, in no position to pursue the free-wheeling lifestyle which was being attributed to them. At that early stage of the war, one of the unwelcome facts that was emerging, was that a large part of the body of reservists and volunteers coming forward comprised married men with families.

The abstraction of married men was in itself becoming a highly contentious matter. In early 1915 comment was made in some quarters that the Tramways Department had engaged 20 able-bodied single men to crew the tramcars in place of married men who had gone to the army. The local authority were quick to respond to the aspersion. At the quarterly meeting of the Town Council on 30 March, Alderman Flint for the Tramways Committee made the point that 'the Tramways have recently been criticised for replacing 22 volunteers with 22 single men. This is incorrect, of the 22 [replacements], four were single men, two were single men who the army had rejected, and 16 were married men'. He then went on to underline the department's position by pointing out that there were 282 tramways men away with the Forces, which constituted a quarter of the entire department, 171 replacements had been found, leaving 111 positions vacant, a situation that was partly being masked by the fact that existing staff were working excessive hours, in many cases without any overtime payment.

The difficulty was also becoming glaringly apparent in most other walks of life, including the police and fire services. In consequence, for the first time in modern history, society was experiencing the creation on a grand scale of what were, to all intents and purposes, single-parent families. This was a circumstance which, as the months wore on into years and the casualties mounted, was to become a permanent situation. In this county alone, thousands of young women, many soon to be widows found themselves to be the sole providers for families. It would be naïve to presume that none of them slid into easy ways, but for a government only four months into a major national crisis, bent on persuading men to leave their homes and fight for their country, to suggest that 'while the cat's away the mouse will play' was the height of untimely folly.

Given that the levels of drinking had, as already

---

1. The War Office backed this up with the very real threat to any woman found guilty of drunkenness or other misbehaviour such as adultery, of the loss of her army pay and separation allowances.

discussed, increased in accordance with the newly-imposed circumstances of the town, a more reasoned explanation to this bizarre allegation nationally is to be found in the fact that by late 1914 and well into 1915, munitions were in short supply. Servicing the artillery batteries which were firing daily barrages into the German trenches was demanding more and more shells. Shells, especially those required for the heavier guns, had to be mass produced and the truth was that industry was not at that stage physically capable of producing them. Douglas Haig, who was shortly to replace Sir John French as commander of the British Expeditionary Force, was swift to point an accusing finger at those manning the Home Front. In a blustering outburst, typical of the man, he informed Lloyd George that the munitions workers were far fonder of their drink and Bank Holidays than they were of serving the nation and winning the war, and that if a few of them were to be taken out and shot, then the munitions would soon be forthcoming.[1]

What became known as the 'Shells Crisis', continued into 1915, and in May, Herbert Asquith, never a particularly strong leader, acquiesced to what had become an untenable political situation and agreed to the formation of an all-party Coalition government. The most immediate step taken by the new administration was to create David Lloyd George the Minister of Munitions. This effectively eroded Kitchener's power base as Minister for War and allowed the politicians to begin the long haul towards regaining a measure of control over the course of the war.

With the Liberal Government already reeling under the pressures being exerted from all sides, the consequent knee-jerk reaction to Haig's hectoring is, with the benefit of hindsight, somewhat unreal. The true dilemma of supply and demand had yet to be seriously addressed. At this juncture, with promises of an impending decisive victory in exchange for political co-operation, the military still held the whip hand – General Haig said that the nation had a drink problem, therefore it must be dealt with.

The Temperance Movement took up the baton with a will. As early as 15 September, a deputation, 36-strong, of the ladies and gentlemen of the Temperance Societies, headed up by the Reverend A. E. W. Mansell, Mr Albert Pickard and Mrs T. R.

Ryder, had presented themselves before Councillor Hincks and the Watch Committee to demand the early closing of licensed premises at nine o'clock for the duration of the war. This latest assertion by the Government gave an unexpected impetus to their cause.

The Watch Committee and Licensing Justices were by no means convinced and not a little sceptical of the patently thin argument, supported by hastily drafted legislation in the form of the Intoxicating Liquor (Temporary Restriction) Act 1914, presented by the War Office. The unanswered question was simple: upon what basis was the claim made? No demographic evidence was presented. Between the first week in August, when war had been declared, and the beginning of December, when the rumblings began, a mere 17 weeks had elapsed. In the time available it would have been physically impossible to identify any such problem (even if the appropriate data had been kept), then collate and quantify it. Had the assertion been made in respect only of Leicester, or a few specified towns and cities, it might have just gained some tenuous credibility. But it was levelled at the entire country. Leicester, along with many other boroughs, decided to wait a while until the issue became clearer.

Although immediate action was postponed, the Government adhered to its position and on 30 December 1914, Leicester magistrates were forced to announce that, in direct compliance with a Military Order issued under the Defence of the Realm Act and effective from that day, all public houses in the borough would close at 9pm. In an obvious gesture of hostility they added that 'in order to comply with the spirit of the Act they had agreed to close all clubs under the Intoxicating Liquors (Temporary Restrictions) Act at 9pm as from 1 January 1915'.

The true government agenda is not clear. Certainly the closure of licensed premises earlier in the evening would have little influence on the perceived problem of drunkenness. Drinking habits would merely shift in order to circumvent the newly-imposed restrictions. In an era which pre-dated even such basic home entertainment as radio, the public house was for many working folk a social focus, and any unwarranted interference was guaranteed to be ill received. With winter nights drawing in, early closure would result in a

---

1. At the end of the war when there was a minor mutiny among troops at Calais returning from leave, who because of the system were long overdue for demobilisation, Haig's solution was to demand that the men be shot. An expedient that fortunately, to Haig's fury, Churchill countermanded.

significant saving of fuel, the garnering of which was fast becoming a necessity. This premise is borne out by the ensuing imposition of lighting restrictions and constraints upon the late night opening of business premises. It is feasible to suppose that if the provisions did curtail the drinking habits of the nation at large, the attendant savings by individuals would result in more available money for donations to the plethora of funds and appeals which were being generated for the war effort. A final possible supposition may be that with the imminent necessity in many areas of industry for the introduction of shift working, this could be a preparatory measure.

Having grasped the nettle, it was left to the magistrates in the various localities to specify the exact permitted hours. In York (the Military Headquarters of Northern Command of which Leicester was a part), as in Leicester, public houses closed at 9pm. In Sheffield it was 9.30pm during the week and 10pm on a Sunday, while in Leeds and Northampton it was 11pm on weekdays and 10pm on a Sunday.

As the cold, depressing winter months drew into early 1915, recruiting locally went into a decided decline. The departure from the town on Friday, 29 January of 900 men of the 4th Battalion, Leicestershire Territorial Reserve saw one of the last of the large contingents to leave. To the intense frustration of the Recruiting Committee, figures fell to a trickle. (This situation was not peculiar to Leicester; after the initial rush to join up during August and September 1914, recruiting nationally had tailed off.) Advertisements were placed in every possible location exhorting men to join a variety of units. A special recruiting campaign was run in the town. Men were addressed in the workplace by recruiting officers, and the dark winter evenings saw a flurry of open-air meetings held wherever people could be gathered. Torchlight processions led by police with recruiting ribbons in their helmets, and bands of musicians, paraded through the town carrying patriotic banners demanding that those who were eligible should examine their consciences and volunteer.

On Saturday, 9 January, a huge military pageant was assembled on Victoria Park. Made up of new recruits for the 4th Leicesters Reserve Battalion and Kitchener's New Army who were under training, police officers, various local bands, 2,000 members of the Leicester Citizens' Training League, a contingent of the Church Lads' Brigade and 1,000 youths from the Leicester Junior Training Corps, the gathering moved off at 1.45 p.m. Processing through the town, the focal point of the procession was a lorry carrying two German machine-guns captured by the 2nd Leicesters in a night attack on German trenches at Richebourg L'Avonne on 19 December. The truck was escorted by eight soldiers of the 2nd Battalion with fixed bayonets. Each of these men, led by Sgt J. F. Cooke, who had lost an eye in the action, had been members of the company which captured the guns and were now convalescing at the nearby 5th Northern General Hospital. On arrival at its destination – the Tigers' rugby football ground – the parade dispersed to the music of the massed bands, and the 20,000 crowd were treated to an afternoon of patriotic speeches, followed by a rugby match in which Mr Crumbie's team defeated a team of Canadians 42-6.

On Saturday, 27 March, on a bitterly cold afternoon, accompanied by intermittent snow showers the process was repeated, a massed procession of every available uniform, band and defence organisation paraded from Victoria Park to the Aylestone Road football ground. The results were disappointing. Recruitment in Leicester was at a virtual standstill. Trade in the borough had now settled down and men who only a short while previously had been in grave danger of being laid off, again found themselves in full employment with firms producing essentials such as boots and clothing. At government level the battle lines were already being drawn between the military, whose voracious appetite for men knew no bounds, and the politicians responsible for servicing the industry which would keep the army in the field. It is little wonder that the man in the street was also now beginning to question just where his best interest lay. There was in Leicester one of the main war hospitals in the Midlands – the 5th Northern General – where convoys of casualties arrived on a weekly basis, disgorging wounded and maimed men. Those of them who were convalescing were to be seen daily in the streets of the town, some walking, some being pushed by comrades in spinal carriages. It would be a most unimaginative man who did not balance the plight of these unfortunates against the heroic promises of the recruiting posters. Feed into the equation the opportunity to earn (probably for the first time in his life), decent wages, overtime and a war bonus by remaining at home, and the average man by the early months of 1915 was becoming less and less inclined to volunteer for the trenches.

The situation was one which afflicted most parts of the country; unfortunately, because of its high profile in the manufacturing field, Leicester quickly fell behind many of the other towns and cities in the recruiting league. At the beginning of February 1915 the Recruiting Committee commented that 'the men of the 4th Battalion having departed, the Magazine is quite quiet – a further 100 men have volunteered and are being trained on Victoria Park. However, between 400 and 500 are still required for this unit'. By March their concern had deepened and they complained that 'during the last week only 20 men have volunteered for the whole of the TF units. In the last fortnight only two men have volunteered for the 2nd Battalion. One hundred men are still needed for the 21st Battery of the Leicestershire Royal Horse Artillery'. Adding to the growing embarrassment of the Town Council, the War Office announced its intention, 'due to the lack of local recruits', to send a recruiting party for the Leicestershire Regiment into neighbouring Nottinghamshire.

The following figures, published at the end of March 1915, did nothing to ease difficulties.

Comparison of towns by population percentage: recruiting percentage.

Newcastle	18.5%
Nottingham	18.5%
Swansea	10.5%
Wakefield	7.6%
Birmingham	7.1%
Hull	7.1%
Manchester	6.7%
Sheffield	6.7%
Leeds	5.9%
Derby	5.2%
Bradford	5.1%
Oldham	4.0%
Leicester	2.6%

Alderman Tollington declared that 'there is great consternation that recruiting in Leicester is below the national average' and called attention to a circular sent by the Local Government Board asking of councils that all work involving capital expenditure be suspended in order to release men

for the Forces. Tollington's difficulty in relation to this proposition was that during the seven months since August 1914, some 600 council employees had joined up and to comply with the directive would put many existing council workers out of jobs. A motion by Councillor Hincks that 'where Corporation men go to join the Colours, their places be filled by men who are ineligible for the Forces and that ten Council members be appointed to the Recruiting Committee to give support', was carried by 35 votes to 23.

Despite the fact that a great number of men had already volunteered, and nationally recruiting was not going well, the above figures, published at the end of March 1915 show quite incontrovertibly that, for whatever reasons, Leicester had about exhausted her contribution of those willing to voluntarily go to war.

Taken many years after the event, this view of Blaby Railway Station shows the refurbished wooden platform and buildings, which in July 1914 were destroyed by the Suffragettes.

June 1913, two Suffragettes take on a predominantly male crowd in Leicester Market Place.

Pictured in Bowling Green Street outside of Joseph Johnson's premises, these Suffragettes prepare for a demonstration in the town centre.

Emmeline Pankhurst, 1858-1928. Secretary of the National Women's Social & Political Union. After August 1914, Mrs Pankhurst elected for the next four years to channel the activities of her organisation primarily into helping the war effort. Not all of the Suffrage Movement accepted this decision, resulting in break-away groups being formed. She died on 4 June 1928, a few weeks after women in Britain were granted full voting rights.

Described as 'Miss Pethick and Miss Bone' two members of the local Women's Suffrage Movement stand outside of their shop premises at 14 Bowling Green Street.

The old Tramways Department Horse Depot in Belgrave Gate was taken over and used as a main local centre for the production of artillery shells.

A group of the women employed at the munitions factory in Belgrave Gate. The object of Douglas Haig's vilification during the 'Shell Crisis' of 1915, these women worked in a most unhealthy environment. Due to the nature of the chemicals used in the industry many workers suffered from depression, nausea and skin problems.

This busy street scene of Uppingham Road on the outskirts of the town is notable – other than a Corporation Tramcar – for it's lack of traffic. It is little wonder that when, in October 1914, Sidney Weston Knight, an outfitter of 81 London Road, was involved in an accident along this stretch of road with a horse and cart, he was described as driving a motorcycle and sidecar, 'at a terrible pace'.

With Leicester being a boot and shoe manufacturing town leather goods were one of the commodities which were to remain in plentiful supply. Pictured between 1911 and 1917 Miss Nellie Wayte stands outside the premises of the Great Northern Boot Stores, of which she was the manageress, at 141 Belgrave Road.

The Three Cranes, 84 Humberstone Gate. Shown standing in the doorway of his premises, Tom Pratt was the licensee on the outbreak of war. The Leicester Brewing and Malting Company seen advertised on the Wharf Street wall of the pub was to be found nearby at 51 Charnwood Street.

Pictured at the turn of the century this town centre pub is the Talbot Inn at 19 St Nicholas Street. The name over the door is William Henry Ganney who was still the inn keeper during 1914 when war broke out.

Seen just after the war one of the best known public houses in the town, The Royal Standard, 21 Charles Street. The name over the door (Alfred Allen), indicates that the premises changed hands during or immediately after the war, as the licensee in 1914 was Ernest Stringer.

Just above the Opera House in Silver Street was the Antelope. Carrying over the door the name, T. Toone 'Importer & Bonder', during the Great War it was under the management of Henry Selvey.

Dealing with the Wounded

ON THE Home Front one of the responsibilities of the Royal Army Medical Corps was the organisation of the military hospitals essential to caring for the needs of the sick and wounded brought back from the front line. To facilitate this, the country was split into regions, Leicestershire becoming a part of the 5th Northern General Region. Territorial Force Medical Officers were commissioned and the search was on for a suitable site for a war hospital.

The old County Lunatic Asylum, later to be the site of Leicester University, on the outskirts of the town was ideally suited to the purpose. Belonging to the County Council, the site could, in the event of war, be turned over to the military for the duration of hostilities. The geographical location could hardly be bettered. Built on approximately 37 acres of ground, some 300ft above sea level, it would be difficult to find a healthier environment so near to all the amenities provided by a busy Midlands town. Bounded by Victoria Park on one side, and by Welford Road, Victoria Park Road, and Victoria Road (later to be University Road), on the other three, it could be accessed easily by vehicular transport. The Midland Railway Station, which was to be the disembarkation point for large numbers of wounded soldiers, was only minutes away from the main gates.

The buildings themselves had been examined as early as 1913 by Major Louis Kenneth Harrison and found to be potentially suitable. Harrison, a local doctor who lived nearby at Holmleigh in Alexandra Road, with a practice at 320 Humberstone Road, had been commissioned into the Territorial Force in readiness five years previously, on 30 September 1909, and given the task along with his CO, Colonel Astley Vivasour Clarke (another well known medical man), of creating the hospital unit. Taking over responsibility for the project in 1911, when Clarke was promoted to the post of Assistant Director Medical Services, North Midlands Division, Louis Harrison was to remain the CO and administrator of the hospital throughout the war.

A lot of work was needed to be done to make the site habitable. Opened as a mental institution in 1837, the premises had been unoccupied for the seven years prior to 1914 and were in a dilapidated condition. However, with so many other factors in its favour, the old lunatic asylum was most certainly an attractive proposition.

Formation of a Territorial Force medical unit had been put in hand early in 1909 as part of Haldane's reorganisation of the army. In peacetime the 5th Northern General Hospital had an establishment of three officers and 43 other ranks, to be increased in the event of war to 109 plus 18 medical officers.

Staff for this, and other such hospitals throughout the country, were to be drawn from the ranks of the Territorial Force Nursing Service and the officers and men of the Royal Army Medical Corps. These were supplemented by Voluntary Aid Detachment nurses and General Aid workers along with the civilian medical practitioners and domestic staff who were drafted in.

As it happened, early preparations were timely and the events of August 1914 did not find Major Harrison and his team wanting.

Taking advantage of the August Bank Holiday, the 5th Northern General Hospital Unit was away at Netley training when Great Britain went to war. Immediately mobilised, the unit returned to

Leicester and took up its posting at the disused lunatic asylum on 5 August.

The nursing service, along with the army, had also been put on a war footing some time prior to 1914. In 1910, the matron of the Leicester Royal Infirmary, Miss Rogers, and members of the nursing staff had been issued with Territorial Forces Nursing Service badges and provisionally attached to the 5th Northern General Hospital. Miss Rogers in fact retired in 1912 and so it was her successor, Miss Clara Elizabeth Vincent, who, having assumed the mantle of honorary matron of the 5th Northern General Hospital was called upon, along with 91 other members of the Nursing Service, to staff the wards of the unit.

Throughout Great Britain, the Nursing Service had been well prepared. When war was declared the Service was able to call upon 46,791 Voluntary Aid Detachment members. This number comprised 40,018 British Red Cross Society nurses and 6,773 members of the St John Ambulance Service.[1]

As soon as the keys to the old asylum had been handed over to the military authorities, work was begun. Colonel A. V. Clarke, now the Assistant Director of Medical Services for the region, along with Mr S. Perkins Pick, an eminent local architect who had a wealth of experience in such projects, examined the situation and building work was put in hand.

A labour force, varying at any one time from 300 to 400 men, was brought in. Outbuildings, trees and the walls of enclosed exercise yards were quickly demolished. While the work was progressing, the Royal Army Medical Corps NCOs, and men, who at that point had no accommodation, slept under canvas on the hospital cricket ground.

By 31 August, barely four weeks after war had been declared, the main work had been completed. The RAMC [Royal Army Medical Corps] had four long, flat-roofed brick-built huts in which to live, an ablution block and latrines, a canteen and a barber's shop. Nurses and medical staff could be accom - modated in the main building along with all the paraphernalia of a working hospital. A catering kitchen ('every endeavour was made to serve an equally portioned, well-cooked and really hot meal to every man – the average cost per man was one shilling and six pence per day')[2], stores for groceries, clothing and linen were all within the main complex. Most important of all, there was bed space for 525 patients.

On 8 August 1914, Harrison was promoted to lieutenant-colonel, doubtless to give him the rank commensurate with the task which he had been allotted – an unenviable one.

Right from the planning stage it was apparent that this site, which was to be known as the Base Hospital, was only a starting point. A further ancillary hospital location nearby, on a similar scale to the asylum would have to be identified as a matter of some urgency.

From a peacetime staff of three officers and 43 other ranks Harrison had to conjure up a war establishment totalling 109 officers and men. In his own words: 'There was some difficulty in making up the numbers – a few of the RAMC were men who had done four days' training and then been discharged at the end of their engagement. The attraction of hospital work was not sufficiently exciting and I had to be satisfied with men of the National Reserve who had no idea of, and were never likely to become proficient in, the work of the RAMC. I had the greatest difficulty in getting hold of a dispenser and a good cook but eventually succeeded. The á la suite staff was up to strength, only one of whom – Capt R. Stamford – had ever seen service. As the hospital was further advanced, all the á la suite officers were called up and the names of other medical men in the borough put forward for commissions.'[3]

Throughout the war the transfer of trained doctors and nurses to active service was to plague Harrison. In nursing staff alone, of the 163 that he managed to recruit, a total of 73, plus 55 untrained nurses, were transferred to various overseas theatres of war.

Initially, the staff at the Base Hospital comprised: Administrator – Colonel Harrison; Registrar – Major R. W. Henry (who had been commissioned in 1908 along with Harrison); Quartermaster – Lieutenant G. Barfield; and 38 other ranks, some of whom had received only one day's training.

Miss Vincent took the post of principal matron (in readiness for the opening of the second hospital.)

---

1. Trained nurses who volunteered for service with the armed forces initially were sent to Haslar Naval Hospital at Gosport to await overseas posting.

2. Report by L. K. Harrison, Leicestershire Record Office.

3. Report by L. K. Harrison, Leicestershire Record Office.

Miss H. Hannath, – who at the time was the matron of the South Staffordshire General Hospital – having been mobilised on 10 August, was given the position of matron in charge of the Base Hospital.

Whilst the builders were still clearing their equipment, Base Hospital accepted its first patient on 1 September 1914. He was not alone for long; the following day the very first convoy of 127 wounded men arrived from the Western Front.

Having completed the initial setting up of the Base Hospital, Colonel Harrison could now move on to the next phase – identifying suitable hospitals and large houses in the county which could be used as auxiliary hospitals. By the end of October, provision had been made for accommodating patients at the Glen Parva Depot Hospital, the Leicester Royal Infirmary and Gilroes Hospital. The end of the year saw Desford Hall, Dalby Hall, Wistow Hall and Charnwood Forest Voluntary Aid Detachment added to the list.

Auxiliary hospitals were to prove tremendously important in relation to the care and treatment of patients. Some, such as the Leicester Royal Infirmary, were large fully-equipped hospitals capable of receiving convoys of wounded direct from disembarkation and performing major surgery; other established hospitals would handle less serious cases. At the other end of the scale of facilities were to be found the numerous country houses belonging to such people as Lady Beatty (wife of Admiral Sir David Beatty), of Brooksby Hall who generously gave over their homes and ensured that 'the men were provided with a particularly generous diet'.

By June 1915, in addition to those listed above, Wicklow Lodge at Melton, Lutterworth Voluntary Aid Detachment and Ullesthorpe Court, had been added to the list. With the arrival of autumn in September of that year, Colonel Harrison and his staff were responsible for the administration locally of 11 auxiliary hospitals. Harrison's responsibilities soon extended beyond Leicestershire. At the end of hostilities, in addition to the 5th Northern General Hospital, he had an involvement with some 60 auxiliary hospitals in Leicestershire, Nottingham-shire, Derbyshire, Staffordshire and Lincolnshire.

As a general rule, patients did not spend more than 60 days in an auxiliary hospital. An apparently sound principle, it enabled a steady turnover of men being rehabilitated and enabled the auxiliary hospitals in Leicestershire to deal with a total of 14,759 patients between October 1914 and September 1919 .

At the end of the 19th century, accommodation and conditions in the workhouse on Swain Street had reached an intolerable level. The Poor Law Guardians, responsible for the management of the establishment decided that the Poor Law Infirmary, at that time a part of the workhouse, should be removed to a more suitable location.

That location was a 62-acre site on the eastern outskirts of Leicester at the top of Gwendolen Road. Completed in 1905 at a cost of £79,575, the new North Evington Poor Law Infirmary could accommodate 512 patients.

In similar fashion to the Base Hospital, the North Evington Poor Law Infirmary was situated on high ground, far enough away from the town to avoid its pollution but near enough to be easily accessible for the delivery of supplies and for ambulances bringing in wounded. Whilst it was not so easy to reach from the town centre on foot, the tramcar service which ran along East Park Road dropped visitors at the bottom of Gwendolen Road within easy walking distance of the hospital. Standing at the top of a hill, in extensive grounds, the hospital would be an ideal place to tend and mend the wounded men who were now beginning to flood in from the Front. A prime consideration was that, as in the case of the Base Hospital, the present owners, the Poor Law Guardians, were prepared to relinquish tenancy for the duration of the war. Once settled, the handover took place on 16 March 1915.

Raising the desired occupancy at Gwendolen Road from an existing 550 to 623 beds was easily arranged. Nurses were accommodated in the main building and the Medical Superintendent's house. Night nurses were put in the maternity block while the RAMC men slept under canvas. The hospital was renamed the North Evington War Hospital.

Under the command of Captain W. M. Holmes, the hospital was staffed throughout by RAMC officers and men transferred from the Base Hospital, and by Territorial Force nurses. The nursing staff was augmented by the recruitment of local women who were quickly trained up by Miss Vincent. Other aspects, such as clerical and domestic work were covered by the employment of civilian workers. Altogether, the work force initially numbered 96 Royal Army Medical Corps and 14 civilians. Miss L.

Barrow was appointed matron, Lieutenant (later Captain), Hedley, quartermaster.

Although the hospital boasted its own laundry (the lack of which, in the early stages caused the Base Hospital some difficulties), other amenities needed to be put in hand quickly.

Quarters needed to be erected for the RAMC personnel. Even though the better weather was approaching, it was undesirable for them to be sleeping in tents in the hospital grounds. The large mortuary was converted into an ablution block and latrines were provided.

On 9 May 1915, the North Evington War Hospital received its first 100 patients who were transferred by motor ambulances from the Base Hospital. Due to a delay in the completion of an operating theatre and an X-Ray room, it was to be another month before, on 18 June, convoys could be accepted directly from the railhead into the hospital.

Further building work was necessary after the hospital was opened. A Royal Army Medical Corps canteen, a chapel, a dining room and a pack store were needed.

Throughout the coming months more accommodation was created. Day rooms were opened up for use as wards, beds were put out on verandas and two marquees were given over to scabies cases. In April 1918 the addition of ten large marquees with wooden floors brought patient accommodation on the site to its wartime maximum of 1,010.

Other responsibilities quickly devolved upon the medical staff. Shortly after the hospital became functional it was designated the 'Morning Sick Reporting Centre' for the region and also undertook the duty of inoculating and vaccinating personnel from local military units. An especially important function of the North Evington War Hospital was its role as the Ophthalmic Unit for the southern part of the Northern Command Area. At the height of the war the Massage Department, treating men recuperating from wounds, was dealing with approximately 200 cases per week. One of the more time consuming chores was the enforced absence from the wards of medical officers travelling to the XIIth Regimental Depot, Glen Parva Barracks, in order to examine army recruits.

At the Base Hospital, construction work of various sorts continued well into the war.

A pack store, essential to any military establishment receiving casualties direct from a theatre of war, was built in the confines of the main building. When a convoy of wounded was admitted, each soldier's uniform and kit was taken from him and fed into the sorting room. From here all items were examined in what was known as the 'dirty room', then passed through the 'Manilove Alliott Steam Disinfector' and out at the other end into the 'clean room' to be returned to the owner in due course. The soldier's backpack, ready for his return to duty on discharge from the hospital, was tagged and retained in the pack store. After much trial and error, by January 1916 the pack store was capable of holding 2,000 packs at any one time.

Meanwhile other matters still needed to be taken care of. Among the buildings yet to be completed were a dispensary, pathology laboratory, recreation hall, chapel, workshops, and all the other requisites of a military hospital.

On 26 March 1915, Messrs Herbert & Son, of Leicester were given a contract valued at £8,350 to build a wing of open-air wards on the south side of the complex. These were to take the form of five long, flat-roofed, single-storey brick structures, each accommodating 51 beds and divided down the middle by a central corridor. The builders completed the work in a total of eight weeks, which was two weeks ahead of schedule and thus earned for the company the princely bonus of £150.

Fitted along the entire length of one wall of each ward were a series of opening canvas screens, not dissimilar to the sun blinds found shading shop windows. These were perceived to be one of the most modern innovations in hospital planning in the country at that time. Whilst being nicely suited to the approaching spring and summer weather, the new wards were to prove unpopular with both staff and patients alike during the winter months, when the single fireplace provided in each, which was intended to heat the ward, proved to be totally inadequate. Having identified the problem the matter was quickly addressed by the residents of the borough who through various donations purchased three slow combustion stoves for each ward.

The original plan of 5th Northern General Hospital, upon which the illustration (overleaf) is based, does not show the location of an operating theatre although one definitely existed on the site.

During December 1915, the War Office, in an effort to standardise procedures and to establish some sort of central control over its budgets, issued

5th Northern General Hospital

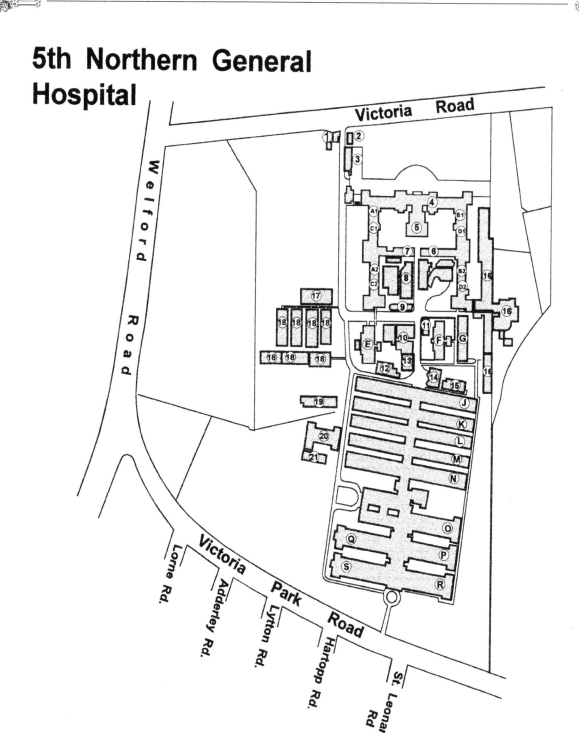

1 Main Entrance & Guard Room
2 Mortuary & Post Mortem Room
3 Garage
4 Administration Block
5 Kitchen & Dining Room
6 Quartermaster's Store
7 Surgery
8 Pack Store
9 Chapel
10 Stores
11 Quartemaster's Office

12 Electrical & Massage
13 Dispensary
14 Observation Wards
15 Pathology Laboratory
16 Nurses Quarters
17 Canteen / Ablutions
18 Royal Army Medical Corps
19 YMCA Hut
20 Recreation Hall
21 Rotary Workshop

A - S = Wards

Based on plan prepared by
Pick Everard & Keay
August 1919

an instruction that the granting of private contracts was to cease and all building work was to be referred through the Barrack Construction Department. This effectively meant an end to the tendering for contracts by local companies.

In March 1916, at the end of the winter, work was begun on five more wards with a view to increasing the hospital's capacity by a further 505 beds. Authorised under the new controls, these were to be wooden structures erected by the Lincoln firm of Thornhills. At the same time, Thornhills were also contracted to build an operating theatre, an X-Ray Department and a large dining hall.

During that year an appeal for funds was launched through the workers in local factories with a view to providing ten spinal carriages, costing £8 8s 0d each for use in the hospital grounds and in the town. Seven local factories in Leicester quickly raised the money for the purchase of nine carriages and three ward chairs. Thereafter the sight of soldiers dressed in their blue hospital suits pushing immobile comrades through the streets of the borough became commonplace.

Base Hospital entered its final building phase in the summer of 1917. Casualties were pouring into the unit in ever increasing numbers and space was at a premium. When convoys of wounded exceeded the number of beds available, casualties were put on mattresses on the hospital floors or taken direct to auxiliary hospitals. The long-suffering Royal Army Medical Corps were evicted from their quarters and put back under canvas while their barracks were converted into wards to accommodate a further 160 light casualties. By now, the total population of the Base Hospital site including, patients, RAMC personnel, medical staff and nurses, was in the region of 2,000. In spite of the sergeants being returned to their original barracks, space was at such a premium that the remainder of the RAMC were billeted out in local homes. (This was often a mutually satisfactory arrangement. For their part the soldiers had the benefit of home comforts, while the householder received a billeting allowance which, although it varied from place to place, was in the region of 9d per day per man. Householders who took several men in could earn up to 21s a week at a time when an average week's rent was in the region of 12s.)

Although the war was coming to an end during 1917, the casualties were not. Increased activity in France meant more men to be cared for at home. The convoys continued, the bed space decreased. November and December of 1917 saw Colonel Harrison examining local hotel accommodation and making arrangements with the police for finding any available billets where patients could be lodged. In April 1918 he seriously considered the use of the Edward Wood Hall on London Road as an annexe to the Base Hospital. Unable to come to an agreement with the Management Committee of the hall, the idea was abandoned.

During the late summer of 1918, Louis Harrison negotiated with the Poor Law Guardians the use of part of the workhouse for what was to be the last of the auxiliary hospitals to be established in the county. In a last-ditch effort to find premises, the Swain Street Auxiliary Hospital opened on 21 July 1918. The experiment was short-lived.

The effect upon injured men, who had spent long periods of time living and fighting in the appalling conditions of trench warfare on the Western Front, now finding themselves consigned upon their return to a workhouse can be well imagined. On 11 December 1918, after only a few months and despite the fact that the other auxiliaries in the county were treating cases well into 1919, the hospital closed its doors. Although 378 patients had been lodged there (the total number of beds was 200), one has to ask if the timing, just before their first Christmas at home was not apposite.

After the signing of the Armistice, the 5th Northern General Hospital Unit began to wind down. The unit accepted its last convoy of casualties on 8 June 1919. During the period since September 1914, a total of 425 convoys bringing in 60,487 casualties had been dealt with by the hospital and its auxiliaries. Along with patients from other sources, a total of 74,652 patients had passed through the North Evington and Base Hospitals – and 7,808 operations had been performed. Remarkably, in view of the nature of its intake, during the four years only 514 patients died. Many different nationalities came through the hospital – officers and men of the British Expeditionary Force, Canadians, Australians, New Zealanders, Belgians and even a small number (59) of prisoners-of-war.

In December 1918, on the instructions of the War Office, 500 beds were made available within the unit in order that the 5th Northern General could be used as a dispersal centre for men being demobilised. Thereafter, up to 120 men per day were being discharged through the hospital. When the demobilisation section was closed down in May 1919, some 3,875 men had received their discharge through the unit. The Base Hospital closed down on 9 September 1919.

An unfortunate issue was to mar the closure of the North Evington War Hospital. In early May 1919 demobilisation of the hospital personnel was commenced and the discharge or transfer to other hospitals of the last of the patients finalised. By 29 May, six months after the signing of the Armistice, almost all the staff had been released and the 50 remaining patients transferred to the Base Hospital. During June and July all medical and surgical equipment, clothing, provisions and other impedimenta were removed to the Base Hospital or returned to the Base Medical Stores at York. The keys to the premises were returned to the Poor Law Guardians on 8 August 1919. There was, however, a deal of equipment, no longer required by the military, still on the site pending its sale by auction. In order to administer this disposal, Captain Hedley (who was now quartermaster and had taken over responsibility since the demobilisation of Captain Holmes) remained on the site. The Poor Law Guardians, who were now in the process of re-equipping the premises as a civilian hospital, were quite amenable to this. By virtue of a local agreement they had been allowed to chose such items as they wished *in situ*, which would be reserved for an agreed sum of £4,500 and set aside from the auction. Doubtless, to all concerned this was a most reasonable gesture of good will in view of the fact that the military had been allowed use of the premises since 1915.

On 1 September 1919 the first sale by auction of equipment realised £2,121 8s 5d. Ten days later, on 11 September, the Controller of the Dispersal Board declared that the items selected by the Guardians were undervalued and must be put up for sale in a second auction. The reaction of the Poor Law Guardians was predictable. They refused to allow the proposed auction to take place on their newly-regained premises and Captain Hedley was required to 'remove his office and records' The equipment was taken to the Junior Training Hall where ironically the subsequent sale by auction realised £3,666 – a deal less than the previously agreed figure.

The 5th Northern General Hospital provided a unique and efficient service from the first week of the war until well after the cessation of hostilities. Harrison – promoted to brevet-colonel on 3 June 1917 – and his staff had carried out their duties efficiently and at times under difficult circumstances. Continuous pressure to find more bed space, combined with a constant drain on trained medical and nursing staff, was a constant worry. Overall, 45 military officers from the rank of lieutenant, up to colonel had served with the 5th Northern General Hospital during the four years. Many of them were lost to the hospital when they were posted overseas to places as far apart as France, Egypt and India. Their individual fields of expertise had been various: general practitioner, surgeon, anaesthetist, pathologist, ophthalmologist, neurologist, aurist and radiographer. As military men were taken away for active duty, so Colonel Harrison had to rely more upon the skills of local medical men drafted in. Royal Army Medical Corps and trained Territorial Force nurses were also constantly being taken away from the unit for active duty. This resulted in a stream of local recruits being brought in to be trained as RAMC replacements. Newly-enlisted RAMC personnel from other areas arrived in order to receive training prior to being posted on active service. Towards the latter part of the war, the unit also undertook the training of officers of the American Expeditionary Force who were en route to France. Between June and October of 1917, five such doctors – all lieutenants – spent between two and eight months attached to the hospital.

At the height of its activities the staff of the 5th Northern General Hospital comprised: 1 administrator (Base Hospital); 1 registrar (Base Hospital); 1 officer-in-charge North Evington War Hospital; 3 quartermasters; 28 á la suite officers; 6 civilian medical practitioners; 1 principal matron; 1 matron (Base Hospital); 1 matron (North Evington War Hospital); 130 sisters and trained staff of the Territorial Nursing Service; 202 Nursing Voluntary Aid Detachment members; 23 masseuse; 271 NCOs and men of the Royal Army Medical Corps. To these must be added the large and varying numbers of civilians employed as domestic and clerical staff.

Conveyance of the wounded from disembarkation at the Midland Railway Station to their dispersal at the various hospitals was also no mean logistical feat. Since the 1800s, Leicester's fire brigade had been responsible for maintaining some form of ambulance service within the town. (A situation which was to prevail until the Second World War, when in 1941 the responsibility passed to the local authority.) In 1914, along with its other duties the Leicester Borough fire brigade could not in time of war also be expected to undertake such a monumental task as the distribution of military casualties to hospitals throughout the county.

This particular responsibility fell not to the hospital unit, but to the civilian authority in the form of Arthur William Faire, the County Director of Voluntary Aid Detachments – commonly known as the VAD. Throughout the war he organised not only the transporting of casualties but also fund raising and charity events to eke out the available budgets in order to provide better ambulance facilities.

Arthur Faire organised the three Voluntary Aid Detachments in the borough which were under his control to create an efficient transport service. (Later, as convoys increased, he was to raise a further two detachments to assist with the task.) Despite the loss of men to the army, Faire managed to keep upwards of 120 men on his active list.

Convoys arrived by rail at the Midland Railway Station at all times of the day and night, so a 'call-out system' was essential. A three-tier procedure was arrived at.

1st During the day time a Volunteer was contacted at his place of work.

2nd Between 6pm and 10pm a 'Calling Man', responsible for a particular area was sent round to individuals homes to alert them.

3rd During the night, owners of private motor cars were responsible for collecting men in their designated area.

When the first convoy of wounded arriving from Southampton completed its six-hour journey, the awaiting transport consisted of three motor vans fitted out to take stretchers, and a large number of private motor cars. As soon as he could organise things better, Faire was able, through fund raising, to provide more suitable transport, his eventual fleet totalling 19 motor ambulances and cars.

The work involved in acquiring vehicles for purposes such as ambulances or fire fighting in this period was far more complex than may be thought. In a climate where the primary form of locomotion was still the horse, choice of motor vehicle

manufacturer was limited, as was availability. Many of the existing vehicle manufacturers were firmly contracted to the production of cars and lorries for military purposes, which in effect meant for use in theatres of war. The problem was often solved by purchasing second-hand, or through owners lending their personal vehicles for the duration.

In the case of the VAD, the majority of motor ambulances were in fact purchased outright. However, in some cases the vehicle chassis was loaned and an ambulance body fitted to it. From existing photographs it can be seen that the end result was a variety of open-cabbed vehicles with a closed rear. These were similar in all respects to the old-fashioned delivery vans used before and between the wars by butchers and bakers. The upkeep of the transport service, including costs for petrol, oil, tyres, repairs and spare parts, was borne by the Voluntary Aid Detachments Transport Fund. The vehicles, not unnaturally, were garaged and maintained at the Base Hospital where a motor mechanic was employed full time. (This joint arrangement, between the hospital authorities and the VAD, potentially fraught with difficulties, appears in practice to have presented few problems whatsoever to those operating the system.)

A room was given by the Post Office near to the Midland Railway Station for the storage of stretchers, pillows and rugs and for the accommodation of Voluntary Aid drivers awaiting the incoming convoy trains which due to delays en route were often long overdue in arriving.

With each convoy bringing in an average of just over 140 casualties, disembarking could be a protracted and complicated business. Incoming convoy trains arrived at the parcel traffic platform in order to allow the unloading of their cargo, often a lengthy affair, to be conducted without the disruption of other services. A difficulty with this arrangement which had to be overcome was the fact that the platform was only 70 yards long and, as such, fell short of the length of the train. To cope with this, two moveable sections measuring 15ft by 10ft and raised 5ft from the ground were constructed and placed alongside the carriages. This arrangement proved particularly effective for the unloading of immobile men who had travelled in cots.

In addition to their work in transferring wounded to the 5th Northern General Hospital from the railway station, the Voluntary Aid Detachment drivers also conveyed patients to and from the auxiliary hospitals around the county. This was often a demanding task such as during the influenza epidemic which hit the country in 1918, especially in the weeks before Christmas when as many as 20 cases a day were being admitted to hospitals.

By the autumn of 1917, the manpower situation nationally had become critical. Such was the need for replacements on the Western Front that throughout the country the remaining able-bodied men were being drafted for active service. Those of Colonel Harrison's Royal Army Medical Corps who could drive had been transferred to the British Expeditionary Force in France. Every fit, adult male was earmarked for other things and Arthur Faire needed to look elsewhere for his drivers. A simple and effective *quid pro quo* was negotiated. In exchange for the use of two of Faire's valuable motor cars, the Army Service Corps (Motor Transport), was prepared to supply him on a regular basis with 'lady drivers'. Thereafter the two cars became a familiar, if uncommon sight in and around the town and county, driven by female ASC personnel.

The work of the auxiliary hospitals cannot be over-emphasised. Of the main hospitals serving the town, Gilroes alone gave 144 beds over to military wards and handled a total of 4,260 patients.

Immediately war was declared in August 1914, the Management Committee of the Royal Infirmary agreed to convert its Out-patients' Department into a 50-bed military ward. Members of the resident staff, nurses and doctors, were called up. Honorary staff were recalled from retirement to work either at the Infirmary or on the staff of the 5th Northern General Hospital.

One of those recalled was Charles John Bond who had retired from practice in 1913. He was given the rank of a colonel in the Territorial Force and made honorary consulting surgeon to the Northern General Region. Military wards at the hospital under the command of Major Blakesley were to include Oliver, Odanes and Rogers. When the military wards at the Royal Infirmary were finally closed on 15 February 1919, they had dealt with 2,790 cases.

Whilst the military were responsible for the medical care and well-being of the wounded men who were flooding into the borough, it was the citizens of Leicester who attended to their other needs.

It was obvious from the outset that a hospital the size of the 5th Northern General, accommodating several hundred patients, many of them long-term, was going to require more than medical supplies and provisions. Men subjected to extended periods of enforced inactivity were going to need those little extras which would make life bearable. On 10 August 1914, under the chairmanship of Councillor Charles Squire, a group of local councillors and businessmen formed the Leicester War Hospital Games Committee. This was, from its inception, to be one of the most important voluntary organisations the borough was to see during the war.

The initial remit of the committee was to ensure the provision of literature and games for the Base Hospital, this was to quickly extend to all areas of welfare for those hospitalised locally and throughout the entire eastern counties, and the supply of parcels to prisoners-of-war. By the end of September 1915 the committee was directly responsible for the needs of all the auxiliary hospitals locally accommodating over 2,000 patients, the Trinity Hospital recreation room, and the Voluntary Aid Detachment rest rooms for wounded soldiers.

Various committee members undertook specific duties. The distribution of cigarettes and tobacco, games and literature at the North Evington Hospital was the responsibility of Mr W. T. Mason of Waterloo Street. Supervision of gramophones was the job of Mr Williams of 101 Bartholemew Street. Treasurer was Mr C. V. Kirby of the Central Library and assistant secretary and storekeeper was Mr T. H. Smith, also of the Central Library.

During the opening months of the war, tobacco and cigarettes were supplied by utilising local tobacconists shops as the collecting points for gifts. This soon became inadequate. Ramsay MacDonald raised the matter at Westminster, resulting in the excise duties on all donated tobacco, cigarettes, tea, coffee and cocoa to accredited War Hospitals and Voluntary Aid Detachment hospitals throughout the country being waived. The existing collection process – initiated by Mr M. Moody, a tobacconist, of Wharf Street – was continued due to the fact that cigarettes and tobacco placed in Voluntary Aid rest rooms, and given out to the wounded soldiers at the railway station when they first arrived on the convoy trains, did not come within the exemption.

Collecting boxes, supplied by J. H. Taylor & Co, were for some time to be seen in tobacconist shops and hotel lobbies. However, by late 1917 it was decided to end the scheme – not from any lack of goodwill but owing to the large increases in customs duty and to general pressures on the public. During the three years that the scheme operated, 115,533 cigarettes, 1,228 ounces of tobacco, 219 cigars and 38 pipes were collected.

To give effect to the excise duty concession nationally, a number of war hospitals duty-free depots were opened in various parts of the country.

On 1 July 1915 one such bonded warehouse depot in Leicester was opened under licence from the Customs and Excise at the Central Municipal Library in Bishop Street. Under the supervision of Mr T. H. Smith, this was to become the focal point of the committee's activities. In the first three months of its existence the warehouse distributed 529 lbs of tobacco and 509,000 cigarettes.

By the end of the war, including the Leicestershire area the depot was clearing goods to 66 war hospitals as far afield as Boston, Bourne, Grantham, Spalding, Worksop, West Bridgford, Mansfield and Nottingham.

During the early period of its existence the War Hospital Games Committee was presented with an Herculean task. With little or no funding they had to rely upon the generosity of the local populace. At a time that was remarkable for the fervour with which people viewed the newly-opened conflict, the response was still quite astounding.

In the first year the citizens of Leicester donated 67,000 sheets of writing paper and envelopes, 20,000 postcards, 16,567 books, magazines and periodicals, 2,049 gramophone records, 1,350 packs of playing cards, 164 table games, 70 pictures, 20 garden chairs, 17 gramophones, 8 pianos plus sheet music, 4 gross of pencils, 4 sets of skittles, 3 billiard tables, 3 bookcases, 1 lawn tent, 1 croquet set, and an 'American Organ'.

Individual contributors were no less generous. Mr Watson, the managing director of Ibstock Collieries, loaned 'a handsome Pathephone Home Cinema'. Mr G. W. Taylor gave 100 boxes to be located throughout the borough, resulting in the collection of 99,291 cigarettes, 251 cigars, 42 pipes and tobacco pouches, 31lbs of tobacco and 15lbs of chocolate. Councillor Baker donated 25,000 cigarettes and 70lbs of tobacco.

Organisations played their part. John Player & Co of Nottingham gave 6,000 cigarettes and 20lbs of tobacco and the London-based organisation 'Smokes, Soldiers and Sailors', was to supply 25lbs of tobacco every fortnight throughout the war.

An invaluable contribution by the Leicester Newsagents' Association, led by Mr Sidwell and the owners of the *Leicester Daily Post*, *Leicester Daily Mail* and the *Leicester Daily Mercury*, was the supply each day of newspapers at wholesale price to the hospitals. By the middle of 1916 some 260 morning, and 276 evening papers to the wholesale value of 5s per day were being supplied to the main hospitals – the Base Hospital, North Evington War Hospital, Royal Infirmary and Gilroes. In the 15 months prior to 30 June 1916 the Newsagents' Association supplied 5,808 penny newspapers and 53,076 halfpenny newspapers. Whilst it was not practicable for them to supply all the papers needed, their efforts saved the committee large amounts of badly needed cash.

The newspaper proprietors had to withdraw from this arrangement at the end of February 1916 due to a national decision of the Newspaper Owners' Federation which had been forced upon them by the shortage of newspaper and pulp imports. As a gesture of their regret, Messrs F. Hewitt & Son Ltd (publishers of the *Leicester Daily Mercury*), and the Leicester Constitutional Newspaper Company, made donations to the committee of £20 and £10 respectively.

Following the 'vast extension to the hospital' [5th Northern General], the new Mayor, Jonathan North, raised a fund of nearly £220 for equipping the new hospital wards with gramophones, games and newspapers. The 1915 Alexandra Day Collection realised £861 which was put to the purchase of much-needed things such as extra gramophones, needles and records, sets of dominoes and board games, ash trays and clay pipes, quoits and skittles, and dozens of other sundry items needed to equip the hospital wards.

During its first year the committee paid out a total of £267 13s 7d. Additionally it was able to send 550 packs of playing cards and 76lbs of cigarettes and tobacco to local men serving in Kitchener's Army and to donate £150 to Lieutenant-Colonel Harrison in order for him to organise the Christmas festivities at the hospital. Nothing was wasted – even the magazines which had been donated were passed on from the hospital to the navy for 'the men on the minesweepers'.

1916 saw the great battles of the Somme offensive and the resultant casualties pouring into the 5th Northern General and its auxiliary hospitals. Demands upon the bonded warehouse, under the management of Mr Smith became more intense. To Leicestershire hospitals alone he supplied 1,912,000 cigarettes and over a ton of tobacco.

Additionally, through the Leicester and Leicestershire Prisoners of War Fund he cleared nearly a ton of tea, one and a quarter tons of sugar, over a quarter of a ton of tobacco, and 300,000 cigarettes. To the men who had been captured on the Western Front and were being held in prison camps in Germany and to those who were prisoners of the Turks, working on the infamous Baghdad railway, these parcels were to become a lifeline.

Each hospital patient was entitled to 40 cigarettes or an equivalent amount of tobacco per week. From 1916 until almost the end of the war the committee were in fact only able to supply each man with a ration of 30 cigarettes or two ounces of tobacco. The frustrations of the chore are apparent in this statement made by the committee in its Annual Report for that year: 'It is difficult for anyone outside of the committee to realise the actual work involved in the distribution of tobacco and cigarettes. To comply with Customs and Excise Regulations, quantities have to be checked and entered in bulk, and detail, and each ward has its separate parcel with the proper quantities for patients in it. To comply with the Excise Regulations all consignments have to be sent to the CO of the hospital, whose receipts go direct to the Board of Customs and Excise. Thus every cigarette and ounce of tobacco is accounted for while the Depot books are carefully examined once a month by the Surveyor of Customs and Excise.'

In an effort to relieve some of the pressure experienced by the depot manager, a system was arrived at whereby, in the smaller hospitals distri - bution was the responsibility of the matron and at the Base Hospital and North Evington War Hospital the CO directly undertook the task.

Every effort was made with the limited resources available to make Christmas a special event. In 1916 it was celebrated by giving to every patient a Christ - mas issue of either, two ounces of Players Navy Cut De-Luxe tobacco, or a packet of 20 Medium Navy

Cut cigarettes. A total of 500 tins of tobacco plus 40,000 cigarettes were distributed at a cost to the committee of £30. On Christmas afternoon, by kind permission of the Picture House Cinema, Granby Street (which in its advertisements boasted 'orchestral music'), Mr Zacharewitsch, 'the great Russian violinist', gave a performance in the Recreation Hall at the Base Hospital. For the 1917 festivities, 3,000 packets of Army Club Cigarettes each containing a seasonal greetings card were distributed.

As the winter of 1916-17 wore on, the need for indoor entertainments increased. In February 1917 Mr W. E. Tyler loaned his Pathescope Drawing Room Cinema along with his film library subscription. Having first been personally checked by Leicester's chief fire officer and found to be safe, it was passed into the hands of Captain the Reverend W. Matthews and his assistants who ensured that it progressed around the wards. (Despite strenuous efforts, the committee was unable to hire or purchase another of these machines and, along with the one loaned by Mr Watson in 1914, this latest addition was a great attraction.)

By 1917 approximately 3,500 relatives and friends a week were arriving at the Base Hospital and some sort of system was required to regulate the huge flow of visitors turning up at the gates. The committee came up with a scheme to control the situation. In October 1915 each soldier who wished to receive a visitor, would fill out a postcard with the person's details and date of the proposed visit. This was duly checked by the hospital administration staff against the numbers authorised for that date. If the visit was approved, the card would be posted off to the prospective visitor, who on the appointed day would arrive at the hospital gate, present the card to the sentry on duty and be admitted.

Financial crisis dogged the committee through - out. Despite fund-raising events such as the Alex - andra Day collections, flag days and a collection by Lady Beatty, taken up among the local hunting community (which raised the not inconsiderable sum of £175 18s 6d), the situation was desperate.

Relying on voluntary support the committee was totally dependent upon individual donors. The money came from sources such as the workers at Messrs M. Wright & Sons, Quorn Mills, who collected through their Employees' War Fund £145, down to the single gifts from such people as Nurse

Garbett who gave 2s 6d. (Workers in Leicester, supported by the Leicester Trades Council, raised £105 5s 11d.)

In September 1917, now known because of its connections on a county-wide basis as the War Hospitals Committee, the group was forced to approach the Alexandra Collections Committee for help. They were given an advance of £1,000 in anticipation of the collections for 1917-18. The Annual Report for 1917 indicates the degree of the problem: 'The outlook is worrying. The fact must be impressed upon the public that there are now over 3,000 patients to keep supplied with tobacco, cigarettes, daily newspapers and other comforts and the cost is £50 per week. During the last year 87 Red Cross trains reached Leicester conveying 14,437 men to local hospitals making a total of 218 trains and 33,722 patients from overseas to this centre since the outbreak of war.'

Although a donation of £20 was sent to the committee in the early part of the year by the British Isles Relief Society of Trenton New Jersey in the USA, overseas donations were now beginning to dry up. Two ex-patriot Englishmen, Mr George Astill of Easthampton, Massachusetts, and his son, William Astill of Providence, Rhode Island, who had been living in the United States for 35 years and had, since the beginning of the war, sent regular cheques to the committee to the value of £93, wrote to the chairman to say that 'regrettably we can no longer help out'.

Since the entry of America into the war earlier in 1917, they would have to contribute to the needs of 'America's own boys'.

By November 1917, all the local hospitals were practically full and the cost to the committee of tobacco and cigarettes alone was £35 a week. New hospital wards which needed equipping were being opened at an alarming rate. At the Base Hospital alone, five new wards were opened in the early autumn, increasing the number of beds by 500. Four Riley miniature billiard tables were bought for £29 – fortunately the maintenance of them was undertaken by the West End Association. Each of the wards had to be supplied with a gramophone costing £15 and records, and W. H. Russell & Son of London Road gifted one to the officers' ward. Meanwhile, replacement board games were becoming difficult to obtain. When the new soldiers' recreation room, provided by J. A. Corah of Oadby, was opened on St Valentines Day 1917, it was the War Hospital Games Committee who supplied it with books and magazines.

Various forms of assistance still came from a generous township. Miss Pearson of the Gable House, Stoughton, and Mr Bennett of De Montfort Street, continued to supply songs and sheet music to the hospital, and the Imperial Typewriter Company in King Street helped out by undertaking considerable quantities of typing and multiple copying free of charge. Victoria Road School donated £13 17s 6d, this being one-third of its Harvest Festival proceeds.

Organisations and local business played their part to the best of their ability. The fire brigade delivered the tobacco rations to each of the hospitals until shortage of petrol supplies forced them to withdraw the service. Oswald Stoll opened up the Palace Theatre during the winter of 1917-18 for the performance of a Sunday charity concert by the Wounded Soldiers Band of the Military Ortho - paedic Hospital, Shepherds Bush. (As with any other such form of entertainment at the time, the express permission of the Watch Committee was required for performances held on a Sunday.)

The closing year of the war was no less difficult. In April of 1918, due to fears of increased casualties resulting from the German spring offensive, the 5th Northern General Hospital was pressured even further. More plans were made for extending its capacity along with all the financial implications for the beleaguered War Hospital Committee. An appeal on their behalf for £5,000 was made throughout the county. By July the needs of the Leicester and Leicestershire Prisoners of War Fund had also become urgent in the extreme and the appeal was closed at £2,750. Yet again, two of their most stalwart supporters, the Alexandra Day Committee and Oswald Stoll, had stepped in with help, the former with cash and the latter with the use of his theatre for a special charity matinée.

In fact the influx from the Western Front was not as great as had been feared. The aggregate of casualties for the last week in April was 2,876. After this the numbers reduced during the first week in July to 1,638 and did not again pass the 2,000 level until the last week in August 1918. In the final week of September the committee was distributing tobacco rations to a total of 2,767 men.

Following the signing of the Armistice things

became much easier, although patients continued to be treated by the 5th Northern General hospital well into 1919.

During the peace festivities in June 1919, 850 patients who were still under the care of the Base Hospital and Wistow Hall, along with discharged soldiers from the Leicester Frith Home of Recovery, were entertained to tea with the Mayor at the Junior Training Hall, in a joint venture organised by the War Hospitals Committee and the Leicestershire Automobile Club, members of which had rendered notable service in the transporting of casualties from the convoy trains. Some 500 of them were first taken out for a motor car ride into the country, while others were allowed free entry into the Leicester Agricultural Show at the County Cricket Ground. The total expenditure for the day of £126 was met by the committee.

When at the end of September 1919 the affairs of the committee were wound up, having given a final gift of £50 to the Ministry of Pensions Hospital to clear its accounts, the work of its members was eventually completed. During the four years since August 1914, the War Hospitals Committee had ensured a constant supply of cigarettes, newspapers and magazines, books and games, and innumerable other small necessities to the wounded men from all branches of the British and Allied forces who had been sent to Leicester for hospitalization.

Throughout its existence, all those involved with the work of the committee gave their time and efforts freely.

Dealing with the wounded at the Front, the officers and men of the 2/2 North Midland Field Ambulance, of which, the Leicestershire section was one of the first to be sent to France in 1914. Seen here outside of the asylum at St Andrea, near to Lille in 1918.

After the first gas attacks by the Germans at Ypres in 1915 it was felt that those who were returned to Britain for treatment in local hospitals, such as here at the Leicester Royal Infirmary would benefit from fresh air and rest.

Arthur Faire's fleet of VAD Ambulances drawn up outside of the 5th Northern General Hospital.

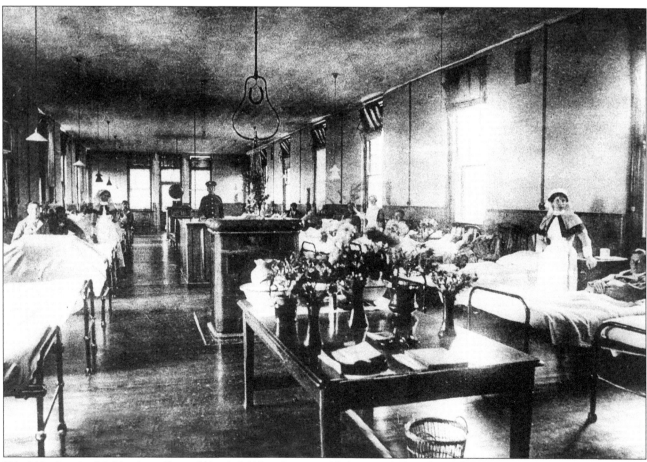

Ward No 4 at the 5th Northern General Hospital. Although a very old photograph the effects of using gas lighting would contribute to the darkening of ceilings and upper walls.

These open air wards at the 5th Northern General Hospital with adjustable shutters were considered to be a great innovation when they were first installed.

Cool in summer but extremely cold in the winter, local citizens contributed to buy slow combustion stoves to heat these open air wards at the 5th Northern General Hospital during the bad weather.

Meals on wheels 1915 style. This medical orderly is about to commence his rounds with hot meals to the wards at 5th Northern General Hospital.

Covered walkways connected the open air wards at the 5th Northern General Hospital. In much later years, these buildings would become familiar to generations of Wyggeston schoolboys as classrooms.

Men of the Royal Army Medical Corps about to move an immobile patient by trolley to another ward.

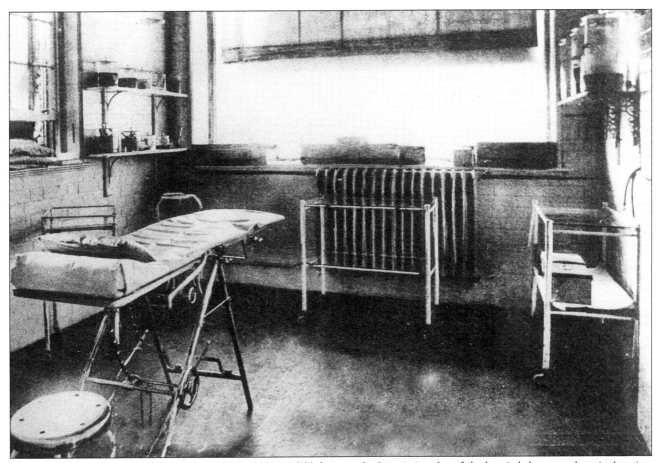

The operating theatre at the 5th Northern General Hospital. Unfortunately, the existing plan of the hospital, does not show its location within the hospital complex.

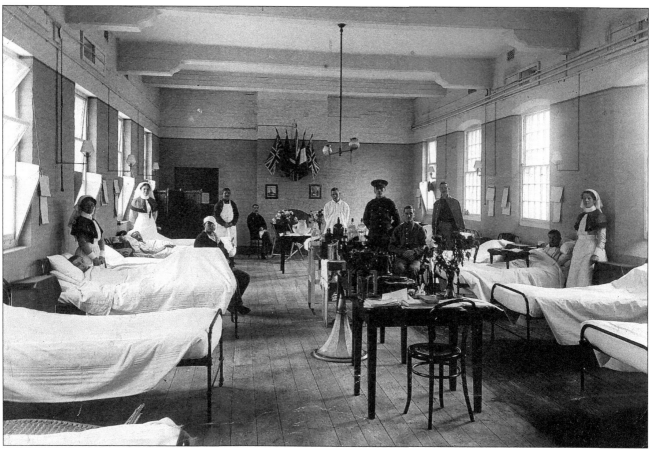

The officers' ward at the 5th Northern General Hospital around 1916.

The recreation hall at the 5th Northern General Hospital.

Waiting near to the church building at the 5th Northern General Hospital this group of men are probably awaiting transfer in the nearby ambulance to an auxiliary hospital for convalescence.

Such was the volume of visitors to 5th Northern General Hospital (by 1917, the figure had reached 3,500 a week) that passes were issued to friends and relatives. The pass was then presented to the sentry on the gate in Victoria Road (in later years University Road) in order to gain entry.

A summer's afternoon in the grounds of the 5th Northern General Hospital.

Originally the Poor Law Hospital administered by the Poor law Guardians, the North Evington War Hospital served from early in 1915 as a part of the 5th Northern General Hospital. Seen here is the main entrance and administration offices. In later years the site became Leicester General Hospital.

A broad view of the front aspect of the North Evington War Hospital. The outside balconies and stairways popular at the time are clearly visible.

A group of soldiers and nurses outside of Wards 1 & 2 of the North Evington War Hospital.

Taking a break from ward duty, these Royal Army Medical Corps men and their corporal pictured with one of the hospital ambulances.

Soldiers waiting for visitors outside of the Lodge to the North Evington War Hospital at the top of Gwendolen Road.

Volunteerism

THROUGHOUT the four years of the Great War the one ever-present concept was that of the volunteer.

While other major powers guarded their interests with conscript armies, Great Britain chose to put its faith in an army of volunteers, under the illusion that it was preferable to rely upon a small force of professionals rather than a large one drawn from the population in general. There has been much discussion surrounding this subject over the years. On the one hand, a substantial standing army, with the potential of an even more substantial reserve gives a nation considerable security. On the other hand, huge numbers of men trained in military skills can pose a grave threat to a government in time of civil disquiet. Irrespective of from which angle the commentator chooses to approach, the inescapable conclusion must be that in the event of a major conflict a small army, with no wartime reserve confers extreme weakness upon the country which it protects. Such was the position of Great Britain in 1914. Since the defeat of Napoleon Bonaparte 100 years previously, the British Army had essentially been responsible for the policing of the interests of the Empire abroad. Certainly its most recent experience of conflict against organised and resourceful resistance – the South African War of 1899-1902 – had not been a resounding success. The British policy of primary reliance upon naval power had led to the maintenance of an army which was sufficient only for her internal needs.

Where conscription prevailed and every eligible male was required to serve in one capacity or another, then inevitably an homogenous cadre of men with common experience was created.

In other words, conscription ensured, albeit unintentionally, that an army benefited from the fact that it encompassed all of a nation's social strata. One particular comment which has been made of the British soldier prior to the Great War is in respect of the actual quality of recruits. During the 19th century, soldiering in the ranks was viewed as a particularly lowly occupation. Thus men who had no trade and could not gain employment, rather than starve joined the army. This is underlined by the pay scales of the day: while a warehouseman in 1914 could earn £2 a week, a soldier's pay in an infantry regiment was 1s a day.

One of the most perceptive observers of the day, Rudyard Kipling wrote:

> I went into a theatre, as sober as could be,
> They gave a drunk civilian room, but 'adn't none for me,
> They sent me to the gallery or round the music 'alls,
> But when it comes to fightin', Lord! they'll shove me in the stalls![1]

It was in this climate that, after every available serving soldier had been shipped off to France with the British Expeditionary Force, the desperate search for volunteers began. On 7 August 1914, as Secretary of State for War, Lord Kitchener launched his initial appeal for 100,000 men to answer the call to the Colours. (Kitchener was no stranger to Leicestershire. His father, Colonel Henry Horatio Kitchener, came to live at Cossington during the late 1880s. Until the death of Kitchener senior in 1894, the future field marshal was a regular visitor to the county.)

The army, however, was only one aspect of the situation. In the time to come, every adult person was to be asked to make some form of contribution to the war effort. Organisations were established at

---

1. Rudyard Kipling, *Tommy*

local level in every town and county to supplement government expenditure on a whole range of matters relating to everything from wounded horses to supplying aeroplanes.

The Leicester Citizens Volunteer Training Corps[1] was inaugurated during the latter part of 1914 with Captain R. M. Pritchard as its CO, Sidney Packer of 2 New Street as its secretary and Councillor John Parsons as treasurer. At the beginning of November, as his first public engagement, the incoming Mayor of the borough, Alderman Jonathan North, addressed the members of the newly-formed group. He told them that their purpose was to 'defend the hearth and home if need arise'. With a membership requirement that a man must be over 35 years of age, in this, one of the first of the Great War's many defence units, can be seen the embryonic 'Dad's Army' Home Guard of later years. The Corps quickly numbered 1,500 men. Within a matter of weeks, by mid-January 1915, the age had been raised to 38 on the promise that men over that age would only be called upon in the case of invasion. In addition to the facilities given to them at the County Cricket Ground, the corps met on four evenings a week at the Drill Hall in the Magazine.

The purview of the Citizens' Volunteer Training Corps covered a wide range. Day drills on the County Cricket Ground commenced at 3pm each day, including weekends. Activities included guard duty and tent pitching, Swedish drill four days a week, training in signalling skills, and, for officers only, from Monday to Friday musketry and arms drill on the rifle range under the tutelage of Colonel Yate MP. Apart from the activities at the Magazine, there were twice-nightly drill sessions at 7.15pm and 8.30pm held at the Empress Rink (later part of the Granby Halls complex), one company of men to attend each session. An Ambulance Section trained in the practice and theory of first-aid every Tuesday and Thursday, and French classes were held once a week. Last, a Mounted Section of two troops of horse, and a Cyclist Section were formed.

By January of 1915 the War Office had started to gather itself and turn its attention towards the vexed question of home defence. At a meeting held at the Saracen's Head Hotel in Leicester at the end of January, the Leicester Home Defence Corps and the Leicester Motor Corps decided that in compliance with a recent War Office directive a consolidation of Home Defence units was called for. All of the disparate units throughout the county would join the Central Association [Volunteer Training Corps], amalgamate into one, and become known as the County Regiment of the Citizens Training Corps. This would result in the co-ordination of the activities of 3,500 men in 19 units throughout the county.[2]

Under the presidency of the Duke of Rutland, the Mayors of Leicester, and Loughborough were installed as vice-presidents. John Parsons and Sidney Packer took office as the overall treasurer and secretary respectively. Captain Pritchard resigned as CO of the Leicester section in May of 1915 when he replaced Major Hamilton as recruiting officer for the district. Pritchard's place was taken by Major W. G. Stanhope Rollestone.

Subscriptions towards the upkeep of the Training Corps quickly reached £4,000 and by January 1915 they were in a position to discuss the purchase of a uniform for their men comprising grey/green breeches or trousers, Norfolk jacket with shoulder straps, brown leggings and boots, and a peaked cap or forage cap. The *Leicester Daily Mercury* for Friday, 30 May 1915 reports that a large crowd gathered in Leicester Market Place to cheer on the 3,000 men of the Citizens Volunteer Training Corps, dressed in their grey/green uniforms and armed with service rifles, as they marched off to the County Cricket Ground.

While firearms training and the carrying of rifles by the corps had been practice from the outset, it was to be another year before the Government, in the following letter, actually regularised the situation regarding firearms.

War Office,
London SW
26 August 1915

Sir,

I am commanded by the Army Council to inform you that those Volunteer Training Corps which are affiliated to the Central Association Volunteer

---

1. In the initial stages of the war reference is variously made to, the Leicester Citizens' Training League and the Leicester Citizens Volunteer League. After May 1915 the sole title is the Leicester Citizens Volunteer Training Corps. The fact that each has the same officers indicates that they were one and the same organisation.

2. Leicester, Ashby-de-la-Zouch, Coalville, Whitwick, Ellistown, Hugglescote, Thringstone, Hinckley, Loughborough, Melton Mowbray, Market Harborough, Kibworth, Syston, Sileby, Lutterworth, Wigston, Blaby, Narborough, East Norton.

Training Corps, may provide themselves at their own expense with rifles, under local and individual arrangements under the following conditions:

a) Rifles should be of a non-Service pattern, but capable of firing Service ammunition. The maximum price must not exceed £2 10s 0d per rifle.

b) The price paid for ammunition must not exceed £5 per 1,000 rounds.

c) No responsibility can be accepted by the War Office in regard to the safety of rifles and ammunition so purchased. They may be of a quality which would not be accepted in the Service.

c) If at any time the labour, machines, or material used for the production of these rifles of a non-Service pattern can be made available for Service purposes, or if it is found that the purchase of rifles and ammunition interferes with the supplies of the Ministry of Munitions, it may be necessary to take steps which would have the effect of preventing the supplies of either article regarding the Volunteer Corps.

Signed,
B. D. Cubitt.

At the end of its first two years of existence, in October 1916, the Leicester Battalion of the Volunteer Corps held its annual general meeting in the hall of the Newarke Secondary School on Imperial Avenue. Eagerly awaiting an inspection within a few days by Field Marshal Viscount French, the Leicester branch of the corps, with a membership of 1,046 (around 50 per cent of whom were also enrolled as special constables), considered itself to be in a state of robust good health.

There is no doubt that the corps was serving a very real purpose in providing a vehicle for the training of men who were either in the process of being inducted into, or had been temporarily deferred by, the army. At this point, two years into the war, they also numbered men who had successfully appealed against conscription and been referred to the corps by a tribunal and men who had attested under the Lord Derby Scheme and were awaiting call-up. The War Office, determined to maintain the momentum nationally of the Volunteer Corps, during the summer of 1917 accepted responsibility for the costs of all equipment, arms and ammunition, training and instruction, and travel to and from courses and drills. The added incentive of expenses was granted – when members of the Volunteers Corps were turned out, in addition to travelling money they were to receive a refreshment allowance and while away at camp free food and 5½d a day out-of-pocket expenses.

The Leicestershire Automobile Association which in August 1914 had solicited 'all owners of motor cars and cycles to come forward', was another organisation which contributed an enormous amount of time and energy to the war effort. Having been incorporated along with the rest of the county units into the Central Association Voluntary Training Corps, the association was by April of 1915 proving to be an extremely useful component of the Home Defence machine.

In April 1904, there were 61 motor cars and 104 motor cycles registered in the County Borough of Leicester.[1] If during the ensuing decade, this number quadrupled, the total number of vehicle owners in the town would still only have been in the region of 240 cars and just over 400 motor cycles.

Figures published in early 1917 show that, in 1914 there were 536,747 motor vehicles on the roads of England and Wales, Scotland and Ireland; this number, during 1915, had declined to 300,62, indicating that 44 per cent of available vehicles were requisitioned for military purposes – a large number of them actually going abroad to the Front.

This requisitioning is yet again a symptom of 'the Devil driving'. The first modern war in history was about to be fought by armies which had prepared themselves on precepts dating back 60 years to the Crimean War. When the British Expeditionary Force embarked for France it took with it to service 120,000 men a total of 334 lorries, 133 motor cars, and 166 motor cycles.[2]

Over Easter 1915 the Leicester Motor Corps,

1. *Leicester Past and Present* Jack Simmons.
2. *Blighty*, G. J. DeGroot.

teamed up with the 25th London Battalion (Cyclists) to spend the Bank Holiday training at the East Coast. Now under the command of C. F. Bray, with F. Webb as adjutant,[1] the men of the corps spent four days learning the techniques of firing machine-guns, drilling, map reading and route marching, night exercises and demolition work.

In his Annual Report for 1915, the secretary, R. Sutton Jnr, makes the following observations:

1 Cars are being loaned for the con-veyance of wounded soldiers from the railways to hospitals and con-valescent homes.

2 The Association has collected for and purchased an ambulance for Loughborough which did not possess one.

3 Two Motor Corps were inaugurated by the Club at the beginning of the war, one in Leicester which is a flourishing unit and one in Lough-borough which has been amal-gamated into the Volunteer Training League.

4 Vehicles and drivers are loaned on a regular basis to various headquarters of Military Commands here and in other parts of the country. Drivers are often away for two weeks at a time on driving duties.[2]

(Perhaps a little tongue in cheek, the report also comments that enquiries concerning touring on the Continent have declined.)

As time progressed, those eligible for the army who left to join the BEF were replaced by others. When the War Office eventually took over the Volunteer Units, the Leicester section became part of the Leicestershire Royal Army Service Corps MT under Major F. B. Roberts.[3]

Despite drastic reductions in its numbers due to members being conscripted (in August 1917 only 50 officers and men were available for the summer camp), the corps continued until the end of the war

performing an essential role in moving casualties and undertaking various forms of transport and despatch work.

The younger element was encouraged to participate actively in the town's endeavours. On Friday, 2 October 1914 the Junior League of Patriots under the auspices of the Recruiting Committee was inaugurated at the Newarke Secondary School. Directed towards unemployed boys between the ages of 14 and 17, its aim was to train them, using the knowledge of the local Boy Scouts Association in marching, drilling, life saving and ambulance work. The Parks Committee granted free use of the public parks while the Corn Exchange was used for wet weather training and displays.

The largest and probably most attractive detachment directed at teenage youths was the Leicester Junior Training Corps. Initiated during the second week of October 1914 and affiliated to the Leicestershire Territorial Association, it invited young men who were 16 to 19 years of age to acquire training in military skills in readiness to join the army once they were old enough. Based at the Leicester Rugby Football Club, with full use of the club's grounds and facilities, one of the most prominent figures in setting up and running the corps was the ubiquitous Tom Crumbie who in common with most of those engaged in the formation of such quasi-military units was given a rank commensurate with their responsibilities – in his case he quickly became Captain Crumbie.[4]

Imbued with the fervour of their patriotic elders, lads rushed to become part of the Junior Training Corps. In September 1915, taking advantage of the late summer weather, the corps mustered between 300 and 400 youths as part of a recruiting parade when it marched out to the home at Glenfield Frith of its president, Sir Samuel Faire.

The growth of the Leicester Citizens Volunteer Training Corps, with its added responsibility for men temporarily deferred by the army, along with the fluctuating membership of the Junior training Corps (as older youths left to join up so younger

1. Most of these original members subsequently left to join the BEF. Amongst them was Webb who was commissioned in August 1915 as a 2nd Lieut., in the 176th Howitzer Battery and later awarded the Military Cross.

2. This paucity of official motor transport is emphasised by a statement made by the Chief Constable of Leicester, Herbert Allen in April 1916 when outlining some of his air-raid precautions, that '20 motorists have volunteered to attend police stations at any time to take Police Officers to any place where they are needed…'

3. During its existence as part of the Central Association Volunteer Training Corps the County Commandant was Lieutenant-Colonel Sarson.

4. As the war progressed, more and more of those responsible for organising voluntary units took military ranks. The titles of Captain and Major abounded. An example is Jonathan North, who as Honorary Commandant of the 1st Battalion, Leicester Volunteer Regiment was given the rank of Lieutenant-Colonel. At one point the question was discussed (rather derisively by those objecting), concerning the validity of certain Councillors turning up for meetings in uniform.

members were enrolled), started to cause serious logistical problems for the organisers. In April 1915, the Estates Committee of the Corporation granted a 20-year lease to Sir Samuel Faire, Evan Barlow and Tom Crumbie in respect of an area of one and a half acres of ground on Aylestone Road adjacent to the Leicester rugby football ground for the erection of a building to be known as the Junior Training Hall. With the additional later responsibility for drilling and training of deferred men awaiting induction into the army, the facilities of the Junior Training Hall became too limited and a further extension became an urgent necessity.[1] At the 11th hour in October 1918 with two additional trustees – Major Rolleston and Lieutenant-Colonel North – to the triumvirate, the Empress Skating Rink was taken over and combined with the Junior Training Hall to create one large facility. Later generations were to know this as the Granby Halls.

Having effectively ensured the readiness of young men who on leaving school were still too young to be accepted by the army, the next step for the Recruiting Committee was to address those still in the school environment. After a deal of discussion it was decided to examine the position of grammar schools in the town and county. Here boys of proven intelligence and application, such as was required for the officer class, were to be found. What better example could be set to them than that of C. F. Jones? In peacetime a master at Uppingham School, he was now Lieutenant-Colonel Jones, CO of the 5th Leicesters.

On 31 May 1915 the announcement was made that the 1st Cadet Battalion of the Leicestershire Regiment was to be founded. Dressed in the service uniform of the Territorial Force – of which it was a part – the battalion would be responsible for educating grammar school boys throughout the county in the intricacies of infantry manoeuvres, King's Regulations and all the other skills of an officer. It is worth noting that at a time when the practice in state-run board schools was for children to leave at 14 years of age, a stipulation was made in respect of members of the cadet battalion that membership must cease when the youth achieved the age of 19. The expectation of the candidate's immediately joining the Colours upon leaving school is obvious. CO of the battalion was Colonel Robert Harvey (Honorary Colonel was C. E. Yate MP.) The role of adjutant, with the rank of captain (later major), was undertaken – not unsurprisingly – by William Allport Brockington, the county director of education.

Brockington, in addition to his position with the education authority, had from the outset been deeply involved in the war effort. Initially, with an office at 33 Bowling Green Street, he worked as county co-ordinator for the Belgian Relief Scheme, then later as vice-chairman of the Leicestershire War Pensions Committee. In October 1915 his application for a commission on active service with the 5th Leicesters was refused on medical grounds. Like so many others he was to lose close family in the war. His nephew, a captain serving with the BEF, was killed in October 1916 while leading an attack upon an enemy trench.

Captain and quartermaster was J. Mantle Hubbard (the vice-chairman of the Education Committee), while the secretary to the battalion was Captain Sarjeantson. The battalion was divided into companies dispersed across the county on a roughly geographical basis. 'A' Company based at the Wyggeston Boys' School provided 190 members of the Leicester Borough contingent. A further 43 from Alderman Newton's and 61 from Newarke Secondary Schools brought the town's contribution to 294.

In total throughout the town and county, 14 schools supplied 850 boys for the cadet battalion. A typical example of the regime followed is that of the battalion's summer camp in 1916 at Burton Lazars attended by 170 NCOs and senior boys.

Leicester Daily Mercury, Wednesday 2 August 1916.

'There are [now] some 950 boys of the county in the battalion. Camp is being held on the Burton Flats Racecourse, cadets sleeping in the stands. The luncheon room is the officers' mess. Offices are being used as the orderly rooms. TA have loaned an army kitchen which is being manned by county council cookery teachers under the command of Miss Fog.

Trainers include: Lieut Forsell (late of 4th Batt. demobilised due to wounds), Mr Bucklar, late of Wellingborough School (musketry expert) and Dr Robinson, county medical officer – M.O. Weather has been very good.'

---

1. The drill instructor was Sgt-Major Jordan who had previously served for 16 years in the Leicestershire Regt.

Sterling work was also done by the YMCA, which quickly formed a Volunteer Corps of its own in order that 'young men 19 years of age or over, who for various reasons cannot go into the army, can be got ready for an emergency – two drills per week, three drills per fortnight compulsory'. Whilst the objectives of this venture were perhaps a little loosely defined, the YMCA made a most profound contribution in another area. Situated in East Street, within sight of the Midland Railway Station, it was impossible for the Management Committee of the YMCA not to be aware of the numbers of servicemen present in the town. Huge numbers of men, awaiting rail connections while en route to other parts of the country were being deposited in the vicinity with nothing to do and nowhere to go. The YMCA was also within walking distance of the 5th Northern General Hospital on Victoria Road (later to become University Road), recuperating patients passing its doors on a daily basis on their way into the town centre. In June 1915 the YMCA announced that its hall in East Street was to be designated the 'Soldiers Hut'.

The Soldiers Hut was to become a focal point for men in transit and wounded men with time on their hands. In a new approach to the needs of its clients, the Hut was opened 24 hours a day and staffed by unpaid volunteers, and like the Windmill Theatre in later years, its motto was 'we never close'.[1] During the daytime it was used by the soldiers as a refreshment and recreation room with facilities such as, bagatelle, table skittles, billiards, chess, draughts and dominoes. Refreshments and cigarettes were available and for those wishing to send home letters, writing materials were on sale. The Hut saw its busiest time during the night. At 10pm it was converted into a sleeping room for men passing through who did not want to spend the night on the open station platform or in the railway waiting room. Twenty beds were set up for early arrivals, with many more being accommodated on blankets and mattresses used as shake downs. For men returning on leave from the rigours of life in the trenches, a night spent on the floor of a warm hall on a mattress was going to be deemed less than arduous. The rest of the YMCA premises (later

known as 'the Working Men's Institute'), were also thrown open until 10pm to any uniformed personnel. Access was given freely to the billiards room, smoking room and reading room. Refreshments were served in the tea room, run by Mrs Kite.

In late January 1917, the association launched an appeal to raise £5,000 to acquire the freehold land next to its existing premises, to permit the extension of the Hut complete with baths and a drying room. The eventual cost of the land was £1,750, building and equipping the undertaking came to a further £2,000. On Tuesday, 15 May 1917, the extension was opened by Lady Beatty[2]. With a 42ft frontage in East Street, it comprised a main hall containing at one end a stage and at the other, a musicians' gallery. Further facilities included a kitchen equipped with gas stoves, and a serving counter, a store room, large bedroom, and a bathroom with showers – all, it was proudly announced, illuminated by electric lighting.

Along with every other available resource, a place was found for the Boy Scout movement to play its part. Formed in 1908 by General Sir Robert Baden-Powell, following the South African War, it was estimated by the beginning of the Great War that the organisation numbered in excess of 100,000 members. Although this represented the lower end of the age scale in relation to the volunteer pool, these youngsters still constituted a valuable resource. Organised on a local basis in small groups, they already had uniforms and equipment combined with an officer-based infrastructure. The boys willingly gave of their time and efforts to take part in the plethora of recruiting parades and processions, unstintingly providing bugle blowing escorts to every group of soldiers, departing from the Midland Railway Station.

Other more focussed work was given to the Scouts. Nationally it was reported that '100,000 Boy Scouts have been employed in security work. They have been guarding main telegraph and telephone cables to ensure that lines are not tapped or cut, also they have been guarding bridges and culverts.'

Local practice certainly adhered to this pattern. Twelve months into the war, in late 1915, the services of the Scouts had been widely utilised. The

1. A later boast, which there is no reason to deny, was that for the duration of the war, someone from the YMCA met every train, day or night, which pulled into the Midland Station.

2. Lady Beatty and Admiral Sir David Beatty, lived locally at Brooksby Hall, which was utilised by the 5th Northern General Hospital initially as an auxiliary hospital, then later as a hospital for naval personnel.

police had employed them as watchers on the railway lines and in October 1914 the Watch Committee had authorised payment of £10 for 'services rendered in guarding Knighton Tunnel'. They had provided packers for the *Leicester Mercury's* Christmas Present Fund, and messengers for the War Relief Fund. Handbills had been distributed on behalf of any group which approached them and orderlies provided for the YMCA Hut, the Magazine, and each of the recruiting offices.

Two rather damp squibs were ignited on the labour front during the war which, despite their lack of impact, are worth mentioning as they are prime examples of 'volunteerism'.

The Women's Volunteer Reserve made a bid in February 1915 for the services of local women to take over the duties at present performed by men. Locally they opened a register of volunteers during the second week of April which after three weeks claimed a membership of 500 women from the town and surrounding district, 'several hundred' of whom paraded on the afternoon of Saturday, 24 April in drizzling rain for inspection by their president Mrs North, wife of Alderman North.

Unfortunately, the Women's Reserve, certainly in the Leicester area, seemed to have an identity problem, or possibly they were attempting to be all things to everyone. On the one hand, a list of names was supplied to Mr Handley at the Labour Exchange of those for whom work was to be found. At the end of April 1915 women are reported as working locally on the land in rural areas. Others had been sent away for training at the Agricultural Dairy College, at Kingston-on-Soar, just over the county border in Nottinghamshire. On the other hand, the women were split up into companies under Major Jenkins to be trained along military lines. The August Bank Holiday camp of 'A', 'B', 'C', and 'D' companies at Thorpe Arnold outside Melton Mowbray was a mixed success. Due to bad weather it was not possible for the women to erect tents and for accommodation they were thrown upon the mercy of nearby farmers, three of whom allowed them to sleep in their barns. Feeding had to be undertaken in the nearby village hall. Undeterred they still engaged in route marches and training in map reading and signalling. A later improvement in conditions permitted the playing of hockey, and a picnic at Belvoir Castle. Probably not helped by a general antipathy at the time towards the involvement of women in almost any sphere of influence, little is reported of the organisation locally after 1915.

In February 1917 the Government launched their National Service Scheme, not to be confused with what in the years after 1918 was associated with military conscription and also known as 'national service'. This was a project aimed at the civilian workforce. Every working man between the ages of 18 and 61 was invited to volunteer for National Service. The notion was to achieve an equal redistribution of labour throughout the country. Based upon a network of local committees, volunteers would be processed through employment exchanges prior to being redeployed.

In Leicester, a forerunner to the scheme was the opening four months earlier, in October 1916, of a substitute office, based at the Magazine. Conscription by this time had taken over the process of providing men for the military. This in its turn presented the ever-increasing problem of securing the release of men from their jobs.

Men were classified as 'A', 'B', and 'C'. Category 'A' was for those who were readily acceptable, while the other two classes comprised men who were either deferred or medically unsuitable. Many of those certified category 'A' were in jobs from which it was not easy to secure their release. Men were no longer so eager to 'do and die', and employers, in an expanding market place offset by a dwindling workforce were desperate to retain every possible hand. Captain Heath, the officer responsible for the 17th Recruiting Area, had high hopes that by swapping and substituting local civilian labour, the possibility existed for him to alleviate his situation in relation to releasing category 'A' men into the army. His proposal was that men who were medically unfit and those over or under military age, could quickly be substituted in the workplace for the category 'A' men. He even conceded a place for female labour in his strategy.

The flaw in this particular idea was the physical shortage of available labour to move around (also to become one of the stumbling blocks with National Service.) In an environment where every able-bodied person could obtain work almost anywhere, no marginal workforce existed.

In January 1917, a 'war work bureau', located in the Town Hall opened its doors from 10am to 4pm daily. (Whether or not this office was in collaboration with Captain Heath's substitute bureau is not clear, however it does not seem likely.) Its purpose appears to have been to provide spare-time employment in areas where the workforce had been depleted.

An early response to the war work bureau resulted in about 200 men being found positions in the Post Office and in munitions work. (This would hardly be a major step forward. In view of the work allocated – munitions work encompassed virtually any factory contracting to the Government, irrespective of whether it was producing bullets or socks – it can be safely assumed that these were men for whom the employment exchange would have easily found placements in the normal course of events.)

The National Service Scheme opened on 6 February 1917; Leicester's local committee, presided over by the Mayor, Alderman North, came into being a few days later. Despite an extensive advertising campaign, the scheme, locally as well as nationally, met with little response. At this late stage in the war the populace was tired and to a great extent disillusioned. The oft-repeated promises made by Haig, that given more men the end was imminent, were no longer believed. Those due to be conscripted awaited their turn while others, not in danger of being called up and in full employment, were not about to volunteer for yet another government plan. The proposed government target of 500,000 volunteers was never achieved and when the review date arrived at the end of March, only 206,000 had signed up for the scheme. It was quietly allowed to fade into obscurity.

One of the more flamboyant gestures made by citizens of the borough was the presentation of its very own aircraft to the Imperial Air Fleet.

Established prior to the war, the prime objective of the Air Fleet was to ensure the equipping of the Empire's overseas units with aircraft. In 1916, Lord Desborough was given the job of canvassing municipalities throughout the land with a view to raising funds for the Air Fleet.

Individual cities and towns were invited to purchase and dedicate an aeroplane which would carry their name into the battle front.[1]

Jonathan North, in his role as Mayor, approached Alec Lorrimer, the president of the Leicester Chamber of Commerce, to organise the fund. Within ten days, Lorrimer and his deputy, O. B. Stannion, had raised 2,000 guineas from 154 subscribers and secured the purchase on behalf of the Canadian Forces of a Sopwith Snipe single-seater, to be named *Leicester*.

This quick response secured for Leicester the position of being the first town under Desborough's initiative to provide a machine. A date of Saturday, 3 June 1916 (Whitsuntide Bank Holiday), was set for the presentation ceremony.

Originally the venue was to be Victoria Park, doubtless on the premise that a good turnout of uniformed men could be supplied by the adjacent war hospital. However, this was vetoed by the War Office as unsuitable. With only a few days left, an agreement was reached that the plane could be flown to Western Park.

Whit Saturday morning 1916 dawned cold and cloudy, which did not bode well for the day's planned activities. However, as the day progressed the weather improved, the sun shone and the seasonal June weather reasserted itself to the extent that during the afternoon, due to the heat there were 37 fainting cases reported among the onlookers gathered on the park. (The only other medical emergency was an embarrassed soldier who sprained his wrist helping to swing the propeller of the aircraft when it took off.)

A vast crowd gathered early in the morning to witness the landing on the hard grassland of the park at 10.30am by the Sopwith piloted by Captain Richardson of the Royal Flying Corps.

Of the eventual 30,000 local people who thronged Western Park that day, it is safe to presume that only a tiny percentage would have ever before seen an aeroplane on the ground, let alone be allowed to approach and inspect it.

The president of the Imperial Air Fleet, Lord Desborough, accompanied by the Canadian High Commissioner and his wife, Sir George and Lady Perley, arrived by rail at the Midland Station at 11am. Met by civic dignitaries headed by the Mayor, the party was conducted on a tour of local factories, followed by luncheon at the Art Gallery, prior to making their way to the park.

The events of the day are probably best described

---

1. For their part the War Office undertook the replacement of any of these aeroplanes which were later destroyed in action.

by a contemporary piece published in the Whit Monday edition of the *Leicester Daily Mercury*:

'How the *Leicester* ascended'

'There was a pronounced lift in the centre of gravity of the population of Leicester in the direction of Western Park on Saturday afternoon. As the appointed hour for the formal presentation ceremony drew near, the Hinckley Road became the scene of a mighty Pilgrimage towards that spot where since the morning the *Leicester* aeroplane had sat in state on the high plateau of the park. The excitement extended as far as the centre of the town, to the two-minute [tram] car service which was specially arranged for the occasion which proved utterly inadequate to convey the crowds that besieged the Western Park [tram] cars at the Clock Tower. When the congestion reached its height, hardly anyone got an opportunity of boarding the cars at the Tower at all, for they were practically filled with those people who were struck with the brilliant idea of walking a little way up High Street and paying for a ride of 50 yards or so to the Tower in order to make certain of a seat on the outward journey. The end of the matter was that the Western Park was thronged with one of the biggest crowds of its history, and the sum total of the good wishes which went with the *Leicester* aeroplane on its journey out to the Front ought certainly to be sufficient to ensure it a distinguished career.

'In front of the small building which adjoins the Western Park cricket ground, a restricted area had been roped off, in the centre of which the aeroplane was guarded by four men of the National Reserve with loaded rifles. The compact, yet graceful lines of the biplane, which bore the name of a famous firm of motor engineers, were duly admired by that comparatively small section of the crowd which caught a glimpse of it while it was still on the ground. This section had in fact plenty of time to admire it, for it was long after the expected time when the ceremony which the crowd attended to take passive part in was brought off. To while away the period of waiting, bands discoursed martial music and national airs from behind the pavilion where was assembled a large contingent of the Junior Training Corps. The Leicester Citizens Volunteer Corps rendered great assistance in dealing with the crowd and preserving order and also provided a Guard of Honour which was in the command of Mr J. Harrison, assisted by Mr Webster and Mr Langley. The police on duty were directed by Superintendent Agar of Loughborough, owing to the indisposition of Superintendent Bowley, in whose division this part of the park lies, assisted by Inspector Freer.

'When the Mayor and the distinguished visitors who took the central part in the presentation of the aeroplane to the Canadian Government arrived, excitement ran high – especially among those who were in a position to see anything of the proceedings – but it was necessary for them to exercise some patience before the ceremony of christening the aeroplane took place. Some consideration was necessary before the time honoured symbolism of breaking a bottle of champagne over the new aircraft could be effectively consummated, for the simple reason that the fore-end of an aeroplane is neither so get-at-able, nor so solid as the bows of an ironclad. The ceremony was well and truly performed, however, by the simple method of tying the bottle, enclosed in a silken bag, over the central boss of the giant propeller and Lady Perley operated upon it with a hammer, then promptly "standing from under" while the sparkling liquid duly moistened the propeller blades. Then amid cheers, the cloths which covered the sides of the aeroplane near the cab were drawn aside and the good old name, *Leicester,* revealed for all folk – including no doubt a few of the country's enemies to see.

'The presentation of the aeroplane then took place in the terms already reported. The speakers used a step ladder as their rostrum, but it is to be feared little of what they said reached beyond the ears of a privileged few, for even those of the public who might have heard, had perforce a large proportion of their attention concentrated upon the words "Stand back there," vociferously used by those engaged in clearing a way for the outward journey of the aeroplane. When the way was clear, the airman, hitherto modestly more or less in the background, became the man of the moment. Taking his seat and good naturedly intimating to those who crowded close upon the rear of the machine that they stood a good chance of being blown away, he soon had the powerful engines roaring and the propeller scattering a great wind that tugged at the hair of those who restrained its premature impulse towards the silent spaces of the air. Subduing the engines to a gentle purr, he climbed down, donned his full pilot's garb, took his seat again, selected the proper section of his map and was ready to start. There was a few minutes delay while the machine crawled as it were, to a more congenial vantage ground and then at last the *Leicester* aeroplane, duly christened, bearing with her the good wishes of a vast concourse of Leicester people, expressed in a mighty cheer, spurned the ground and was at home in the bosom of the air…'

On completion of a full circuit of the park the aircraft then flew away towards the South Coast and France.

In a ceremony held at Hendon Aerodrome on 21 January 1919, the aeroplanes, *Leicester*, *Huddersfield* (a DH9 two-seater), and *City of Glasgow* (a two-seater Bristol fighter), were handed over from the Imperial Air Fleet by the Air Ministry to the Canadian Government.

From the very early days, right through to the end, the Government was beset by the problems of financing the most expensive war to date in history. One solution was the proliferation of a number of War Loan and War Bond flotations. A look at some of those on offer gives an idea of the general tenor of such schemes.

On Wednesday, 7 July 1915 the War Loan Stock plan was floated. The proposal was fairly simple. The working man, who for whatever reason was not about to personally go and fight, was to be encouraged to take a financial stake in ensuring victory. The first step was for major employers to purchase large blocks of the newly-released war stock. Employees would then purchase small amounts of the stocks in £5 blocks, paying 2s per block per week to the employer, who effectively acted as the Government's broker. The employees received for their investment a half-yearly dividend.

Should the employee fall sick and be unable to meet their repayments, then the employer took over the commitment on a loan basis. On final payment, each £5 block became the property of the employee. Unofficial figures locally indicated by the end of the first week in August, some 71 firms in the town had purchased £52,000 of stock in support of the 'National War Loan'.

In common with most strategies aimed at raising large sums of money, it had its share of attractions sprinkled with the appropriate potential pitfalls. From the Government's viewpoint, anything which eased its cashflow problems was to be welcomed. A bonus was that in the immediacy, finance was being supplied by many of those businesses which were reaping a harvest from Government contracts, thus closing a rather tidy fiscal circle. Companies and local authorities who bought in, established an unprecedented hold over their workers. The downside to this was that, in some cases, relying too much upon the continuing boom in production, firms overstretched themselves with dire financial results. For the man and woman in the workplace who was prepared to part with some of their hard-earned cash, there existed for the first time an opportunity to discover the joys of being a small investor. Implicit in this was, of course, the linking together of the management and staff into a stable workforce – if you owe money to your employer you are hardly in a position leave – drawing yet another nicely interlinking circle.

Nine months later, in April 1916 at the behest of the Government that local authorities needed to do more to attract revenue, Leicester Corporation launched the Leicester War Savings Association. A Management Committee chaired by Jonathan North (under the watchful eye of Theodore Chambers representing the interests of the National Council), was formed with a view to being under way in time for Easter. This particular enterprise, based upon the sale of Exchequer Bonds and War Savings Certificates, aimed nationally to secure £1.325 million by the end of the year. Exchequer Bonds could be bought in £5 blocks, with a guaranteed return of five per cent. War Savings Certificates, however, were sold at 15s 6d with the promise that they would be worth significantly more in five years. There were certain restrictions on the purchase of these certificates – no individual was allowed to hold more than 500 certificates and anyone with an annual income in excess of £300 was specifically excluded.

January 1917 saw the nation at a low ebb: the war had become interminable, casualties were off the scale, fuel and food at home were at a premium. It was now that the population were invited to take shares in the Great War Loan, also referred to as the Victory Loan. Similarly to the launch of the previous year, this was split into two separate issues. The first, a five per cent loan, with interest paid half—yearly, was subject to income tax. With an issue price of £95, repayable on 1 June 1947, the shares were promised to yield on redemption £4 2s 3d after tax. The second leg was a four per cent loan which was exempt from tax. Available only through banks, the issue price was £100, repayable at £100 on 15 October 1942, with a yield of £4.

Confident in the knowledge that the offer was being shared throughout the Empire by the citizens of Canada, New Zealand, Australia, India and South Africa, the Corporation on behalf of the borough snapped up £10,000 worth. These were sold to residents in tranches of £50 to be paid for in instalments of 10s over a two-year period with the stocks remaining the property of the Corporation until paid for in total by the purchaser. Administered by the Corporation treasurer, William Penn Lewis, the shares were marketed by Messrs Arthur Wheeler & Co of the Bank Chambers in Town Hall Square, and generally through banks and Post Offices.

A final push was made in the summer of 1918 with a National Tank Week, aimed at raising money towards paying for tanks and aircraft by the now rather hackneyed process of a further issue of bonds and certificates.

At a more mundane level, cash was raised on an almost weekly basis by various charities and groups putting on events, or simply shaking tins under the noses of passers-by in the streets of Leicester. Despite one common aim – to continue the war effort and alleviate suffering – the actual diversity of appeals was very wide. Among requests to the Watch Committee for permission to hold one-day collections were: the French Fund; the Blue and Purple Cross Societies for wounded horses; the societies supporting Belgian and Russian refugees; distress in Serbia; the Mission for Seamen; the flag day for Russian wounded; the British Red Cross; and innumerable other good causes. Not all requests were granted. Mr Cook of Biddulph Street was refused permission to use his dog as a street collector on behalf of wounded horses, and Mr Crewe's permit to 'parade a few dogs to collect for the Wycliffe House for the Blind' was withdrawn when it was discovered that he had already received a contribution from the Alexandra Day Society for the same cause. The annual Alexandra Day Committee collection, selling roses produced by the Cripples' Guild in Colton Street, was always a main event resulting in substantial donations to a host of charities across the board.

Among those in need of immediate cash subscriptions was Arthur Faire, the director of Voluntary Aid Detachments, who held collections to provide the ambulances needed to transport casualties around the county. The Leicester War Hospitals Games Committee, responsible for the provision of materials to the growing number of auxiliary hospitals in the county, was also to be found among those shaking their tins.

Leicester Cattle Market was the scene in 1915 of a massive charity auction on behalf of the British Farmers' Red Cross Fund. Held on Wednesday, 13 October under the auctioneer's hammer of George Tempest Wade, the sale attracted a packed throng of market day bidders. Items on sale included 42 head of cattle donated by Admiral Beatty, 369 sheep and lambs, 48 pigs and 725 geese, duck, turkeys and other fowl. In the less likely categories were 34 Stilton and Leicester cheeses, a donkey, several goats, a rubber-tyred Victoria, a bull mastiff and a cooking stove.

Sadly, one of the most enterprising ventures during the early to middle years of the war could not be sustained until the end. The Leicester Soldiers and Sailors Christmas Present Fund, run by the *Daily Mercury* (the Shilling Fund), to ensure that servicemen from Leicester received Christmas presents, ran into difficulties from 1915 onwards.

After its immense success in 1914, a decision was taken in September 1915 by Francis Hewitt & Son Ltd, the owners of the *Mercury,* to run the appeal for a second year. Projections indicated that with the escalation of manpower in the various theatres of war, a sum of between £4,000 and £5,000 would be needed to finance the project for a second year. Hewitt initially approached E. C. Kemp, the secretary of the Alexandra Day Committee, whose offices were in Horsefair Street, with a view to that committee helping to organise a flag day to start off the fund. Kemp agreed, but with the proviso that half of any proceeds should go, via the Alexandra Day Committee, direct to prisoners-of-war held in Germany.

In an open letter published in the *Mercury* on Monday, 27 September, Hewitt outlined the terms which had been presented to him, leaving no doubt as to his feelings on the matter. Hewitt's stance was that this was not in the spirit of the fund and that it would be grossly unfair to send half the proceeds to a few hundred men, leaving the other half to be divided between several thousand. He shrewdly added the rider that his newspaper would gladly support any independent initiative to organise a separate fund directly for the benefit of prisoners-of-war.

Undeterred by this initial snub, the *Mercury* set to, as in the previous year, seeking donations from its customers on the 'shilling a reader' principle. An early declaration of intent set out the objective of despatching presents to all those serving on the Western Front and in the Dardenelles, Mesopotamia, Egypt, India and the colonies.

Despite regular pleas in the pages of the *Mercury*, the £4,000 target was never reached. At the closing of the appeal just before Christmas 1915, the fund (including £380 plus bank interest held over from the previous year) stood at £3,099 9s 1½d. Although presents were sent both to those serving overseas and at home, it is obvious that compared to the £8,000 raised by a similar fund in Nottinghamshire, Leicester's had not been a resounding success. In October 1916, in answer to enquiries as to his intentions for the third Christmas of the war, a disenchanted Hewitt announced that the fund would not be run again. In publishing his decision in the newspaper, he briefly cited the following reasons: that the paper now had insufficient manpower to run an appeal; labour shortages in the industry prevented the assembling of parcels; shortage of paper for the printing of news restricted advertising space. His final and probably most succinct comment was that charity calls on the public were becoming excessive.

Voluntary Aid Detachments were central to the nation's ability to maintain a Home Front. Both men and women were members, giving their time to a whole range of activities ranging from clerks and kitchen hands to nurses and ambulance drivers. In Leicester the co-ordinator was Arthur Faire, who had prime responsibility for arranging the transportation of wounded from the railway convoys arriving at the Midland Railway Station to the various hospitals in the district. The fact that 'Salonika' is included on this poster would indicate that it dates from sometime after October 1915.

With the trains carrying convoys of wounded often being delayed for several hours facilities were needed for the volunteers waiting to meet them. This group is seen in the rest room at the Midland Railway Station. The soldier on the right is from the Leicestershire Regiment and is probably taking a break and some refreshment whilst waiting for a train. On the window to the right, it is possible to make out the words, 'VAD' and below that 'Rest Station'.

Wounded men were brought up by train from the south coast to the Midland Railway Station where they were met by Voluntary Aid Detachment personnel

Loading the wounded onto ambulances from the incoming trains.

Due to the platform being too short to accommodate the disembarkation of casualties, two moveable sections measuring fifteen feet by ten feet and raised five feet from the ground were constructed and placed alongside the carriages. This arrangement proved particularly effective for the unloading of immobile men who arrived on cots.

During the period prior to the introduction of conscription, every available space was utilised to exhort men to join the Colours. Seen amongst this group standing outside of the Town Hall is one of the local Boy Scouts who performed duties as 'runners', taking messages between the barracks and various recruiting offices around the town.

A group of Tramways motormen and conductors along with the department's manager pictured during the period between the end of the Boer War and the outbreak of the Great War. After 1914, this department in particular was to experience the difficulties created by the release of a high ratio of its manpower to the army.

With the few motor cars in production being needed by the army, the moving of goods within the borough remained firmly within the province of the horse-drawn vehicle. Tramcars, such as this one on the Stoneygate route provided the primary link between the suburbs and the town.

Throughout the course of the war the slopes of Western Park were used for many purposes. In the early days, volunteers to the Leicestershire Regiment were given training whilst awaiting a place in the regiment. The top slopes at Whitsuntide 1916 saw the presentation of the 'Leicester' aeroplane to the Imperial Air Fleet. During the last days of the war, from April 1917, the golf course area was given over to the growing of grass for animal fodder.

The bandstand and pavilion on Victoria Park. Apart from being a place to stroll and relax on a pleasant afternoon, Victoria Park was used on a regular basis as the marshalling point for the large parades which aimed to increase the flow of recruits to Kitchener's New Army.

In the full regalia of a Field Marshal, Horatio Herbert Kitchener. Distrustful in 1914 of the locally-raised Territorial Force battalions, he set to at an early stage of the conflict to raise a second army to be known as 'Kitchener's Army'. Always seen politically as a 'loose cannon', Kitchener was killed in June 1916 when the *HMS Hampshire* on which he was travelling to Russia, was sunk off of the Orkneys.

Jonathan North (1855-1939). The managing director of the boot and shoe firm of Freeman Hardy & Willis, he was elected to the Town Council in 1898 and became an alderman in 1909. From the end of 1914 until two days prior to the Armistice in November 1918, North served as the Mayor of Leicester. Serving as a member of the Education Committee from 1903 (for the greater part of the time as chairman) until 1935, he had the distinction of having a school, Sir Jonathan North Girls' School named after him. (*By permission of Sir Jonathan North Community College.*)

Private John Walter Protheroe of the 4th Leicesters. A tailor's cutter employed in Leicester by the firm of Levy & Hart, he was one of the thousands of men who volunteered from the town for active service. He was killed in action at Passchendaele in 1917.

Well known for his connections with the Leicester Rugby Football Club, Thomas Henry Crumbie was one of the most prominent figures in Leicester during the Great War. In business as a stationer in Halford Street, he spent the war years raising and organising training units and additional contingents for the Leicestershire Regiment. A sufferer of diabetes, Tom Crumbie died in March 1928 at the age of 60.

Frank Vernon Hewitt, proprietor of the *Leicester Daily Mercury* from 1911 until 1939. The *Mercury* undertook during the first two years of the war to organise the 'Shilling Fund' in which readers were asked for contributions to send Christmas gifts to Leicestershire men at the Front. Due to shortages after 1915 the scheme was closed down.

Conscription

BY THE middle of 1915 the sheer logistics of feeding men into the war machine at the level demanded by the generals had become an impossibility. The Secretary of State for War declared that he required an army of 70 divisions, which in practice meant an average of 35,000 men a week, almost double the number of those volunteering. Herbert Asquith already forced to accept the necessity of a Coalition government and unable to escape from the incessant demands of the military finally acceded to the inevitability of conscription.

The decision posed many problems, mainly of how to organise such a massive venture. The primary objective was to decide who was liable to be conscripted and then, how were they to be pro-cessed? Whilst Kitchener envisaged a roll call of every man in the country, who, once identified, would belong to him, others realised that a balance would have to be arrived at. A balance which facilitated not only the building up of the army, but also left behind a workforce capable of maintaining that army in the field.

Logistically, the most pressing matter was the identification and location of those to be conscripted. With this in view, at the end of July 1915 the announcement was made that a National Register was to be compiled.

The compilation of such a register was not only a huge undertaking, it needed to be completed most expeditiously. A National Registration Act was rushed through and local authorities charged with obtaining the requisite information. Responsibility for implementation of the Act in Leicester fell to Herbert Arthur Pritchard, the Town Clerk. The requirements were:

1. All persons, male and female aged 16-65 years obliged to register, except: those in HM Forces, prisoners held in HM prisons, residents in Poor Law institutions, prisoners-of-war and internees.
2. Every person must furnish full details of their name, address, age, marital status, dependents, occupation (including whether skilled or unskilled), their nationality and place of employment.
3. Any change of address must be notified within 28 days.
4. Employers must furnish details of all person in their employ.

Anyone failing to comply with the requirements of the Act was liable to an initial fine of £5 with a running penalty of £1 a day until the information was supplied.

By the middle of August, Pritchard had set in place an elaborate system for procuring the information required. In respect of the borough, 540 enumerators (389 men and 151 women), all of whom were unpaid volunteers, were assigned to different areas of the town. Their task was to visit every household and record details of the occupants in a book of returns. Where a household comprised in part temporary occupants (lodgers or simply friends and relatives visiting), then that persons details were to be taken down and forwarded to the area in which they normally resided.

On 19 August all the enumerators, along with 110 appointed supervisors, reported to the 12 centres which had been designated in the town for the returns to be checked.

Throughout the country 100,000 volunteers, mainly women, worked at amassing the data for the register. An estimated 23 million forms and explana-tory leaflets, published by His Majesty's Stationery Office, were distributed.

Once safely gathered in and checked, the

procedure for managing the information was clearly defined and split into three stages:

Stage One:

1 Faulty/defective forms will be returned for the enumerator to revisit the address.

2 Forms relating to non-residents who were in the borough during the census will be forwarded to the local authority for the area in which that person permanently resides. Difficulty is anticipated at seaside resorts where, due to the time of the year, there will be a large number of temporary residents.

3 Each enumerator will supply details of addresses where details were refused.

4 Completed forms will be taken to the Town Hall in motor vans.

5 Any forms which the enumerators failed to complete but which have now been completed by the householder should have been returned by post direct to the Town Hall. They will now be married up with the returns in the book for the correct area.

6 Forms received from other local authorities relating to Leicester residents temporarily in other parts of the country will similarly be placed in the relevant area returns.

Stage Two:

57 banks, warehouses, [and] societies have been approached asking them to undertake the follow-up clerical work. 54 have agreed (the other three have declined due to shortage of staff.)

Next Mon. they will receive the completed forms for:

a) Coding under 46 occupational headings for males and 30 for females. The headings are in relation to potential employment capabilities.

b) Listing of males between the ages of 18 and 41 years.

c) Printing of Registration Certificates for return to individuals by the enumerators.

(250 enumerators and other volunteers have agreed to pick up the inevitable overflow of work from these organisations)

Stage Three:

The forms will be sorted into occupational headings and lodged at the Town Hall. Statistics will then be supplied to the Registrar General.

Having been thus far successful, the primary object of the exercise was to transmit to the military authorities details of those men subject to conscription. This in itself required a substantial amount of effort.

Details of men who were liable for call-up were recorded on pink forms which in turn were split on to register sheets and cards. These numbered some 60,000. Yet again, unpaid volunteers from organisations such as the Leicestershire and Rutland Recruiting Committee, the Women's Voluntary Reserve, the Green Ribbon League, and many others, set about the task. Working at the Assembly Rooms, loaned by the County Council for the purpose, 160 men and women laboured from 9.30am to 9.30pm, checking and indexing every form.

As the job of indexing progressed, the forms were then double checked and numbered by the town's school teachers, working in the evenings in their respective elementary schools. Finally the information was forwarded to the War Office.

Given the scale of the undertaking and the time constraints imposed – by the third week in October, details of the Derby Scheme, as it became known, were already being advertised. It is a tribute to the abilities of civil servants such as Herbert Pritchard, that the register was completed in the time available. The sheer logistics are unenviable. With virtually no motor vehicles at their disposal, the enumerators had to physically visit every dwelling in the borough. Communications between various towns were limited to a relatively small number of telephones or reliance on the postal services (telegrams were reserved for dire emergencies.) Every piece of information had to be processed and recorded manually prior to storing either in files or card indices. When all of this was completed, each set of details needed to be despatched to the correct governmental department for central co-ordination.

On 5 October 1915 Asquith appointed Lord

Derby as Director of Recruiting with a brief to mount a last-ditch campaign to ascertain if sufficient recruits could be obtained voluntarily. This appointment was without doubt a poisoned chalice. Asquith and the Government knew perfectly well that manpower on the scale demanded was not going to be forthcoming without coercion. The Derby Scheme was doomed to failure. However, in that failure it would secure the administration in its assertions that conscription was inevitable. It is still, however, worth examining the Derby Scheme which was to affect many Leicester men.

The basis of the scheme was that with the aid of the National Register, all men considered to be fit for the army were to be canvassed to 'attest' their willingness to serve. Those who wished to join the Colours immediately could do so, others would continue in their employment until required. Those who attested were divided into 46 groups. In the first 23 groups were single men, grouped according to age. In the second 23 were married men, again grouped according to age. The promise (which was not to be kept), was that married men would not be called upon until the resource of single men had been exhausted. Those in employments which were designated as protected would be classified as 'starred men' and only called upon as a last measure. (This was in itself to be highly problematic.) The final persuasion was that while all men would go to whichever units needed them, married men would in preference be sent to the Army Service Corps or Royal Army Medical Corps – another patently impracticable proposition.

Two weeks after his appointment, Lord Derby wrote the following letter to Manchester City Council:

'We are at a dividing of the ways and in order to get the men must either make voluntary recruiting a success in the next six weeks or revert to other methods. I would beg all your members to put themselves in the position of employers in other countries where compulsion is part of the Law of the Land and endeavour as far as possible to make such arrangements as will allow for their employees enlisting under the voluntary system.

'Nobody sees clearer than I do the necessity for interfering as little as possible with the industrial life of the country, but the scheme I have put forward will, I believe, reduce the inconvenience to a minimum, especially as machinery is being constructed whereby men called up who can prove that their services are indispensable to their employers can be relegated to later groups.

'The success of the scheme must depend not only on the total number of men obtained but on the number of young unmarried men who now undertake the obligation to serve their country when called upon to do so.'

Irrespective of individual suspicions as to the viability of the Derby Scheme, in Leicester those responsible for the promotion of recruiting entered eagerly into the fray. Many still genuinely believed that it might yet be possible to stay the hand of compulsory conscription. Ward committees, co-ordinated by W. J. Arculus and T. W. Smith, were set up to canvas for recruits. (Ironically the first call was for 1,000 canvassers in order for the committees to function.) Having scrutinised its administrative staff, the Corporation declared that of 3,500 workers, only 70 men could be listed as indispensable. Among the 4,000 men employed by the Education Department, 3,500 attested almost immediately.

Premises all over the town were designated as Recruiting and Attestation Centres. In the weeks prior to Christmas, the Corn Exchange in the Market Place, the Foresters' Institute in St Nicholas Street, the Drill Hall at the Magazine, and the Shoe Trades Hall in St James Street processed men at a rate comparable with the heady days of August 1914. At the Town Hall six doctors were engaged in conducting medical examinations of candidates. On 6 December, the Recruiting Committee reported that 1,200 men had enlisted in the newly-raised Leicester Pioneers Battalion, with a further 400 required to fill its ranks.

Not to be deflected from its agenda, the Government issued a statement on 12 November that '...if recruiting figures are not met by 30 November then compulsory measures will be taken. No marriage contracted since the compilation of the National Register will be recognised as changing the status of a previously single man.'

At the end of the first week in December, prior to the closing date of the Derby Scheme, men were being processed at the Corn Exchange in groups of 30 to 40 at a time. Such was the volume that medical examinations had to be dispensed with.

Not unexpectedly, when the Director of Recruiting's report was issued on 4 January 1916 it declared the scheme a failure. Although approximately 2.3 million men nationwide had attested, this was an insufficient number to stave off conscription.

Conscription was a nettle which Asquith's Coalition government grasped unwillingly. Well into 1915 a large proportion of the Liberals on the Government benches, along with the Labour members and some Conservatives, were strongly opposed to the move. However, bowing to necessity, the Military Service Act, conscripting single men between the ages of 18 and 41, was put before Parliament in January 1916. The first reading on Thursday, 6 January despite threats of Labour support being withdrawn from the Government, was passed with a majority of 298. Herbert Asquith managed to prevail upon the Labour Party in the form of Arthur Henderson to remain in the Coalition. Thereafter, the second and third readings went through with majorities of 392 and 347 with a view to being enforced by the second week in February.

Apart from being focussed upon drawing single men into the army, the Act obviously contained explicit guidance as to whom it did and did not encompass:

1 All British subjects, resident in Great Britain on 15 August 1915, or who have been resident since that date.
2 Men who were 18 or over on 15 August 1915, and under 41 on 2 March 1916.
3 Men who were on 2 November 1915 single or widowers without dependent children.

Except:
1 Men temporarily resident in GB or the Dominions solely for the purpose of education or some other special purpose.
2 Members of the Regular or Reserve Forces, Dominion Forces, or Territorial Force, who are liable for foreign service.
3 Men serving in the Navy or Royal Marines and men recognised as exempt by the Navy.

4 Men in Holy Orders or Ministers of the Church.
5 Men who have been discharged from the services on grounds of ill health or as disabled.
6 Men holding a certificate of exemption and men who have offered to enlist and been rejected since August 14th 1915.

Exemptions:
1 Men in reserved occupations.
2 Cases where severe hardship would be caused to domestic or business situation.
3 Ill health or infirmity.
4 Conscientious objection to undertaking a combatant role.

A further enactment, the Revised Schedule of Occupations was quietly slipped through at about the same time in order to lay the ground for assessing the impending avalanche of applications for deferment of service. Because of the fact that many would inevitably contest their liability to be conscripted, a Local Government Board circular allowed as early as November 1915 for the establishing at local level of tribunals to decide on individual cases.

One of the more unpleasant facts of life which lay in wait for the average man in the street was that there were not sufficient (and never had been) single men to fill the army quota. In April 1916, the Military Service (No 2) Act, extended conscription to married men with immediate effect. Despite the ensuing uproar, the promises made by Lord Derby – that no married man who attested would be called up until every single man had gone – were proved false. Conscription was universal.

Following the rush of men in Leicester to attest, the turn around by the Government in what was viewed as a betrayal of faith by embracing married men at such an early stage of the process was met with considerable dismay. In mid-November 1915, Ramsay MacDonald, speaking at Mantle Road School, with a deal of prescience, warned his audience that Derby had originally asked for 30,000 men a week with the rider that failure would bring about conscription. In his [MacDonald's] opinion, this was a smoke screen and the Government would not be satisfied until every man had been enlisted.

The *Leicester Daily Mercury* in a pre-Christmas

edition on 22 December 1915, appeared to be equally sceptical concerning the Government's intentions. The Premier, it stated, had asked for a further one million men for the army. Looking back to the end of November 1914, the Government had voted an army strength of two million. The agreed number for the current year, 1915, was three million. Mr Asquith's present demand brought the figure to four million. Lloyd George, it pointed out, was asking for 80,000 skilled and 240,000 unskilled men to work in the munitions industry servicing an agreed army of three million. Presumably, an army of four million men would proportionately increase the burden on munitions. Where was all of this manpower to come from?

Leicester's other MP, Gordon Hewart, had, in common with MacDonald, reservations concerning the ethics of conscription. However, adhering to agreed policy, in an address to a meeting of Liberal Party supporters in the town on 26 February, he asked, albeit grudgingly, that the citizens of Leicester support the move.

The townsmen, however, were not about to acquiesce gracefully. On 9 March the Corn Exchange in the Market Place was packed with married men who had attested. The protest meeting, chaired by Councillor William Hincks who was flanked by Councillors John Stanton Salt and Walter Wilford, was, in view of the emotive issues at stake, quite orderly. Demands included, that the Government be presented with a motion to release all married men from their attestations and in the interim there be a 28-day moratorium on the call-up of married pending the Government' response. A hurriedly devised Leicester and County Attested Married Men's Society was formed, to be chaired by Councillor Hincks. Admission to meetings of the society would be on production of an attestation card. The group, of course, was a formed in vain; it made absolutely no different to the outcome.

Appearing before a tribunal, however, could alter the outcome for an individual. After the passing of the Military Service Act, tribunals, chaired by Alderman Albert Sawday, sat locally at the Town Hall twice a week until early 1917. The grounds for appeal had to fall within the exclusions of the Act, the most popular being that of conscientious objection, or being in a reserved occupation. As was to be expected, applications for deferment were legion. In one day's sitting in March 1916, the Leicester tribunal issued (including 82 on grounds of conscientious objection) 159 Exemption Certificates. This continued through the summer of that year, at a rate of up to 60 a day.

Eventually, the outcome in Leicester, as for every other town in the country, was the same. Every available man, single or married, who fell within the ambit of the Military Service Acts, was conscripted.

Herbert Henry Asquith, (1852-1928), leader of the Liberal Government during the early years of the war, he was replaced as leader of the Coalition Government in December 1916 by Lloyd George.

Taken during the war, this picture of Sergeant Hill of the Leicesters provides an excellent example of the Leicestershire Regimental cap badge which earned the regiment the nickname of the 'Tigers'.

Five of the men who for the major part of the war controlled the destinies of those fighting for the Allies. From left to right: General Joseph Joffre, the French commander-in-chief; Raymond Poincaré, President of France; King George V; General Ferdinand Foch; and General Sir Douglas Haig.

This photograph, taken in 1910, is of two of the men destined to be closely involved in the conduct of the war. On the left is David Lloyd George (1863-1945), who having held various ministerial posts became Prime Minister of the Coalition Government formed in 1916. On the right, a strong advocate of conscription, is Winston Leonard Spencer Churchill (1874-1965). As First Lord of the Admiralty, Churchill was instrumental in the disastrous Gallipoli Campaign of 1915. During 1915-16 he resigned from the Government to serve as an army officer, commanding a battalion in France before subsequently returning to Westminster as Minister of Munitions under Lloyd George in 1917.

MP for the Borough of Leicester, by his unyielding stance against the Government and the voicing of his anti-war sentiments at every opportunity, James Ramsay MacDonald (1866-1937) brought unpopularity upon the town and himself. Although a future Prime Minister, MacDonald lost his Leicester seat in the 1918 General Election.

'On War Service', the coveted lapel badge worn by men engaged in reserved occupations to declare that they were still part of the war effort. One of the origins of this was to avoid the attentions of women who made a practice of accosting men not wearing the King's uniform and handing to them a white feather as a token of cowardice.

A group of men who in 1916 refused to be conscripted into the army on grounds of conscience or religion and chose to appear before the Leicester Tribunals. Many elected to serve in the forces in non-combatant roles such as stretcher bearers – by no means a safe option.

1915

THE new year of 1915 opened dramatically with the death of Frances Handley at her lodgings in Belgrave. 'Fran' Handley, who was also known as Frances Swain, was 32 when she met her untimely end. Prior to Christmas 1914, she had lived at 50 Mansfield Street with John Charles Yousson, a 46-year-old labourer. After their relationship ended, Handley took a room as a lodger in the home of Mary Jane Alfonzo, at 17 Britannia Street, in Belgrave. Over the lunchtime of Tuesday, 9 February, Handley and Yousson met and spent time together drinking in the Britannia public house. About 3pm, Fran Handley returned on foot and alone to her nearby lodgings. At the house she spoke to Florence Emma Gamble, a 13-year-old girl who cleaned for Mary Alfonzo. Fran told Florence Gamble that she was going upstairs to have a nap. Shortly afterwards, John Yousson arrived and told the girl that 'he was going up to see Fran'. Around 4pm, a friend of Fran Handley's, Elizabeth Manders, went to the house to call for Fran. On going up to her room, Manders found Frances Handley fully clothed, sprawled across the bed, dead. She had been stabbed several times in the chest. Laying at the foot of the bed, having attempted to cut his throat with a clasp knife, was Yousson. A passing constable, PC Newman, was summoned from his beat in Belgrave Gate and John Yousson was arrested.

When interviewed by the police, Yousson told them that having gone to see Fran Handley, he was cutting some tobacco with his clasp knife when she attacked him. A scuffle ensued in which Handley was stabbed with the knife. Yousson was tried in June before Mr Justice Horridge. Despite the evidence of Dr Spriggs, the police surgeon, that he had found no less than seven stab wounds in the body, the jury brought in a verdict of manslaughter. Disregarding Yousson's pleas that he be allowed to enlist and go to the Front (he had previously seen service in the army), Judge Horridge sentenced him to ten years' penal servitude.

In general the town was booming. One of the great interests of the day was cycling. A Leicester engineer, Henry Curry, had in 1884 ventured into the production of cycles. Now with over 50 shops nationwide, Curry opened a branch at 24-26 High Street on Saturday, 13 February. For the more affluent citizen who cared to cross over the road, Campion's at 83 High Street were offering BSA motor cycles for £63. A brand new delivery van could be purchased from Central Motors in Belgrave Gate for £120, or a two-seater motor car for £115. (This was actually more opportune than may appear – the majority of newly-produced motor vehicles were being appropriated by the army.)

By now the munitions industry was booming. Contracts for the production of everything from shells to underwear abounded and local factories struggled to keep up with the demands made upon them. The boot and shoe trade, along with hosiery, were particularly engaged, with at least 29 local firms specifically contracted to the Government. Some of these, probably around 20 per cent, pooled their resources to work together in order to improve production.

This abundance of direct work had, of course, an indirect effect upon other sectors of industry. Contracted firms required expanded sources of materials which in turn generated business for those supplying them. Factories required machinery which, when operated at full capacity over extended periods of time, needed added maintenance and eventual replacement – and local engineers were hard pressed to meet the demand. In mid-summer of 1915, the *Boot and Shoe Trades Journal* announced apprehensively 'that in order to keep up with the present demands for boots by the army, excluding leather for soles, the trade will need nationally, 35,000 hides per week. How will this impact upon the beef supplies?' Disapprovingly, the *Shoe and Leather Record* in June, criticised Leicester manufacturers for adding two and a half per cent to their invoices to cover the cost of war bonuses being paid to employees. Later in the year it commented: 'Several army boot repair shops have now been established in France to mend the soldiers' boots. The army now needs 200 tons of sole leather within the next 18 days. There exists in manufacturers' warehouses in the United Kingdom some four million pairs of boots. At the time of Mons, boots were lasting six to eight weeks. Now, because of the changed nature of the warfare, a pair will last five to six months and can be refurbished in France.'

For men engaged on war work to move about between employers was not a given right. Once trained by a company, an employee needed to secure a certificate entitling him to change employers. Conflict was inevitable and in August 1915, chaired by Alderman Thomas Smith, the first War Munitions Act Tribunal in Leicester sat to hear cases. Two such stories from September of that year are typical. In the first, Aaron Nuttall, an iron moulder employed by Messrs Taylor and Hubbard in Kent Street, appealed against their refusal to grant him a certificate. His case was that he presently earned £2 a week plus 3s war bonus and was being prevented from bettering himself by moving to another company.

The second case illustrates how attractive employment in Leicester had become. An employee of the British United Boot and Shoe Machinery Company, A. Wagstaff, appealed against the withholding of his certificate by his employers. Wagstaff's plea was that he had come to Leicester from Burton upon Trent to work. He could not now support his family in Burton and live in Leicester. In the prevailing climate it is not surprising that the tribunal, in both instances, found for the employers.

It was around about this time that the question of the employment of women began to come into focus. Prior to the war, on leaving school a working or middle class woman would take some form of employment until she married. By far the largest sector of employment was domestic, although other areas such as teaching or secretarial work were available for the socially better qualified. Upon marriage the majority of women ceased to work. This created a fluid, short-term labour market,

which by its very nature tended to be low paid. If there were any doubt about the level of wages, it was universally accepted, by employers and unions alike, that in any given situation a man would be paid at a higher rate than a woman.

With the massive draining away of the male labour force, employers were now compelled to accept women into the workplace. Leicester was no more eager than other towns, but by the middle of the summer of 1915, the presence of working women was becoming a fact of life.

Agricultural volunteers were being trained at the Kingston Dairy College, middle class ladies were to be found manning the booking offices at the railway station, while their working class counterparts were employed as carriage cleaners. In many banks now, the traditional celluloid-collared gentleman clerk was replaced by a smartly dressed young woman. A great novelty was the sight of women and young girls working as grocery assistants, or driving bread and milk carts.

On 8 July, the *Leicester Daily Mercury* rather primly commented that 'the practice of employing women in the Postal Service as clerks and to deliver letters has not yet been adopted in Leicester. Women are not being employed as drivers and conductors on tramcars as this is not seen as a suitable occupation for women.' The latter situation was to alter within the next four months. During September the Corporations of Birmingham and Cardiff announced their intention to employ women conductors, with the promise that Nottingham was soon to follow suit. In Leicester during the first two weeks of November, an initial group of 16 'lady conductors' was trained and sent out on the platforms of local tramcars. Factory owners throughout the borough, desperate to maintain production levels, bowed to the inevitable and opened their doors.

There is something of a misconception that the Great War resulted in the total emancipation of females. This is not strictly correct. It is true that for the first time, some women took the opportunity to become involved in long-term career employment. However, these were not in the majority. In allowing women a place in industry, the ground rules had been very specifically laid down. The employment of female labour was a temporary measure. As and when men came back from the war, their places would be unconditionally returned to them. An example of this determination is shown in a motion put forward at the Boot and Shoe Trades conference in July 1915. The Manufacturers' Association and the Operatives' Union agreed wholeheartedly that 'as a war measure only, women may be employed in the industry to fill places where no men are available'.

It was about this time that cracks began to appear in the relationship between employers and workers. As an incentive for those manning the Home Front, a system of war bonuses had been implemented to cover long hours and increased workloads. It is in the nature of the beast that once the climate of substantially increased earning power had been established, people began to study who was getting what. Whilst at management and professional levels little had improved, on the shop floor pay scales had increased substantially by virtue of overtime work and bonuses being paid. Combined with an unprecedented rise in the cost of living, this inevitably led to a degree of industrial unrest.

Among the first in the town to flex their muscles were those members of the unions employed by the Corporation. Due to the Corporation's unstinting support of the war effort from the outset, manpower in various departments had been stripped down to almost unworkable levels. An instance is the Gas Department which had become so depleted that it had to refuse to release any more skilled men unless a replacement was readily available. At the end of April 1915 the Amalgamated Association of Tramway and Vehicle Workers, the Gasworks and General Labourers' Union, and the Municipal Employees' Association, put their case to the Corporation. They asked for a general level of war bonuses to be paid across the board. The suggestion was that men earning less than 30s a week should receive a bonus of 3s a week, men earning 30s to 35s should get 2s and those earning more than 35s should have 1s.

Councillors debated the situation long and hard. They were acutely aware of the inherent problems involved. The cost of living index had indeed soared by an estimated 22 per cent. And despite the industrial boom, many Corporation employees had not been in a position to benefit. For example, the weekly wage of a gardener in the local authority employ was still only between 25s and 30s.

If the Corporation acceded to the requests, then an increase in rates would be necessary, resulting in a further escalation in the cost of living. If it refused, then those not so well off would suffer a lowering of living standards and probably ill health, followed by loss of working hours due to sickness.

After taking five weeks to review matters, the following formula was agreed. A war bonus would be paid to full-time Corporation employees[1] with the exception of the police (who were subject to a separate agreement), and Asylum staff. Those earning less than 30s per week would receive a bonus of 2s while anyone earning 30s to 35s would receive 1s.

At this point, 11 months into the war, the Corporation had to take the first of many long hard looks at its finances. With the war bonus scheme applying to approximately 2,371 men, the projected cost, to be absorbed by the rates, would be an estimated £9,000.[2]

On 18 May a dispute centring on a group of about 150 scourers in the dyeing and trimming trade led to a general lock-out of 2,500 men. Earlier in the month, on 4 May, the Leicester Hosiery Union (of which the dyers and finishers were a part) had asked the employers for a pay rise of a penny in the shilling for men on earnings up to 48s a week and for women on earnings up to 30s a week. (An indication of wage levels for factory workers at this point is that men who were earning more than 48s were actually employing helpers.) For their part, the scourers demanded an increased war bonus or a pay increase of 20 per cent.

The employers' stand was that a month previously, in April, they had agreed a war bonus for all employees of 1d in the 1s. An *impasse* resulted and on Saturday, 15 May the scourers came out on strike and the employers retaliated by imposing a lock-out from 12 noon on the 18th.

Central Government quickly drew the attention of all concerned parties to a Government circular concerning industrial disputes: 'With a view to preventing loss of production caused by disputes between employers and work people, no stoppage of work by strike or lock-out should take place on work for Government purposes. In the event of differences arising which fail to be settled by the

1. This created an anomaly in respect of certain employees such as lamp lighters who were excluded by virtue of the fact that they worked only 30 hours a week.
2. Doubtless the Corporation were also influenced in their decision making by the fact that during May a strike by tramcar drivers in London resulted in the authorities having to bring horse-drawn trams out of retirement.

parties directly concerned or by their representatives, or under any existing agreements, the matter shall be referred to an impartial tribunal nominated by His Majesty's Government for immediate investigation and report to the Government with a view to settlement.'

The tribunal was indeed hastily convened. At the Town Hall on Wednesday, 2 June, seven representatives of the unions, and seven from the Leicester Hosiery Manufacturers' Association, presented their case to the appointed arbitrator, Alderman Thomas Smith. Having heard the evidence, Smith found against the scourers, ruling that they must accept the now agreed general increase of seven and a half per cent.

Meanwhile, the war machine continued to demand more recruits to replace the alarming losses of the British Expeditionary Force in France. At the end of April a further two rooms at the Town Hall were set aside for recruiting. A survey of local factories and businesses by the Leicester Labour Bureau indicated that there still remained approximately 2,000 men aged between 19 and 38 years of age who were eligible for the army. However, the decline in recruiting had by now set in. Captain Mosse reported to the Recruiting Committee that during the last week of April, only 106 men had volunteered for the local regiment, plus 70 to the transport regiments. Prominent townsmen continued to lead by example and from the Leicester Cripples' Guild, their honorary surgeon, Dr Pemberton Peake, and their secretary, Percy Groves, both volunteered and departed for the war.

In a vain effort, Captain Pritchard, who had taken over from Major Hamilton as the town's recruiting officer, together with five NCOs newly-returned from France, set off on a recruiting drive into Derbyshire. They in turn were only relatively successful, returning with a total of 105 men. It is worth noting here that recruiting in rural areas such as Derbyshire and surrounding counties was not without its difficulties. In July 1915, at Ryedale in North Yorkshire, a recruiting party fell foul of local feeling. Private Tom Harland of the 5th Yorkshire Regiment, while trying to persuade a young lad to enlist, was set upon by George John Sigsworth, a local farmer. Rushing up to the men, Sigsworth shouted at Harland: 'You have no business recruiting here. You ought to be at the Front, you want

punching out of town.' Fined £25 by Helmsley magistrates on a charge of 'making statements likely to prejudice recruiting to His Majesty's Forces', Sigsworth, who owned 365 acres of farmland, told the court that he could not find labour due to the war.

On 13 May, the Leicestershire Yeomanry suffered severe losses in France. While being deployed as unmounted infantry in the trenches at Ypres, the Yeomanry came under heavy bombardment, sustaining 200 casualties. Among those killed were their CO, Lieutenant-Colonel Percy Cecil Evans-Freke, and the adjutant, Major William Francis Martin.

Born in 1871, the son of the 8th Baron Carbery, Colonel Evans-Freke of Bisbrook Hall at Uppingham was, prior to the war, Deputy Lieutenant of Rutland. Major Martin had been the chairman of the Mountsorrel Granite company. Both had served as members of the Yeomanry for nearly 20 years and had seen action with the 7th Company Leicestershire Imperial Yeomanry in South Africa during the Boer War.

Ironically, the dreadful losses of May provided a spur to recruiting. Within two weeks, volunteers had filled the depleted ranks of the Yeomanry, and recruiting for a new unit of artillery was quickly set in motion. The indefatigable Tom Crumbie set about raising 800 men for the 176th (Leicester) Royal Field Artillery Howitzer Brigade. With its headquarters, depot and stores at the Leicester Tigers' clubhouse, and brigade battery offices at the Nurses' Institution, business was brisk. (Gunners needed to be 19-40 years of age, height 5ft 7ins to 5ft 10ins, minimum chest measurement 35½ins. Requirements for drivers were the same except that the height requirements were 5ft 3ins to 5ft 7ins.) Nine days after launching the appeal, the brigade was half full and two 18-pounder guns, courtesy of the War Office, had arrived for training purposes. Following in his family's tradition, one of its first officers was Second Lieutenant Tom Crumbie Jnr. At the end of June the 'Recruiting Barometer' on the Town Hall showed that during that month some 1,200 men had joined the Colours, 600 of whom had enlisted in the Howitzer Brigade. A further 43 volunteers had presented themselves for recruitment at the newly-opened Royal Navy offices in Market Street.

In late September, with the inevitability of

conscription looming ever closer, the town raised one last volunteer unit. To be known as the 11th (Service Battalion) Leicestershire Regiment (Tigers Pioneers), it was a general infantry regiment with responsibility for road and railway building. Men who joined the new unit were paid 2d a day above the infantry rate. Ambitiously, the battalion aimed for 1,350 men plus 30 officers, with a second Depot Company of a further 250 men.

The members of the Recruiting Committee conscientiously continued working right up to the day that conscription relieved them of their task. In October 1915 the committee reported that during the previous six months it had arranged for the following: 742 men to receive dental treatment; 247 men to undergo minor operations at the Royal Infirmary, of whom 201 had subsequently been accepted by the army; 535 men to attend training classes at the YMCA to improve their physiques, of whom 376 were accepted for service, plus a 'miscellany of others'. Overall, out of a grand total of 782 candidates with remedial needs, 577 had been brought up to the required standard.

Meanwhile, the new-found prosperity in Leicester did not extend to everyone. Women left at home to bring up a family on an army separation allowance found things exceptionally hard. Prices that had soared to previously unseen levels were not going to come down as long as the nation was at war. Generally the increases on individual items were relatively small, but the overall result for those on a fixed income was soon to become a heavy burden.

Due to the exporting of grain to France and Belgium, a loaf of bread which had cost 6½d in August 1914 was selling for 8½d six months later.[1]

A scarcity of eggs forced the price up to 1s for seven. By the autumn of 1915, granulated sugar, which two years previously had sold for 1¾d a pound, had almost doubled to 3¼d. An increase in Excise Duty at the end of April raised the price of a bottle of whisky from 4s 6d to 6s 6d.

A small respite came when violent thunderstorms throughout the county during June threatened to wipe out the local strawberry crops. The result was that for a short period, market stalls and shops in Leicester were overwhelmed with cheap produce. The weather, though, brought more problems than it temporarily solved. During the last week of June and the first week of July, violent thunderstorms caused damage to property throughout the town. Two shops, one on Welford Road and another in Eggington Street, were damaged by lightning. Narborough Road near to the railway bridge was flooded for a distance of 30 yards to a depth of two feet. Twenty soldiers of the 3rd/4th Leicesters training on Victoria Park were affected by lightning strikes, two of whom had to be hospitalised. The storms reached a peak on Sunday, 4 July when many houses in the town were flooded and a house at 26 Lothair Road, in Clarendon Park, was struck by lightning. Manhole covers were forced off and in Draper Street and Dashwood Road garden walls collapsed.

In July the cost of a tramcar ride on the Stoneygate-Aylestone-Clarendon Park route rose by 50 per cent, from a penny to a penny ha'penny. This increase, disguised as an experimental scheme, created a huge controversy. Because the route in question was well patronised and ran through the better class suburbs of the town, it had been decided by the Corporation that the increase would be accepted with a minimum of fuss. This was a complete miscalculation. Although they persisted with the new fares, the attendant publicity and public furore created for the embattled Corporation a highly embarrassing situation.

The early months of 1915 heralded, another hard winter. The first snowfall of the year arrived during the afternoon of Thursday, 18 March. A blizzard which deposited four inches of snow over the town and surrounding county brought movement in the streets to a halt. Throughout the following day, 305 men and 74 carters were employed by the Corporation to clear the streets. Usually taking on between 200-300 men as casual labour for this task, the local authority was now able to find a total of only 55 able-bodied men available to augment their workforce.

Shortly after Christmas concern began to grow over the welfare of those children whose circumstances were only just above the bread line. The Elementary Schools Sub-Committee was well aware that irrespective of the present industrial prosperity which the town enjoyed, there were still many families in need. The children of those women existing on army allowances, and such part-time work as they could find, were experiencing great

---

1. This was exacerbated due to bakers in Leicester being paid at a higher rate than those in the surrounding counties.

suffering in the cold grip of winter. In the second week of January two school meals centres were set up to feed the children of poorer parents who were unemployed. About 40 children were fed at Elbow Lane, at the back of Sanvey Gate, and another 40 at Catherine Street. Provision was also made for a meal allowance for other poor children, enabling them to be fed at home. By the end of the month 80 families representing 245 children were benefiting from the plan.

Whilst prompted by humanitarian motives, the Elementary Schools Sub-Committee was quite pleased to point out to the Corporation that, if successful, the scheme would prevent some families from seeking Poor Relief. The implicit message being that, while school meals were funded by the Board of Education, Poor Relief came out of the rates.

Despite the constraints which the war placed on peoples lives in Leicester, as in hundreds of other townships throughout the country, the daily round continued. Recruiting posters adorned every billboard and lamp standard. Women worried over the cost of food, and men bemoaned the price of fodder along with the lack of horses to feed it to.

During April, the celebrated creator of Sherlock Holmes, Sir Arthur Conan Doyle, paid a visit to Leicester. In an evening's visit to the De Montfort Hall he gave to a packed audience '… an inspiring lecture entitled *The Great Battles of the War*", in which he explained British strategy and the events of the Battles of Mons and Ypres'. For those seeking less intellectual entertainment, in the same week Vesta Tilley gave a Saturday night concert at the 5th Northern General Hospital.

At the end of April, news was received from France that Private 6276 William Buckingham of the 2nd Battalion Leicestershire Regiment had been awarded the Victoria Cross. The citation read that the award was: 'For conspicuous acts of bravery and devotion to duty in rescuing and remaining with and rendering aid to wounded while exposed to heavy fire, especially at Neuve Chapelle on 10 and 12 March 1915.'

In the ensuing months William Buckingham was to become a huge local hero. Born in 1886, he had been taken into the care of the local authority when he was six years old and spent his childhood in the Countesthorpe Cottage Homes. In 1901, as a 15-year-old, he joined the Leicesters as a regular soldier,

serving in Egypt and India. When the regiment was mobilised in August 1914, Buckingham went to France with the Indian Expeditionary Force. Whilst in action at Neuve Chapelle, over a period of three days his conspicuous gallantry won him the VC. During three days of battle, Buckingham acting as a courier, went back and forth with despatches. At one point he rescued, under heavy fire, a German soldier whose leg had been blown off. On the third day he himself was shot in the chest. The bullet, entering from the left, was deflected by a packet of postcards in his pocket and exited through his right side. It was deflected for a second time by his cartridge case and lodged in his right arm where it remained until removed by surgeons at South Manchester Hospital. On his return to France, William Buckingham, while serving as orderly to Captain Mosse (the son of the CO at Glen Parva), was killed by machine-gun fire on 15 September 1916.

Other locals also returned home with tales to tell. One such was Harold Robotham, the son of the toy shop owners in Belvoir Street. Harold, described in the local press as 'a 21-year-old youth of slight build', had sailed from New York on 1 May aboard the Cunard liner *Lusitania* as secretary to the chief steward. One week later, 1,198 passengers and crew lost their lives when the *Lusitania* was torpedoed during the afternoon of 7 May off the coast of Ireland by the German submarine *U20*. Thrown into the water as the ship went down, Robotham, a non-swimmer, managed along with another crew member to scramble into one of the ship's life boats. They were joined by 12 more survivors including three women and later rescued by *HMS Heron*. The young survivor must have reflected upon his fortunes when he discovered that among his companions in the lifeboat was a stoker whose previous two vessels had both sunk – one of them being the *Titanic*.

In May a grand new hospital, the Gilroes Sanatorium, was opened for the treatment of consumptives by the octogenarian councillor, Alderman Windley. Boasting electricity supplied by dynamos and gas for cooking and heating, the hospital cost a princely £11,000. The following month saw the arrival on the news stands of a brand new newspaper. With its first edition appearing on Saturday, 12 June, the *Illustrated Leicester Chronicle* was on sale at 16 pages for a penny.

As the year progressed, the Leicester Poor Boys'

and Girls' Summer Camp and Institute was taxed with the question of what should be done in respect of those children who were annually given a free holiday at the seaside. The Poor Children's Holiday Home at Mablethorpe had been taken over by the army in order to billet troops. It was felt that due to the activities of the German fleet, and the bombing raids on the East Coast, a safer location should be sought.

The Manor House, Little Stretton, was leased from the owner, Mr Porter, and on Saturday, 12 June the first group of children arrived for their holiday in the country. Although not as large as the Mablethorpe premises (the Manor catered for 30 children as opposed to 78 at the coast), the new venue was to serve its purpose admirably. The extensive cream-coloured building, framed by a large sturdy tree and deep wide lawn, and looking on to a backdrop of open countryside, was an ideal location within easy reach of the town. Throughout the summer, poor children from the borough were given a two-week holiday – girls during the early summer, boys during the later months.

For the remainder of the war, children who otherwise would not have had a holiday each spent a fortnight at Little Stretton. In 1916, the number was 120, while in 1917 it doubled to 240. Somewhat to the children's dismay, the Board of Education, at an early stage, elected to provide staff, ensuring that 'a teacher was present to conduct lessons'.

Along with Private Buckingham and Lord Kitchener, a further celebrity and local hero was Admiral Beatty of Brooksby Hall. A charismatic figure, David Beatty joined the Royal Navy in 1884 as a boy of 13. As a young lieutenant he first came to notice while serving as a gunboat commander during Kitchener's campaign of 1896-98 in the Sudan. Whilst at the bombardment of the Dervish stronghold at Hafir, he was awarded the DSO when his CO was wounded, and taking command he ensured the success of the action. After further mention in despatches by Kitchener for his work with the gunboats on the Nile and at Khartoum, at the age of 27 Beatty was promoted to the rank of commander. Then came the Boxer Rebellion in China, resulting in his becoming the youngest captain in the Royal Navy. The advent of another war found Beatty as Officer Commanding Battle Cruisers at Rosyth. In this role he was responsible for the sinking in the North Sea of the German warships *Blücher* and *Königsberg*. It was to the great delight of the local populace that on 9 August 1915, David Beatty was promoted to the rank of vice-admiral.

Despite everyone's best efforts, Christmas was not the festive occasion of previous years. Men who had been expected home a year earlier were still away. When the Leicester Ragged School Mission gave its annual Robin Breakfast on Christmas Day to 500 of the town's poor children, a show of hands confirmed that the majority had fathers absent at the Front.

Shopping was made difficult during the early evenings by the newly-imposed black-out regulations. Street lamps were doused, shops were constrained from presenting extravagant displays. There was, as one newspaper, with a degree of understatement, commented, 'a noticeable absence of German clockwork toys in the shops!' Food prices, where the commodity was indeed available, were still rising. Turkeys had gone up from 1s a pound at Christmas 1914 to 1s 4d; ducks from 9d a pound to 1s; pheasants had gone up from 5s 6d a brace to 8s 6d; rabbits, the staple diet of the poor at Yuletide, were now 1s 6d each as opposed to 1s the previous year.

Whatever the strictures imposed upon people, in the spirit of the season, every effort was still made by those who could afford it to assist those who could not. The Wesley Hall Robin Breakfast Society fed 300 children at its Christmas Day breakfast. One of the helpers declared that '…Gargantua would have envied the fare provided. In addition to large quantities of pressed beef, there were 100lbs of bread, 28lbs of cake, 300 oranges and 300 mince pies. Mr Charles Wood, the chairman of the Society, Mr H. Carlisle and the Reverend W. J. Ball with a host of helpers put on a great deal of labour in order to carry on the good work as usual'.

Oxford Street Chapel provided a dinner of roast potatoes, beef, mince pies and oranges for 600 children. School masters and mistresses supplied details of sick children missing from the school registers in the poor districts and hampers were sent to 160 homes. Seventy aged and poor widows received clothes and hampers of meat and groceries.

As the year had begun, so it ended. The winter of 1915-16, which was making such a misery of life for the men in the trenches of the Western Front, extended its grip across the Channel. On Boxing

Day, Leicester was subjected to a series of ferocious gales. Roofs were blown off houses and garden walls demolished. In the later part of the day, around 8pm, several people were admitted to hospital suffering from broken bones caused by being blown off their feet. Considerable damage was caused to trees in North Evington and Clarendon Park, one in particular in Melbourne Road requiring several horses to remove it. Communications were disrupted due to the damage caused to telephone and telegraph wires. The gales continued throughout the coming week. On New Year's Day a telegram boy was injured in Highfield Street when winds blew him off his cycle and under the wheels of a passing motor car. On the same day, such havoc was caused to stalls in the Market Place that traders abandoned business at lunch-time and went home.

This was only a precursor of what was to come. Conditions continued to deteriorate. By the end of February 1916 Leicester was subjected to the fiercest winter it had seen for 25 years. Two days of continuous blizzards had, by Friday, 25 February, blanketed the borough. A foot of snow fell in 24 hours. Over the weekend a further six inches fell. The Borough Surveyor, E. George Mawbey, turned to the military for assistance. Mawbey's 138 Corporation men, along with 20 casual employees, were supplemented by 1,200 men recruited to the Pioneer Regiment at Leicester. Their CO, Colonel Canning Turner, divided his men into gangs of 40 or 50 under the control of NCOs and Corporation gangers. These were later supplemented by 350 artillerymen who had been drafted in.

Carting the snow away also proved to be a problem. Due to their shoeing, the horses of the army's Remount Division, which had been loaned to the Corporation, were unable to maintain their footing on the slippery ground. In the end the work of clearing up had to be left to the 35 carters employed by the local authority.

And the chaos was not restricted to the confines of the town. In the surrounding area, snow closed roads and at Whitwick Colliery haulage was stopped and several hundred miners had to be brought back above ground.

The conditions persisted until the end of the following month. On 28 March snowfalls nationwide caused serious dislocation to transport and communications. Railway lines into and out of London were blocked, effectively isolating the capital, and most of England south of Chesterfield was brought to a standstill.

In Leicester the heaviest snowfall of the year came during the night of Monday and Tuesday, 27-28 March, effectively closing all the roads into and through the town. Vehicular traffic ground to a halt, tramcars became stuck in drifts and had to be abandoned.

With all telegraph and telephone systems rendered useless there was no communication with other areas. Extensive drifting closed the Midland Railway lines, preventing trains from running. Linesmen reported that the track to the north, between Leicester and Nottingham, was blocked by fallen trees and telegraph poles. South of the town, the two trains which attempted to make the journeys to Market Harborough and Desford became stuck in drifts and had to be dug out. Commuters hoping to travel the short distance between Leicester and Syston found themselves stranded overnight in the cold and cheerless conditions of the waiting room on the Midland Railway Station. No information of the conditions beyond Thurmaston to the north and Knighton to the south was available.

The blizzard during the night caused the clock on the Corn Exchange in the Market Place to stop at 3.15am. Three and a quarter hours later the one on the Town Hall succumbed at 6.30am. At 3am, snowploughs and scrapers were set to work in an attempt to re-open contact with the outside world. Matters were not helped by the fact that the blizzards continued throughout Tuesday until around 4.30pm, when freezing temperatures rendered working conditions intolerable.

Life began to assume a semblance of normality during the latter part of the week. On Wednesday the Tramways Department, using three large snow-ploughs to bulldoze the snow and spray brine on the tram rails, succeeded in getting the cars moving again. In order to keep the points clear, men were stationed at each set clearing away the snow as it fell. By Thursday, rail services were in the process of being restored, much more slowly however. Fallen trees and debris had to be cleared in the most difficult conditions. A fallen telegraph pole could take a gang of engineers up to a day to clear and replace. The first line to become operational was the one from Melton Mowbray to Leicester, and then onwards to London.

This German machine gun, captured in France just before Christmas 1914, was displayed in a recruiting pageant in Leicester during January 1915. One of those escorting the gun was Sgt J. F. Cooke, who having been part of the unit involved in its capture, was recovering form wounds (he had lost an eye in the attack) at the 5th Northern General Hospital. The plaque reads: 'Captured by the 2nd Battalion (17th) The Leicestershire Regiment near Richebourg L'Avoue during a night attack on the German trenches on the 19th December 1914.'

Private 6276 William Buckingham, 2nd Battalion, Leicestershire Regiment. A regular soldier long before the war, Buckingham was awarded the Victoria Cross for rescuing wounded men under fire at Neuve Chapelle, during a three-day period in March 1915.

During an action on 12-13 May 1915, the Leicestershire Yeomanry suffered severe losses in France. While being deployed in the trenches at Ypres as unmounted infantry, they came under heavy bombardment, sustaining 200 casualties. Among those killed was their Commanding Officer, 44-year-old Lt Colonel Percy Cecil Evans Freke. (An old picture taken at the time of the South African War.)

An increase of 50 per cent in tramcar fares on the Stoneygate Aylestone-Clarendon Park routes provoked a public outcry in July 1915. A trip into town on a tramcar such as this one pictured at the junction of Victoria Park Road and Queen's Road jumped from a penny to a penny ha'penny.

Despite considerable resistance to their presence in the workplace, the employment of women to fill the places of men away at war was inevitable. On 8 July 1915, the *Leicester Daily Mercury* announced: 'Women are not being employed as drivers and conductors on tramcars as this is not seen as a suitable occupation for women.' As this group of Tramways Department staff clearly shows, that presumption was to be quickly overturned.

A group of men from 'A' Company, 8th (Service) Battalion, Leicestershire Regiment, being trained in the art of digging trenches, at Wokingham in England, prior to going to France.

The winter of 1915-16 was particularly hard. At the end of March 1916, blizzards cut off all road, rail, telegraph and telephone communications, isolating Leicester for several days. A resident of Billesdon, the elderly gentleman with his dogs is Dr Williamson, seen here making his way along Uppingham Road on the outskirts of town.

Emergency Services

DURING the Great War there were essentially two official emergency services – the police and the fire brigade. Originating from the concept of the Metropolitan Police Force which was created in 1836, boroughs and counties throughout the land followed suit in establishing police forces during the years immediately after. The Leicester Borough Police came into being in 1838 with a presumed responsibility to provide from its ranks a fire-fighting service. The impracticability of this was soon realised and by 1872 the town had a Borough Fire Brigade separate from its police. One anomaly, however, was that the fire brigade also had the responsibility for providing an ambulance facility within the borough. This situation was to pertain until August 1941 when the local authority took over the responsibility.

With the benefit of hindsight, it can be seen that in August 1914 the attitude adopted by Leicester Corporation towards the war was, to say the least, naïve. Britain was involved in an issue, the magnitude of which few people grasped. Deluded by totally unfounded promises of a short war, local authorities, Leicester included, released – irretriev-ably as it transpired – essential personnel.

From an authorised establishment of 295 police officers, the Watch Committee in August 1914 immediately permitted 87 men, almost a third of its police force, to go to the Colours. They were in fact obliged to release only 19 officers who were subject to recall as reservists. Similarly firemen, in addition

to those reservists who were bound to return to their regiments, were allowed to leave the brigade. By the second day of the war, Leicester's fire brigade had signed up four new men to replace those leaving and were seeking more. During the next two months the police took on 40 new recruits. (The result was that these organisations were quickly placed in an invidious position. By releasing able-bodied men they depleted their ranks and in the process of engaging replacements opened themselves to accusations of hiding men who were eligible for the army. Also, by agreeing to treat absent men as still serving as employees, they created for themselves severe long-term financial difficulties.[1]) Retirement, other than due to ill-health, was stopped with immediate effect by the Watch Committee in an attempt to maintain a level of experienced man-power in the essential services.

One of the steps taken to bolster the police reserves was the swearing-in of special constables. The Watch Committee minutes for 4 May 1915 show that '608 special constables are now sworn in, of whom 382 are now performing occasional duty'. This seems to be an exceptionally high figure and should be taken in conjunction with a prior offer by the Citizens' Training League to assist – the pre-sumption being that this figure in fact represents large numbers of the Citizens' Training League being sworn in *en masse*. Performing a four-hour tour of duty once every two weeks, each special constable wore a brassard on his arm to identify him in his

---

1. From the outset married men's wives were paid the difference between their Separation Allowance and their husband's pay. Single men received one third of their pay in addition to any army allowances. In June 1915 it was agreed that constables who were away at war should receive a war bonus of between one and two shillings a week – this was withdrawn in June 1917. Firemen who went to the Colours as reservists were also regarded as being temporarily absent and put on half pay.

role, and after ten duty periods he was allowed 5s for boot allowance. The 'specials' paraded for the last time at 10pm on Saturday, 2 January 1919. Having sung *Auld Lang Syne* at the end of the shift, they dismissed and, for the time being, disbanded.

While the fire brigade, under Chief Officer Henry Neal, had a brief to prepare and hold itself in readiness for any eventualities, the police force took on an immediate responsibility for various activities from the outset of the war.

The initial flurry of activity which engaged the attention of the police in August 1914 was centred upon the enemy within. Under the terms of the Aliens Restriction Act of 1914, all German, and later Austrian and Hungarian, nationals were declared to be hostile aliens. Having been peremptorily rounded up, about 50 people – who had been previously regarded as good citizens, even though foreigners – were shipped off to York for the military authorities to deal with. These were followed a month later by a further dozen men who, being classed by the German Government as reservists, were arrested by Leicester police and sent up to York under military escort.

So far as Leicester was concerned, the question of the enemy within was never to be a particular problem. Having initially identified those to whom the Act referred, the matter was effectively dealt with. As could be expected, over the subsequent months a little tidying up was necessary. Acting on various items of information, a final round-up was conducted in July 1915, when 24 men and six women found themselves in custody due to their nationalities. Of the men, 20 were sent to Handforth Internment Camp in Cheshire, while the other four went to Lofthouse Camp at Wakefield. The women were deported.

As time progressed, a more realistic threat was posed by the potential for escapees from the nearby prisoner-of-war camp at Donington Hall to make their way into the borough. Situated close to the north-west boundary of the county, a short distance from the village of Castle Donington, this was one of the principle 'officer' camps in the country. While there were several unsuccessful escape attempts, only one of the German officers managed to evade recapture and make his way back to Germany.

Oberleutnant-zur-See Günther Plüschow had, prior to being captured, created for himself quite a history. When war was declared he was serving at the German Yellow Sea naval base of Tsingtoa on the South China coast. As an extremely important strategic location the base was soon under attack from a combined Japanese, British and Indian force. The only pilot on the base (with responsibility for artillery spotting), Plüschow made good his escape in a monoplane when the Germans surrendered to the Allies on 10 November 1914. Eventually arriving in the United States, Günther Plüschow took ship for home. Unfortunately his identity was discovered when the vessel put into Gibraltar, resulting in his arrest. Sent to England as a prisoner-of-war, he eventually ended up at Donington Hall.

In July 1915, Plüschow, along with another officer, Oberleutnant Oscar Treppitz, executed a carefully rehearsed escape plan. On the morning of Sunday, 4 July both officers reported sick and stayed in their quarters all day. Late that night, during one of the heavy thunderstorms which beset the county during July, they avoided the sentries and climbed over the perimeter wire. Having changed into civilian clothes[1] they walked into the nearby village of Castle Donington and eventually made their way to Derby. Here they parted company at Derby Midland Station, ironically having just walked past the Midland Road premises of a Derby photographer, W. W. Winter, who had earlier been employed to take photographs of the German prisoners at Donington Hall.

Plüschow bought a ticket to Leicester. At Leicester he changed trains and continued on to London, from where he eventually stowed away aboard a steamer, the *Princess Juliana* bound for Holland, and thence went by train to Germany. On his return he was promoted to *kapitänleutnant* and awarded the Iron Cross (First Class). Treppitz did not make it. He was arrested at Millwall docks and returned to the camp. Günther Plüschow was one of only four POWs to successfully escape from prisoner-of-war camps in Britain during the First World War.

As the war progressed, so others tried to emulate Plüschow's feat. During the night of Saturday, 14 July 1917 three more officers escaped through a hole cut in the perimeter wire of the camp. Two of them,

---

1. In a book which he wrote after the war, Plüschow maintained that at no time did they have any outside help. This is difficult to credit. Both men were able on the other side of the wire to change into civilian clothes, complete with macintoshes and hats. Later while in London he had money to sustain him in the city for several days before he finally escaped from the country.

Carl Spindler and Max Ernst Winkelmann, were German naval officers, the third, Arpel Hern, was an Austrian army officer. Again as in the case of Plüschow and Treppitz, civilian clothes were waiting for them on the other side. This time all three were quickly recaptured. A few weeks later, in September, 22 prisoners-of-war, including Karl von Müller, the captain of the *Emden,* tunnelled out of the internment camp between Sutton Bonington and Kegworth. A massive police alert followed in Leicester, Nottingham and Derby. Local police officers and volunteer forces men armed with rifles and shotguns scoured the towns and countryside. A dozen of the fugitives were rounded up within hours, the remainder soon followed.

A never previously encountered danger was now to manifest itself for the first time. Warfare reached middle England, from the skies, initially in the form of Zeppelin airships and later by the Gotha bombers. The civilian population was for the first time subjected to aerial bombing raids. Towns situated along the South and East Coasts had always been vulnerable to attack from the sea. In December 1914, the Kaiser's Navy had taken the opportunity to stand out to sea and bombard Scarborough and Hartlepool resulting in over 700 casualties, including 137 killed. However, this was the first time in history that inland targets could be attacked from the air.[1]

The first raids, carried out by fixed-wing aircraft, took place over Dover and the mouth of the Thames on Christmas Eve and Christmas Day 1914, when no casualties were reported. During the following months, regular visits were paid by Zeppelin crews over the East Coast and Norfolk. By May 1915, their activities had extended to the outskirts of London.

Once the potential of the aerial threat was appreciated, the Government set about minimising the risks. In view of the fact that this was the first time that anything of this nature had been encountered, the precautions arrived at were basic, but none the less were in the main realistic. (In some cases early estimates were grossly inaccurate. The Lord Lieutenant of Leicestershire was warned in late 1914 to expect, as a consequence of Zeppelin activities, a possible 134,000 refugees fleeing from Lincolnshire, accompanied by 27,000 horses and 19,000 vehicles.)

With a slightly more pragmatic approach, the Watch Committee gave its attentions to ensuring the safety of the borough. In collaboration with Henry Neal and Herbert Allen, the Chief Officers of Leicester Borough Fire Brigade and Leicester Borough Police respectively, they set about the task of making specific preparations.

In February 1915 the issue of warning posters to be distributed throughout the town was put in hand. A month later, during the third week of March, the task was made easier by the promulgation by the War Office of specific instructions.

Military Order re Zeppelin Raids issued by Officer Commanding 11th Northern Division.

'I, Major General F. Hammersley, being a competent Military Authority in exercise of the powers vested in me by Regulation 12 of the Defence of the Realm Consolidation Regulations 1914, do hereby order and direct as follows:-

That all lights other than light not visible from the outside of any house shall be kept extinguished between the hours of sunset and sunrise in all places mentioned in the Schedule hereto; except such lights as are not contrary to the following Regulations:-

(1) In all streets and public places and on bridges, a portion of the lights must be extinguished in such a manner as the Chief Officers of the Police shall direct so as to break up all groups or rows of lights, and the lights which are not so extinguished must be made invisible from above by shading or by painting over the tops and upper portions of the globes.

(2) Sky signs, illuminated fascias, and lights used for outside advertising or illuminating of shops must be extinguished.

(3) All interior lights (except in factories), must be partially shaded by blinds being half pulled down.

(4) In factories in which night shifts are working, the upper windows must be shaded so that no lights are visible from outside, and such of the lower windows must be similarly shaded as may be settled

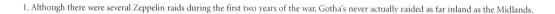

1. Although there were several Zeppelin raids during the first two years of the war, Gotha's never actually raided as far inland as the Midlands.

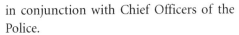

in conjunction with Chief Officers of the Police.

(5) The lighting of Railway Stations, sidings, and goods yards, must be reduced to the intensity sufficient for the safe and prompt conduct of business.

(6) The sides of lights along the water front must be painted or obscured so as to prevent the reflection of the light upon water.

(7) The aggregation of flares in the street markets is prohibited.

(8) The interior lights of tram cars and omnibuses must be so obscured by curtains or otherwise as to be invisible from the outside, or if not obscured no more than one light shall be used. No outside lights shall be carried except a red tail light and a head light of moderate intensity.

(9) All public lamps under the control of the local Lighting Authority shall be extinguished and kept extinguished from 10 o'clock until sunrise.

SCHEDULE LEICESTER

The Police and Military Patrols have received orders to enforce the above Regulations. Any person contravening the Regulations commits an offence and becomes liable to be tried by a Court of Summary Jurisdiction or by Court Martial.

Made and published at Grantham
on the 15th March 1915.
(Signed), F. Hammersley.
Major General.

The Order must be enforced at once. Shopkeepers whose lights shine into the street must be warned to cover them and any refusal to do so must be reported so that the information may be forwarded to the Military Authorities for any action they choose to take.

(Signed) H. Allen
Chief Constable

The emergency regulations were not necessarily well received by all. In the absence of any airships overhead, many of those who felt that their business or lifestyle was threatened baulked, while others who were simply careless fell foul of the new constraints.

A month after the restrictions became law, Thomas Mortimer, a confectioner of 5 Applegate Street, when reported for showing a light at his premises by Inspector Clark and PC Matthews, told the officers that '…he hoped the Germans would come and shoot Major General Hammersley'. Taking a serious view of his comments, the magistrates at the Town Hall made it clear to Clark that they were in a position to send him for court martial, fine him £100 or send him to prison for six months. Having stated their options, because this was the first prosecution under the Regulations to be brought before them, the bench fined him 15s plus costs.

Similarly, in June, John Henry Burbidge of 42 Gwendolen Road was fined 10s for showing a light which he had left on to illuminate his wife's way home – and for being abusive to a constable.

In London that early summer, with the reality of war suddenly being brought to their doorsteps, the people of the capital took to the streets. In the second week of May, riots broke out in London's East End. The targets were those premises owned by Austrian's and Germans, all of whom had lived and worked in the city long before the war. Seventy shops were looted and 26 people injured. The disturbances were quelled by mounted police and special constables.

As a provision for an early warning system the Watch Committee arranged that air-raid hooters be installed at various locations around the borough. In the town one was manned at the Midland Railway Station, while on the outskirts there was one at the Power Station and another at the Wheatsheaf factory on Knighton Fields Road East. In order for the system to work, it was necessary for all factory owners in the town to co-operate by agreeing to suspend indefinitely the use of their factories' steam-driven hooters.

The signal of approaching Zeppelins or aircraft was four short and one long blast. After September 1916, if an alert was initiated during the late evening or early hours of the morning, one short blast was given in order to alert police officers who were on duty, but not disturb the slumbering citizenry.

Once the alarm had been raised, all off-duty police, special constables, St John Ambulance men and women, and Volunteer Corps personnel were required to report to their stations. Volunteer motorists reported for duty and parked their cars outside the Central Police Station at the Town Hall

COUNTY BOROUGH OF LEICESTER.

POLICE NOTICE.

AIR RAIDS.

The public are requested to make themselves acquainted with the following instructions with regard to the steps that will be taken in case of raids by hostile aircraft. They are earnestly asked to assist the Authorities by remaining calm, and by willingly and strictly complying with these instructions. They can greatly assist in safeguarding the Town by always strictly observing the Lighting Orders, and using the darkest curtains they can obtain.

Should it become known that hostile aircraft are approaching the neighbourhood, the following steps will be taken:

HOOTERS.– Steam hooters will be blown for a period of five minutes (if safe to do so). This warning will consist of a succession of five blasts - four short ones, followed by one long one.

As no steam hooters are now sounded after 4-0 p.m., the alarm may be recognised when a hooter is heard in the evening.

TRAMS.– The electric trams will be stopped immediately, and remain stationary until all danger is believed to be passed.

GAS.– The gas will be reduced to a minimum, and householders are earnestly requested to extinguish what light remains, taking great care to turn off the taps at the gas jets and the meter, to avoid danger in case of fire, or of explosion or suffocation after the pressure is restored.

ELECTRIC LIGHT.– The electric light will be gradually reduced to a minimum, and in this case also the public are requested to switch off what light remains.

FLASHLIGHTS.– The use of flashlights at such a time is strictly prohibited.

MOTORS AND OTHER VEHICLES.– Drivers must reduce their lights as low as possible, and proceed at a walking pace, and with the greatest caution. They must stop if requested. Motor horns must not be sounded unless absolutely necessary to avoid accident.

The Police have had strict instructions to report any driver who disobeys this Order.

If the drivers of vehicles are not bound to proceed they are requested to draw into side streets, extinguish their lights, and remain stationary. It should be borne in mind that the position of a town is likely to be located by the noise of traffic.

PUBLIC.– The public are strongly advised to remain at home. The windows and doors of the lower floors should be closed to prevent the admission of noxious gases in case of poisonous bombs being dropped etc. A supply of water or wet sand should be kept ready so that a small fire could be promptly and effectively dealt with.

FIRE ALARMS. Inhabitants should ascertain the position of the nearest Fire Alarm.

STREET LAMPS.– Householders opposite street lamps that are lit are requested to assist by turning them out.

SPECIAL CONSTABLES, Auxiliary Firemen, St. John's V.A.D., Citizens Training League, and other bodies, should assemble according to arrangements in force.

H. ALLEN,
Chief Constable

14th February 1916

in readiness either to transport police officers to strategic points or to be used as ambulances. Vehicles at the 5th Northern General Hospital and the War Hospital were put on stand-by. Police and volunteers went to high buildings to listen for the engines of the approaching dirigibles. All on and off-duty firemen (plus those of private brigades), reported to their respective stations and a gas engineer in a motor car toured the streets.

Although the air-raid warnings were sounded with regularity (12 times in 1916, seven in 1917 and five in 1918), Leicester itself was never the subject of a raid. The nearest town to be attacked was Loughborough. During the early evening of Monday, 31 January 1916, a force of six Zeppelins arrived over the Midlands, dropping 220 bombs over a wide area of several counties, including Derbyshire and Leicestershire.

The airships appeared over Loughborough about 7pm and dropped several bombs on the town. Shops, houses and a pub were damaged and ten people killed, as well as several others being injured.

Zeppelin raids virtually ceased by the end of 1916, although sporadic attacks by aircraft continued until late 1917. The crew of one ship remained to spend a large part of the war in the county. Whilst participating in a two-squadron raid on the Eastern Counties, Zeppelin L15 was hit by gunfire and came down 15 miles off the coast of Kent near Margate. The captured officers, having initially been taken to Chatham, spent the remainder of the war at Donington Camp.

Henry Neal had started his working life as a naval engineer. Leaving the sea he had joined Grimsby's fire brigade as chief engineer in 1901, being promoted to its chief officer in 1903. Neal then came to Leicester as head of Leicester Borough Fire Brigade in 1909 at the end of the horse-drawn era. A progressive man, he combined his engineering skills with a high degree of ability as a fire officer to bring the brigade into the 20th century and the age of petrol engines and electricity. The onset of war and all its potential for disaster provided Henry Neal with an unexpected opportunity to push through his plans for maximising the efficiency of Leicester's fire-fighting force. The fact that Leicester escaped enemy attacks should not detract from Neal's work. He laid the foundation for a fire brigade which would take Leicester through the inter-war years.

In 1914, Leicester's fire brigade comprised 29 permanent firemen with headquarters in the middle of the town and branch stations at Clarendon Park, Aylestone, Belgrave and North Evington. Of the first three, each maintained a hose truck and fire escape with a telephone line to the Central Fire Station. Opened in October 1899, North Evington branch station, situated in Asfordby Street, had three resident firemen, a motor pump and six retained firemen. The latter were paid £5 per year retainer in 1917.

The Central Fire Station was a relatively new building. Having shared accommodation at the Town Hall with the police since 1876 (when it was built and known as 'the New Town Hall'), Leicester Borough Fire Brigade moved to its new home at 31 Rutland Street on 30 August 1892. Complete with engineering and blacksmith's shops, paint stores and carpenter's workshops, almost all the brigade's maintenance was undertaken by the firemen themselves. The stables at Rutland Street were altered at the end of 1917 to provide garages for motor ambulances.

One of the first improvements to be achieved during late 1914 and early 1915, was in the realm of communications. The use of telephones was still restricted in the main to business and professional use. Neal first had a new call-out board installed at North Evington, then proceeded with the upgrading of on-street fire alarms directly linked to the Central Fire Station. Shrewdly, he offered the shared use of these telephones to the police at night time – provided the police bore the maintenance costs. The British United Shoe Machine Company was offered, for a fee, a 'direct communication' with the Central Fire Station. In March 1915, Messrs W. A. Bates of St Mary's Mills and The Imperial Picture Theatre on Green Lane Road were connected to Rutland Street by direct fire alarms linked through the street alarm system. Rental for this facility was charged at £2 per annum.

The on-street system was, without doubt, most effective. On the night of 14 June 1915, a large fire in a box store at 90 Brunswick Street was quickly notified from the post in the same street. A large fire in the three-storey building of Knight and Mobbs boot factory, which severely damaged the premises along with an adjacent shop and house, was called in from the Checketts Road post. Turning the system around, Neal also charged Associated Fire Alarms Ltd, the company who installed the alarm systems in premises, a fee for allowing their equipment to be set up at the Central Fire Station. In January 1917 the company made a plea for a reduction in the charge of £2 on each installation of their system at the fire station as they had 53 of them which came to £106 a year.

Water supplies were the next thing to be addressed. With the threat of aerial bombardment, the Corporation needed little convincing of the premise that fighting-fire required an adequate water supply. In November 1914, Neal arranged for an underground water tank to be installed at the junction of Granby Street and Chatham Street. This was accompanied by a promise from the local authority of further tanks during the next six months in Jarrom Street, King Street and Evington Valley Road. (The Corporation were somewhat tardy and despite their promises, the first tank – at the Clock Tower – was not installed and tested until March 1916.) Exploiting his advantage, in February 1915, the fire chief gained acceptance of one further improvement in the delivery of water at hydrant level. Using his engineering skills, Neal persuaded the Corporation to review the number of hydrants in the borough. By linking up various dead ends of water mains it would be possible to reduce the 1,500 existing hydrants to a total of 500, which would be needed by the fire brigade. The scheme was agreed upon, dependent upon the fire brigade budget paying to the Water Board a sum of £750 in five instalments of £150 for the work to be done.

During 1915 the fire brigade, in addition to dealing with 1,568 ambulance calls, attended 146 fires in the borough and assisted at ten in the county. Some, such as the one at the boot and shoe factory of Messrs Swan and Preston in early June, were serious and extremely time consuming. This set Henry Neal reflecting upon the quality of the existing system of fire-fighting in the county and its reliance upon the services of his brigade. The presumption was that Leicester Borough Fire Brigade, with its modern equipment, would in times of need attend conflagrations in outlying districts. This not only left the town at some risk, it also cost time and money. Neal, deciding that the future is not necessarily a continuation of the past, put a proposal to the Watch Committee:

BOROUGH FIRE BRIGADE
Rutland Street,
Leicester.
23 June 1915

Gentlemen,
I most respectfully recommend your

Committee to consider the existing arrangements respecting the attendance by the Brigade to fires outside the Borough.

At the present time the County of Leicester pay a retaining fee of £50 per annum, under a resolution passed by them dated January 1882. At that time the Brigade consisted of volunteer men with scarcely any equipment at their command, and the amount appears to have been paid for the protection of property just outside the Borough amounting in value to over £100,000, without reference to villages outside or in any way stating what service was expected of the Brigade.

According to a list prepared many years ago by my predecessor, we undertake to attend, if possible, fires at 65 villages within a radius of eight miles, which does not include Wigston Magna, Syston, and several others, but no mention is made respecting any of these places in the County Council resolution.

During the last 5½ years the Brigade attended 46 fires outside the Town occupying men and appliances 226 hours. In addition to the retaining fee, £430 0s 6d was received from Insurance Companies or the owners of property for out-of-pocket expenses. Out of this amount £100 19s 6d was paid to Hackmasters for Horse Hire, leaving £329 1s 0d for the department, which averages £7 3s 0d per fire and is in my opinion most inadequate for the services rendered.

At two recent fires 425 feet of hose was used, and on each occasion the water had to be driven a long distance, putting tremendous pressure on the lines of the hose near the pump which shortens its life very considerably. This is an important matter, as hose costs £50 per 1,000 feet.

I have considerable information obtained from other Cities and Boroughs and most places have a fixed agreement of some kind, but in nearly every instance the arrangement varies and in my opinion none are suitable for this District.

If your Committee decide to continue this work I respectfully recommend that the arrangement with the County Council be determined and that the Urban District Councils and Parish Councils in the neighbourhood be approached and informed that if they desire to secure our services, a charge of £1 0s 0d will be made for every £1,000 or portion of £1,000 on their rateable value as a retaining fee for the Brigade, also that the Council concerned will be asked to become responsible for the payment of expenses in accordance with the following scale:-

Motor Fire Engine	£6 6s 0d for first two hours or any portion of two hours. £2 2s 0 per hour thereafter.
Steam Fire Engine	£3 0s 0d for first hour and £1 0s 0d per hour after.
Horses	£1 5s 0d each
Officer in Charge	£3 3s 0d
Firemen	3s for first hour and 1s 6d per hour after.

In the event of a turn-out and services not required, the first hour scale to be charged.

> I am Gentlemen,
> Your Obedient Servant,
> Henry Neal
> Chief Fire Officer.

The members of the committee did not need much urging, the matter was quickly approved and a minute entered that 'those Authorities which are invited and do not accept these terms not be considered in the event of a fire call to their district'.

In common with his opposite number, the Chief Constable, Henry Neal was constantly at odds with the Government in his efforts to preserve his dwindling manpower resources.

In December 1915 he and other chief fire officers received a War Office memorandum assuring them that, with immediate effect, no man engaged as a full-time fire-fighter would be required to join up. The letter stated that the authorties '...fully recognise that these men are engaged in the protection of life and property from fire and are of the opinion that they are doing as good work for their King and Country in their present occupation as if they were serving with the Army in the field'. Where a fireman had already attested and been placed in the army reserve, a chief fire officer was to issue a certificate which, on presentation to the recruiting officer, released the man from his obligation to the army.

Heavy losses abroad over the following months quickly revealed the hollowness of this promise. The weeks following December 1915 saw the evacuation of the defeated Allied forces from Gallipoli. Further east, General Townshend's contingent of 3,000 British and 6,000 Indian troops was about to be taken prisoner at the siege of Kut-Al-Imara in Iraq. In France, the German attack on the little village of Verdun, which heralded the supreme losses during the summer of 1916 in the Battle of the Somme, was begun in February.

Fresh instructions issued by a desperate War Office were soon circulated to local authorities.

> War Office
> London SW
> 14 April 1916

Sir,

With reference to previous correspondence from this Office regarding the enlistment of men employed permanently on Fire Brigade duties, I am directed to inform you that men are now urgently required for service. It is hoped that arrangements may be made to find substitutes to replace the single men of military age at present employed on your Staff, in order to release such men at the earliest possible date for service in the Army.

> I am, Sir,
> Your obedient Servant,
> (Sd) NOEL FRENCH,
> Maj.
> for Director of Recruiting.

Henry Neal Esq.,
Chief Officer, Chief Fire Station,
Leicester.

> War Office,
> London SW
> 29 April 1916

Sir,

Adverting to this Office's letter of the 14th instant No. 27/Gen N0/4507, I am commanded by the Army Council to inform you that in accordance with the revised lists of Certified Occupations, single men under 25 years of age who are engaged permanently on Fire Brigade duties will not be exempted from military service on account of their occupation on and after 1 July 1916.

I am Sir,
Your Obedient Servant.
(Signed) B. B. Cubitt.

The Chief Fire Officer,
Chief Fire Station,
Fire Brigade. Leicester.

With a dearth of new recruits, Henry Neal and Herbert Allen were constrained to optimising their existing resources and steadfastly refusing to allow any of their older staff to retire for the duration of the war.

Intent upon bringing the fire brigade into the 20th century, Henry Neal's final efforts were directed towards replacing the now outdated horse-drawn transport facilities with motorised appliances. This process had been commenced in 1906 with the purchase of the brigade's first 'self-propelled appliance', capable of speeds up to 20mph.

Neal began the building of his fleet proper in 1912 with the addition of two 55hp motorised fire engines, three motor pumps, a motor turntable, a two-seater motor car and a motorised ambulance van. In November 1916, the Watch Committee agreed to the fire brigade entering into a 12-month contract with the Shell Marketing Company for the purchase of petroleum fuel at 2s 6d a gallon. This expansion was curtailed during the middle years of the war, due partly to activities in other areas and partly to the fact that the military had first call on the production of motor vehicles.

It was not until 1917 that, with the assistance of the Watch Committee, a bid could be made to acquire new vehicles. In the summer of 1917, Neal reported that the horse which was employed with the ambulance and prison van was, after 13 years in the traces, no longer fit for work.[1] As it was not possible at that time to purchase a motor vehicle for such purposes, he would examine the availability of buying a second-hand chassis and adapting it. The difficulties in this are illustrated by the fact that tenders for such a chassis were solicited without success from Messrs Straker-Squire, Wolseley

Motors, the Sunbeam Motor Car Co, Daimler, Siddely Deasy, Austin Motors, and the Clement Talbot Motor Co. All, with the exception of Austin, declined to tender as they were under government production controls. The Austin tender was not accepted by the Watch Committee (it is not clear why), so the net had to be cast a little wider.

Eventually, a Siddely Deasy vehicle – obviously overlooked by the military – which was for sale, was discovered at Cleethorpes, in the possession of Mr J. Ross, of Filey House. It was brought down to Leicester and purchased for £350, having been 'thoroughly tested on the steepest hills in the county' in the presence of Watch Committee members, the Chief Fire Officer and a motor engineer. The workshops at the Central Fire Station then set to about stripping down the engine and rebuilding the vehicle's existing body. In February 1918 Neal announced to Councillor Hincks and the Watch Committee that the new motor ambulance had been completed at a total cost of £521 8s 2d. More important, its current value was about £850. Also, that the 'old horse' had been sold for £35 to a Mr Hill of Wigston.

Throughout the war, the rank and file of the fire brigade and the police force, both locally and nationally, were constantly at odds with their employers over money. In common with the factory worker and shop assistant, their cost of living was rising at an alarming rate.

In January 1915 a fireman, depending upon his grade, earned between 27s and 50s a week. A police constable 28s to 35s, a sergeant 45s and an inspector 56s to 58s.

The following four years were punctuated by applications and petitions to the Watch Committee, each of which was deflected with promises of substantial pay increases once the war was won. At the beginning of 1919, fire brigade pay worked upwards according to rank, from 53s a week for a district officer to 72s 6d for a second officer. The police force, balanced precariously on the edge of a national strike, earned from 40s for a constable to 73s for an inspector.

A central factor in the equation was what should happen to the war bonus at the end of hostilities. In early 1915, Leicester police officers received 2s a week. It is most probable that fire brigade employees received the same. One month before the

---

1. One of the anomalies in the distribution of responsibilities at the time was that the fire brigade provided the horse-drawn 'Black Maria' used to transport prisoners in police custody.

end of the war, in October 1918, both organisations were in receipt of a weekly allowance amounting to 16s. (By March 1918, Leicester Corporation were paying out the huge sum of £161,982 a year in war bonuses to its employees.) The moot question was: would they be allowed to keep the allowance as part of their salary, thus making it a pensionable matter? In the aftermath of the war, the ensuing struggles resulted in much acrimony – and even a police strike – before either group succeeded in resolving matters.

As regards the heads of the two emergency services, there was a considerable disparity between their individual salaries. Herbert Allen, who had taken office as Chief Constable in February 1913, was granted in December 1917 a salary increase of £100 a year, taking his earnings up to £700, while Henry Neal in July 1918 was in receipt of only £500 a year.

Much has been made of the artificially high earning potential of Leicester's factory workers during this period. To put into context the pay of those on a fixed income, it is appropriate at this point to look at a snapshot of the wages and salaries paid to Corporation employees in Leicester.

During the period, 1915-17, Tramways Department staff – motormen, conductors, maintenance staff, cleaners – earned an average of 31s 6d to 32s 6d per week. A glazier employed by the Lighting Department received 36s a week, while a lamp cleaner, employed to clean the lamps during the summer months was paid £1 a week. Women cleaners for the Police Department received an increase in June 1917 from 16s to £1 per week. Wages of female attendants and searchers at police stations increased from 20s to 25s per week

An elementary school teacher aged 21 to 31 received £65-£85 a year, an assistant of 35-45 earned £150-£160. Temporary female teachers were paid 32s 6d to 35s a week. Elementary schools were graded from one to five, 'one' being the smallest. A head teacher's salary ranged from £150 for a Grade I school to £330 for a Grade V (County) school. All school teachers were required to retire at 65 years of age on a yearly pension of £1 per year for every year of service, plus 10s a week supplementary, which was contributed from their salaries.

Below is a list of Corporation employees' salaries for the period February to July 1918.

Town Clerk	A. H. Pritchard	£1,500
Electrical Engineer	T. R. Smith	£900
Medical Officer of Health	Dr Millard	£800
Water Manager		£800
Chief Constable	Herbert Allen	£700
Tramway Manager	A. F. Lucas	£500
Fire Officer	Henry Neal	£500
Police Surgeon	Dr N. I. Spriggs	£225

As in most instances of crisis, the full-time emergency services were supplemented by volunteers and auxiliaries. Special constables reinforced Leicester Brough Police, private fire brigades were on call to assist the Borough Fire Brigade. Casualties were transported by the local Voluntary Aid Detachments.

There were, however, variations upon the rule. The St John Ambulance Association was one such. With their own private horse-drawn ambulance, kept at Mr Dawson's mews at 84 London Road, they were able to provide a limited private ambulance service. In the three years from 1913 to 1916, the St John Ambulance trained 5,775 people in first-aid. Under the auspices of Colonel Harrison of the 5th Northern General Hospital, the organisation maintained a Voluntary Aid Hospital at Knighton House (loaned by Geoffrey Stibbe) for the duration of the war.

On Saturday, 9 October 1915, a part of two convoys of motor ambulances visited the town and county. Organised by a coal owner, H. Dennis Bayley, the vehicles, a gift from the Nottinghamshire and Derbyshire Miners' Association to the British Red Cross and St John Ambulance, were en route to France. Each convoy (costing a total of £70,000, with the Coal Trades Association undertaking to pay £5,000 a year for upkeep), comprised 50 motor ambulances, three lorries, four motor cars, seven motor cycles and a field repair lorry. The group visiting Leicester under the command of Captain Murray (British Red Cross) was only a portion of one of the columns. The ambulance accompanying the motorcade – which stretched along Granby Street from Halford Street to Chatham Street – was built on a one-ton Buick chassis with a large red cross emblazoned on its canvas sides. On leaving the town, the motorcade set off for the north east of the county, passing through Moira, Donisthorpe, Swadlincote (Derbyshire) and as many other mining villages as could be pulled in.

Whilst the majority of nurses who joined the BEF were inducted and sent to the Naval Hospital at Haslar, not all chose to follow this route. One such was Sister Flora Scott.

Prior to 1915, Flora Scott's history is somewhat sketchy. A single woman, she is shown by the British Red Cross archives to have lived in Nottingham after the turn of the century. Described in the *Leicester Daily Mercury* as 'a well-known surgical nurse in the town', she had until 1911 worked in several hospitals before going to work for Miss Pell at The Home Hospital in Princess Road. Twelve months later Miss Scott was the proprietor of her own nursing home in Tichborne Street, progressing shortly after to opening The Nursing Home in Victoria Road.

It is not clear whether the business venture was unsuccessful, or if it was for purely altruistic motives that a few months after the beginning of the war The Nursing Home was closed down and patients distributed among other institutions while Flora Scott went off to war.

Recruiting had begun for a hospital unit organised under the auspices of the Red Cross to serve in Serbia. The prime mover in this enterprise was Lady Leila Paget, the wife of Sir Ralph Paget, a former British ambassador to that country. Lady Paget had returned to Serbia in October 1914 with a hospital unit under the command of Dr H. G. Barrie. Comprising six doctors and 12 orderlies, the hospital, set up at Skopje, was in desperate need of trained nurses.

Along with, Miss L. Chuley and Miss I. Pickering, two of her nurses from Victoria Road, Flora Scott joined a contingent led by Dr Berry of the Royal Free Hospital, London, at Avonmouth on Friday, 15 January 1915. Sailing aboard the *SS Dilwara*, the party arrived at Valetta harbour, Malta, two weeks later. From there they took ship for Piraeus, the port of Athens, aboard the *SS Caledonia*, and thence by rail to the 3rd Military Hospital at Skopje.

Shortly after their arrival at Skopje, Scott was separated from Nurses Chuley and Pickering when she was transferred from the 3rd to the 7th Military Hospital where there was an outbreak of typhus. In a letter, published in the *Leicester Daily Mercury*, in April, Flora Scott graphically describes the conditions which she encountered.

'Around Skoplji [Skopje], there are 3,000 Austrian troops, who throughout the winter have been sleeping rough in the basements, cellars and outhouses of the old Turkish barracks about two miles from here in the mountains.

'Some five or six weeks ago we found out that they were dying at the rate of 20-30 a day of typhus. Lady Paget said that something must be done and got permission to use three pavilions of the barracks to nurse them. Each pavilion has 100 beds. Two sisters and I volunteered to go and nurse them. No one could believe the state of these poor men.

'In one building, living and dying were lying together, the living too ill to move and had not had water for three or four days. The weather is bitterly cold, thick snow and not even straw to lay on. It was a ghastly business sorting out living and dead and more than terrible to see the plight of these poor men. However, we have now got our hospital in a little order and the poor men have at least got sacks of straw to lay down on.

'A few days after we commenced work, Lady Paget was taken very ill with typhus. Then one of the Doctors fell ill two days afterwards, so one Sister had to go to nurse them. Three days after, the other Sister also took ill and for about ten days I was left alone with only the convalescent Austrians to nurse these poor souls.

'I could get little else done than just give medicines, drinks and other necessities – but these men are so grateful. Although I seemed to be the only woman about the place, neither day nor night did I feel in any way nervous...'

As the situation in the Balkans deteriorated, the Red Cross hospitals, which had been tending to allies and enemies alike, were obliged to withdraw and Flora Scott's unit, along with the other medical teams in the region, was forced after a relatively short stay to return home.

Like so many others who were to return from the various theatres of the war, once back in the town, Sister Scott appears to have quietly picked up the threads of her former existence. The last time that she comes to notice is late in 1916, where she is reported one winter's evening in November, 'giving a lecture at the St Stephen's Presbyterian Church Hall, on nursing typhus in Serbia'.

Henry Neal, Chief Officer of the Borough Fire Brigade throughout the war. Having been educated at Waltham School in Lincolnshire and later at the Technical College, Grimsby, Neal went to sea as a marine engineer. In 1901 he changed direction and joined the Grimsby Fire Brigade, where, having been promoted to chief officer in 1903, he served until 1909. Coming to Leicester in that year as chief fire officer of the Leicester Brigade, Neal was responsible for the technological improvements which took the brigade into the inter-war years. He retired from the fire service in 1939.

The crew of an early appliance pose during the pre-war years outside of the North Evington Branch Station in Asfordby Street. The driver of the machine (seated next to the officer) is Fireman Walter Sturgess. Serving with the brigade throughout the war, Sturgess was later to achieve the honour of being the oldest living fireman. Born on 10 March 1883, he died on 7 April 1987 at the age of 104.

Being demonstrated at the side of the canal at Painter Street, this Merryweather pump is put through its paces for the benefit of the Mayor, John Frears and local councillors, 12 months prior to the outbreak of war, in July 1913. Equipped with a 50ft escape ladder, this was to be a part of Henry Neal's motorised wartime fleet of vehicles.

Pictured outside the Central Fire Station in Rutland Street during 1913, these Deasey pumps and appliances were the pride of the brigade's motorised fleet. The figure standing in the centre of the picture is Chief Officer Neal.

With responsibility for both ambulance work and the transporting of prisoners in police custody, the Fire Brigade needed to move on. Replacing the horse-drawn ambulance with a newly-built motor ambulance in February 1918, the Chief Fire Officer was able to tell the Watch Committee that 'the old horse had been sold to a Mr Hill of Wigston for £35'.

Gradually replacing the older horse-drawn ambulances, this wartime motorised vehicle bears on its side the Borough Fire Brigade badge below the words 'Fire Brigade Ambulance'.

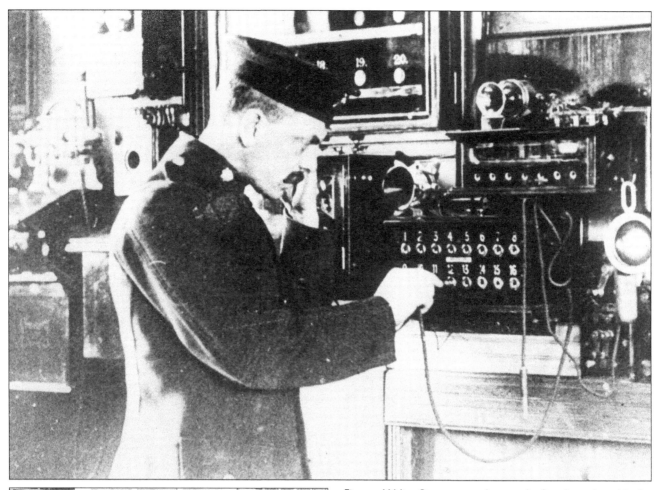

Fireman Walter Sturgess seen here at the fire alarms board in the Central Fire Station. One of Henry Neal's innovations, the plug-in section which the fireman is working on was the link to the street alarm system. The numbered board above his head carries the connections to private alarms installed in commercial premises.

These two photographs show German officers at Castle Donington prisoner-of-war camp during the Great War.

1916

By 1916 the stresses of war were becoming a very real burden upon the population of Great Britain – as indeed they were for all the other nations involved – and despite a degree of overall increased prosperity, the pinch was felt equally in Leicester. Weather at this time tended to follow more traditional patterns than in later years of the century. Long warm summers were punctuated by flash rainstorms which often caused serious flooding. Winters began well before Christmas, bringing biting cold, gale-force winds and heavy snowfalls extending over several months into late March and even April. The new year of 1916 promised little difference to other years, with the addition that now it was not only the poor who suffered privations. The shortage of many basic commodities, such as food and fuel, was a great leveller.

As early as the second week in January, the *Board of Trade Labour Gazette* was commenting dolefully on the situation.

'There has been a shortage of labour throughout 1915 in most trades. This has been dealt with by paid overtime, transfer of workpeople from job to job, the dilution of traditionally skilled labour by unskilled labour and high levels of female employment.

'At the beginning of 1915 the rising cost of living caused higher wage demands. In February 1915 a sharp upward movement began, largely in the form of war bonuses, or of special wartime pay increases being paid. Initially the main industries affected were those directly involved in the war effort – munitions, transport of troops, supplies, engineering, shipbuilding, railway service, dock labour, carting. Gradually over the year the wage increases spread to almost all areas of industry and by the end of the year, overall pay increases exceeded any previous year.'

Even with the facility for some sectors of the community to improve their earnings, the task of keeping up with the cost of living was becoming increasingly onerous. Those on a fixed income, or in occupations not attracting higher rates of pay, were in dire straits. Food prices, a reliable barometer, were overall 45 per cent higher in January 1916 than in August 1914. Staples such as butter, flour, meat, tea and sugar, where available, were the hardest hit. Conversely, the cost of such things as house rent had changed little.

An added hardship of this particular winter was that just before Christmas 1915, a particularly virulent strain of measles broke out in the North Evington district of Leicester. Despite the closure of several schools in the worst affected areas, the infection reached epidemic level. At the quarterly meeting of the Town Council on 29 March 1916, members were informed that since November there had been 2,709 cases reported, of which 166 had proved fatal.

March 1916 saw severe hardships among the population due to a lack of coal for domestic consumption. Commercial users had by now almost exhausted any stockpiles which they may have amassed. A reduced labour force resulted in difficulties for the mining industry hewing coal. The manpower problems were reflected in other areas too. Transporting coal by rail and the storage and delivery of it by merchants and suppliers became more problematic by the day. Whilst coal was not formally rationed, it was a common sight at the local wharf to see men and women buying quarter-hundredweights (28lbs), of coal and carrying it away home in tin baths and old prams.

At a time when the principal mode of transport,

both urban and rural, was the horse, a major blow to trade was inflicted in April when the Government issued instructions severely limiting the supplies of animal fodder. A circular, promulgated by the Army Council on 31 March under the ubiquitous Defence of the Realm Act, stated: '…all hay, oats, wheat and straw, standing on farms or in warehouses, is now requisitioned by the Army Council. All applications for domestic use must be passed through the District Purchasing Officer.' This was followed by the closure of all hay markets, the implication being that any fodder purchased – after military quotas had been met – must be under the direct supervision of, and at prices fixed by, the Government.

The implications for local traders, totally reliant upon horse-drawn wagons and carts, were bleak. As in later years, when petrol supplies were limited, a shortage of reserves plus higher prices equalled increases in the cost of living. On Friday, 14 April an open meeting of hay dealers and consumers, under the chairmanship of F. E. Randle, a local auctioneer, was held at the George Hotel in the town to discuss the matter. Not unexpectedly, there was nothing constructive to be achieved. The Local Purchasing Officer (based in Nottingham), Captain Pickering, was unsympathetic. In fairness he had his own problems in acquiring stocks to fill his quotas. From now on, hay worth £5 to £6 a ton was going to cost £10 – when it was available.

The restrictions imposed on the sales of wheat also had serious implications for Leicester's bakers. By the end of the year, government controls were in place regulating the amount of wheat, mixed with other additives, which would in future constitute a loaf of bread.[1]

One of the paradoxes of the First World War, which has been discussed at length by many historians, was the ethic of 'business as usual'. The philosophy was based upon what was essentially a correct premise – that the nation which could maintain its own economic stability, while destroying the stability of the enemy, would be the eventual victor. One of the many pathways leading to this goal was the capture of export markets formerly controlled by the enemy. Thus evolved a complex and often shadowy web of business dealings, mainly directed through neutral countries. A bi-product of this process was a startling piece of litigation concerning the firm of Standard Engineering, based on Evington Valley Road. In May 1916, when the war was being conducted with the utmost vigour by both sides, a patents dispute arose involving two British companies, one of which was Standard Engineering, and the firm of Machinen Fabrik Meonus of Frankfurt-am-Main in Germany. The complaint, made by the Germans, was that the British Patents Office had granted a patent to the British firm in relation to an improved pulling lever in a machine. The legal appeal was heard by Mr Justice Sarjeant, who summarily dismissed it. The irony is not that a Leicester company had acted contrary to German interests, which in the circumstances one would have assumed to have been well within the bounds of reason, but that the mechanics remained in place for the Germans to bring the matter before a British court of law.

All of this was ammunition for Ramsay MacDonald, whose fulminations against Great Britain's involvement in the conflict continued unabated. A regular speaker at events in his constituency, his appearance at the 1916 annual May Day meeting of the Leicester Trades Council in the Market Place resulted in a tense few hours for police and public alike. Accompanied on the platform by local luminaries such as Alderman George Banton and Councillors Amos Sherriff and George Kenney, MacDonald delivered to the crowded Market Place a diatribe against the Government's policies. Despite the fact that by no means all those present were adherents of MacDonald (at one point he apologised to the police officers present for the behaviour of opposition parties in the crowd), his words fell upon all sections of the gathering. Among the points he made was the fact that compared with two years previously, the sovereign was now worth 11s 2d – just over half its previous value. If the war continued for a further 18 months, the National Debt would be in the region of £4 billion, a sum which those present and their children's generation would be forced to repay. With uncannily clear foresight into the necessities of another war yet to come, MacDonald advocated that it was now time for the Government to take control of the management of the railways, shipping, coal and supply industries.

There still persisted a love-hate relationship between employers and employed. The employment

---

1. At the same time, in November, the 'Price of Milk Order 1916' fixed the price of a quart of milk at 5d.

of women conductors by the Tramways Department was still a contentious issue which was not helped by events elsewhere in the country. In London, the South Metropolitan Tramways Company went on strike during April because two women were given instruction as drivers. When the dispute threatened to spill over into the Croydon Tramways area, the Government, following the old adage of 'speak quietly and carry a big stick', ended the matter by threatening to withdraw the motormen's privilege of being in a reserved occupation.

In the middle of the summer the boot and shoe industry was thrown into a state of consternation by the change of status previously enjoyed by its workers. As from 25 September 1916, boot and shoe repairing and manufacturing would cease to be a reserved occupation for any single man or any married man under 25 years of age. Prior to that date clickers, sole cutters, lasting machine and screwing machine operators of whatever age had all been reserved. Much to their chagrin, authorisation to wear the coveted 'War Badges' displayed by those exempted from conscription was withdrawn

During September a quarrymen's dispute arose resulting in stoppages in the district. The strike was prompted by the installation of mechanical time clocks, which the unions saw as jeopardising the jobs of men employed as timekeepers. It cannot be coincidental that this move by the quarry owners came shortly after a new appeal for men to join labour units at the Front. During the last weeks of August all local quarries had suffered reduced workforces due to men answering the call for volunteers to serve in non-combatant battalions which were engaged in quarrying stone to build bridges and repair roads in France. The union's rather debatable, not to say lame, response to the time clocks issue was that with so many men away in the army, this would not be a good time to change working practices.[1] With the two sides unable to find a compromise, the system was installed at the Mountsorrel Company's quarry at Stoney Stanton. Finding themselves trapped in a corner, 105 men at the Mountsorrel quarry came out on strike. They were quickly joined by 108 workers at Groby Granite and a further 70 from Croft Granite. The dispute lasted for only a week before the employers agreed to discontinue the system and resume the use of timekeepers pending the Government's arbitration.

It was during this middle year of the war that the disparate bodies who had taken responsibility for the well-being of those local men unlucky enough to become prisoners-of-war amalgamated to form one composite group.

Initially, in May 1915, the Leicestershire Regimental Committee had begun to send parcels to members of the regiment who had been taken prisoner. In the first week of June that year, a new association was formed and took over the responsibility of looking after any prisoner from the regiment living locally. During the early days for some reason – probably as simple as a lack of communication between the borough and the county authorities – this association only covered those men who were resident in the town. The situation was remedied at an early stage and the organisation became known as the Leicester, Leicestershire, and Rutland Prisoners-of-War Committee. Where notification was received that a man had been taken prisoner, his home was visited by a committee member. It was found, certainly in the early days, that often, at some considerable hardship to themselves, the family, probably consisting solely of his wife who was attempting to live on her army allowances, would be sending parcels to the man at a cost of around 6s a time. The association, having talked to those concerned, then undertook to maintain the contact on behalf of the family. This arrangement became mandatory when the War Office issued an Order prohibiting private individuals from sending parcels to prisoners. Whilst this was done with the best of intentions – to prevent espionage – a certain degree of double standards was allowed to prevail as the restriction was not extended to those sending packages to officers.

At the end of the first six months of its existence the Leicester, Leicestershire, and Rutland Prisoners-of-War Committee, under the chairmanship of William Hincks, was in a sound financial condition, buying foodstuff and provisions at wholesale prices and negotiating duty relief on excisable goods such as tea, sugar and tobacco.[2] At the end of 1916 the association had despatched a total of 32,900 parcels to Leicestershire men via the International Red Cross in Berne. (The record was a consignment of

1. Those affected were mainly set makers, kerb dressers and loaders.
2. All such regional organisations were tied into a centrally based committee in London. However, no financial aid was envisaged and each regional committee had to rely upon local charities for funds

1,830 in one week.) Although the parcels were originally intended to supplement the meagre rations provided in the prison camps, it was soon understood by those at home that the problem was a much wider one. When a man was taken prisoner in action, he almost without exception lost all his kit, which meant that he went into captivity with only the clothes in which he stood up. As a consequence the parcels sent via the Red Cross were augmented over a period of time to ensure that each man received at least one pair of boots and slippers, a greatcoat, jacket, a pair of trousers, two shirts, two undershirts, two pairs of underpants, four pairs of socks, a muffler, cap, kitbag and gloves or mittens.

When the association held its annual general meeting at the Town Hall on the afternoon of Monday, 2 April 1917, with slightly over 300 prisoners on its books, it was sending packages to 236 men at a monthly cost of just under £500.

Additionally, the committee had taken on the task of sending parcels to the dependents of refugee families living in the town, who were interned in various camps. One of the organisation's proudest achievements was to send the wives and mothers of ten prisoners to see their men on an arranged visit in Switzerland.

The effect of the 'Great Satan' conscription was now being felt in the town. Employers were as desperate to retain men in the workplace as were the workmen to remain there. Despite keeping their forges alight 14 hours a day, local blacksmiths were unable to cope with the work of shoeing the town's horses. In August 1914 there were 27 farriers' shops operating in Leicester with 30 employers, 36 journeymen, eight lads and some 'casuals'. By May 1916 there were 20 forges with 21 employers, 22 journeymen and eight lads. Giving precedence to the shoeing of working horses, the trade managed – except for those single men under 25 – to maintain its status as a reserved occupation.

Hoping to stave off political disaster, the Government now promised grants of up to £104 a year to both single and married men whose families encountered severe hardship due to their absence. The offer was accompanied by the ominous rider that each claim would be 'secretly investigated by local commissioners'. In order to maintain an edge over those attempting to avoid conscription, on the evening of Thursday, 14 September raids were made on places of entertainment in Leicester's town centre.

A combined force of police officers under Superintendent Cornelius Carson, and the military commanded by Majors Heath and Garnett, descended upon the first house of the Pavilion Music Hall, and the second house at the Palace Theatre of Varieties, both in Belgrave Gate. While the exits were guarded by policemen and armed soldiers, all the women and elderly men were allowed to leave before identity checks were made on those males remaining. Unfortunately, existing records do not show how successful this operation was, other than to state that several men had their names taken and a few were removed to the police station. Doubtless as a deterrent to backsliders, this was to be a case of the process being as important as the result.

While events such as the 1916 Easter Rising in Ireland – an occurrence of such magnitude that its repercussions will continue to echo through history for generations – made concerned reading in the Press, it was more parochial matters which really caught the attention of the people of Leicester. In the bleak early days of the year, local newspapers regaled their readers with details of a visit paid by Alderman Jonathan North, along with other civic dignitaries from around the country, to the Ypres sector of the Western Front.

On 17 June, the town and county suffered a sad loss when, at the age of 56, Lieutenant-Colonel John Mosse, the CO at Glen Parva Barracks, collapsed in the orderly room and died. Having served for 37 years as a regular soldier, Mosse was recalled to the Colours at the outbreak of war and had shortly afterwards taken over the command of the barracks which were being used as a troop staging post. Private Buckingham VC, who was killed in action in France later the same year, was orderly to his son, a captain in the 2nd Leicesters.

The visit by Field Marshall French (whose command of the BEF had been terminated with the appointment of Douglas Haig) to inspect the Leicestershire Volunteer Force on 30 October was quickly eclipsed by the forced landing, two days later in a field at Aylestone, of a military plane with a fuel leak. Having been guarded overnight by the recently inspected Volunteers, the plane, its leak duly repaired, took off again the next day for 'a secret destination'.

The main event of the latter part of 1916 was a massive pageant held in the Market Place to collect money for the Lord Mayor's Fund. It was held on Thursday and Friday, 27-28 September and described as 'Ye Olde English Faire'. The business of Leicester Market came to a standstill for the duration of the event. Officially opened at midday on Thursday (taking advantage of a spell of very fine weather many stallholders were reported to be selling prematurely from 11am onwards), all the stallholders were dressed in the costume of various periods from Elizabethan to Georgian. Working throughout the previous night, 100 young ladies under the guidance of Miss Hall of the Newarke Secondary School had decked the Market Place out with hangings and decorations to give atmosphere. Amidst diverse entertainments put on by local elementary schoolchildren, stallholders (counting among their numbers many of the town's population of refugees), busily sold vast quantities of Belgian lace, fans, shawls, dolls, toys and a myriad of other goods.

Having reached what was to prove the mid-point of hostilities, the people of Leicester prepared for their third wartime Christmas and, hopefully, a better new year in 1917.

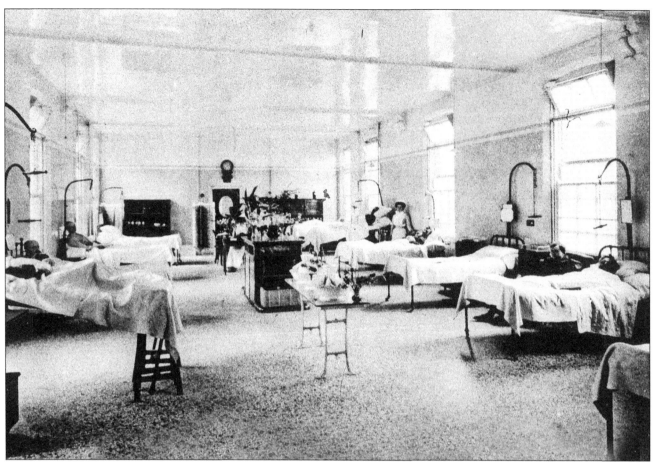

During the winter of 1915-16, a particularly virulent measles epidemic broke out in Leicester. Between November 1915 and March 1916, of 2,709 reported cases 166 were fatal.

Fielding Johnson Ward at the Leicester Children's Hospital. It was not until a much later era that provision was made for parents to remain with their sick children in hospital.

Ramsay MacDonald in Leicester Market Place addressing the Leicester Trades Council May Day meeting.

Ramsay MacDonald addressing the 1916 May Day meeting of the Leicester Trades Council. The grim faces of many looking up at him give a clear indication of the mood of the crowd.

A minor scuffle being broken up by the police at the 1916 annual May Day meeting of the Leicester Trades Council held in the Market Place outside of the Corn Exchange.

Relaxing in camp, men of the BEF take time out from the trenches. As steel helmets were not issued to British soldiers in large quantities until just prior to the Battle of the Somme, this picture is probably taken during the early summer of 1916.

A group of 'Leicester Tigers' pictured behind the lines during the Battle of the Somme (July-November 1916).

A rare picture of Lord Kitchener in civilian clothes, inspecting a contingent of Boy Scouts at a Leicester rally. His father, Henry Kitchener, who had been a colonel in the army during the 19th century, lived locally at Cossington from the mid 1880s until his death in 1894. He is buried at All Saints' Church, Cossington. Lord Kitchener was therefore in his younger days no stranger to Leicester and the surrounding district.

Private William Buckingham VC, of the 2nd Leicesters, seen here with a group of children at the Countesthorpe Cottage Homes, where prior to joining the army in 1901 he had spent his own childhood. On his return to France, Buckingham was killed in action by machine-gun fire on 15 September 1916.

1917

IN TERMS of civilian morale, 1917 was probably the low watermark of the entire war. In order to fully appreciate what life in Leicester was like during that year it is necessary to look at the position of the country as a whole.

There are many different aspects to the conduct of a modern war. The two critical areas of influence will always be, on one hand the actual activities of the military forces involved, and on the other the prevailing economic situation which allows those forces to operate. The deterioration of either of these factors in the equation will always have a most detrimental effect upon the end results. It was as much the virtual collapse, in 1918, of the German economy which brought about the downfall of the Kaiser as any great military victory by the Allies.

During the century preceding the outbreak of the Great War, Britain had allowed her commercial position in the world to decline. By 1914 Germany and the United States had outstripped Great Britain in the production of steel, thereby securing a better manufacturing position. Unable to provide all her own food, Great Britain imported 80 per cent of her wheat supplies and 40 per cent of her meat. With an overall import-to-export ratio of 5:3, the country could, according to estimates, be self-sufficient for a period of only 125 days. Britain having been dependent for two and a half years upon supplies from America being delivered by sea across the Atlantic, the commencement on 1 February 1917 of unrestricted submarine warfare by the Germans posed a grievous threat to the island's ability to continue the war. (Conversely, the German situation had reached a state where it was imperative that the submarine blockade should succeed.) By Easter of 1917 one out of every four British merchant ships was being sunk, with a consequent loss of invaluable cargos. The balance was redressed to a certain extent by the entry, on 6 April 1917, of the United States into the war and by the adoption during that summer of a convoy system as a defence against the U-Boats.

An impending food crisis had prompted the Premier, David Lloyd George, in December 1916 to establish a Ministry of Food under Lord Devonport. Soon after the commencement of the U-Boat campaign, details of a self-rationing campaign to be managed through local Food Control Committees was released. It was proposed that each adult should restrict themselves to four pounds of bread, two and a half pounds of meat and three-quarters of a pound of sugar a week.

In April 1917 Devonport was replaced by Lord Rhondda, a 61-year-old Welshman who undertook the responsibility for preparing a plan to institute formal rationing by the beginning of 1918.

Despite the entry of America into the war, morale was at its lowest ebb and Lloyd George's Coalition Government was deeply concerned over the possibility of civil unrest. Major developments abroad served to underline their disquiet. In March the Russian Revolution began the process of dismantling that country's establishment and placing power in the hands of the workers. The situation abroad was actually graver than realised. After a particularly hard winter at the Front[1], and sustaining extremely heavy casualties, the French army under General Nivelle was for a period of about six weeks during the spring and early summer of 1917 in a state of mutiny. Worn out and demoralised, units refused to obey orders and, in sympathy with their Russian counterparts, waved red flags and demanded peace. So well did the French authorities succeed in concealing these events that neither their

---

1. On the night of the 4/5 February 1917, following three days of heavy snow, Leicester recorded 21 degrees of frost – the severest cold since records commenced in 1908. The winter conditions prevailed until after Easter.

allies nor their enemies were aware of the extent of the problem until much later when control of the situation had been regained.

It was in this climate of low morale and shortages that Leicester entered the penultimate year of the war. In February the price of a ton of potatoes was pegged at £10 10s 0d wholesale, with a retail price not to exceed £11 10s 0d. A Government Order made it compulsory for millers to extract no less than 81 per cent of flour from their wheat supplies. Before being made into bread it was acceptable for a further five per cent of rice, maize, barley, semolina, oats, rye or beans to be added. In March, due to bad weather affecting crops and transport, a potato shortage occurred in the town.

At a meeting of the Poor Law Guardians during the third week of January, Draconian alterations to the catering strategy at the Workhouse in Swain Street were mooted by Councillor Amos Sherriff. Prefacing a formal motion with the assertion that 'the manner in which inmates have hitherto been supplied with food, there might not have been a war on...', he proposed what he considered to be acceptable alterations to the paupers' diet. On one day a week, tripe should be substituted for meat. Butter supplied to the Workhouse cost 1s 8½d per pound, making a total outlay of £21 7s 6d, a week. The equivalent amount of margarine could be purchased for £11 11s 0d per week – a saving of nearly 50 per cent. (In relation to butter, he added the rider that pre-war, if butter was sub-standard it could be returned to the supplier, now you had to keep it!) A further saving of 30s a week could be made by substituting condensed milk in the inmates' tea in place of fresh milk. One meal of meat at the Workhouse worked out at £13 15s 0d; by the substitution of tripe, the sum of £6 14s 2d would be saved on that one meal alone – and 'if tripe suppers are so good, then a tripe dinner will be much appreciated by the inmates!' A rather sad indictment on the Management Committee is that Sherriff's motion was carried unanimously.

The ever-vigilant Temperance movements now added their weight to the wheel by running advertisements in local newspapers urging townspeople to save the money which they might spend on supporting the brewing industry and channel it instead into the war effort. One such advertisement prompted an irate reply from an unidentified citizen to the effect '...let those that don't drink look to their own ends, and leave alone them that do!' One of the more bizarre drink restrictions related to a prohibition upon civilians from buying beer or spirits for wounded soldiers who were convalescing in the town. On 20 January police went to the home of Louisa Pridmore, a 37-year-old single woman, where they found her 'entertaining' two soldiers from the Base Hospital, having previously been out to purchase a jug of ale for the men. At the subsequent hearing, where Pridmore was fined £1 for the offence of 'procuring ale for wounded soldiers contrary to the Defence of the Realm Act', the magistrates, were told by the Chief Constable, Herbert Allen, that between 500-600 posters had been put up around the town prohibiting the practice.

The situation among Leicester's poorer elements had in reality become quite desperate by this time. Following the lead of places such as London, Bradford, Leeds, Edinburgh and Belfast, soup kitchens were set up in some of the most needy areas of the town. In April the Salvation Army established a kitchen in Darker Street, open from 12 noon until 2pm to supply cooked meals such as hot pot, potato pie, rice, beans and soup to working families who could no longer support themselves. About the same time the locally-established Food Control Committee[1] opened a kitchen in Sanvey Gate, which was closed during the summer months as it was felt that during the warmer weather the need would not be so great as in the winter. On 22 March 1918 the committee organised a further food kitchen at the premises of Henry Walker and Son in Oxford Street. This particular location, however, was run on a slightly different basis. This was not to be viewed as a charity, rather as a business enterprise capable of producing and selling, 2,000 meals a day for home consumption. Run by J. S. Winn, a well-known Leicester café owner, the kitchen served its purpose until its closure in April 1919. A further centre, again under the direction of Winn, operated for a short space of time, between January and April 1919, at 70 Narborough Road.

In August 1917 the establishment of Food Control Committees, responsible to central government, was formalised. Leicester was required to have a committee of 12 independent people whose task it would be to prepare the borough for

---

1. This would appear to have been an *ad hoc* arrangement, superseded by the official Food Control Committee set up in August 1917.

rationing.[1] Once formed, the committee set to work immediately to deal with the first commodities that were to be rationed – sugar and meat. Around 60,000 ration cards were hastily prepared for use by householders, while a register was compiled of commercial caterers along with the town's various institutions. During September flat rates of food prices were proclaimed. Bread was to cost 2½d for a one pound loaf and 9d for a four pound loaf. Milk from November would be 8d a quart. Examples of the prices of some cuts of meat, commencing on Monday, 3 September were: best steak 1s 10d a pound; leg of mutton 1s 6d; shoulder of mutton 1s 5d.

Throughout the year, the authorities set out to make an example of any tradesman flaunting the new regulations. In May the magistrates imposed fines of 10s each on William Henry Cole of Waterloo Street for adding almonds to a cake, and Tom Miller and Elizabeth Garner, both confectioners of Granby Street, for adding to their cakes whipped cream and almonds. Those retailers who sought to impose conditions of sale on their customers were viewed in a most serious light by the Justices. In July, Harry Lawrence, a fruiterer and greengrocer, was fined 40s for refusing to sell to Marion Brooker two pounds of potatoes unless she bought other goods as well. At the same sitting, the magistrates fined Peter Bailey, described as a shop manager of 40 Chatham Street, 40s for refusing to sell to a customer a pound of sugar with only a quarter of tea.

The summer saw the dark shadow of penury extending yet again over the meetings of the Tramways and Electricity Committee. The committee were addressing two problems by the middle of the summer. The first was lack of funds, the second that the tramcar system was literally grinding to a halt – the power supplies being generated were now inadequate for the amount of trams on the rails. They came up with some suggestions to alleviate the first problem, suggestions which not unexpectedly caused a furore among the fare paying public.

1. All free travel passes other than for wounded soldiers, blind persons and cripples would be withdrawn. (This primarily affected such people as VAD workers and nurses.)

2. Officers in uniform to pay full fare and not half as at present.
3. Return tickets to be increased from 1½d to 2d.
4. Outer return tickets to be abolished.
5. Outer transfer tickets to be increased from 1½d to 2d.
6. New increased fares to be implemented.

The second problem demanded a more complex resolution. It was decided that a new converting plant was needed in the North Evington district to deal with the drop in voltage to the tram rails in order to save losses in existing cables and to enable the generating plant to cope with the constantly increasing power load in the district. The committee arranged the purchase, for £200, of a site comprising 322 square yards from Sir John Rollestone on the north side of East Park Road. It was proposed to erect a building to house a new 1,000 kilowatt rotary converter at a cost of £3,100 from Messrs Siemens Bros, and switch gear at a further £410 with provision at a later date to install transformers. Messrs Glover and Co of Manchester undertook to supply the cables for a cost of £3,452, while the building work added a further £1,580 on to the overall cost.

It was little wonder that the increase in tram fares was not well met by the citizens of Leicester.

At the end of the year, with coal costing the householder between 28s 6d and 35s a ton, the Government brought, in for the first time, a restriction on the use of motor vehicles.

Coming into force on 1 November 1917 the Motor Spirit Restriction Order No2 1917 specified the permitted usage of vehicles.

1. [Motor vehicle may be used] in the conveyance of a person or a person's goods, to or from the nearest convenient railway station in connection with a railway journey and where no other means of conveyance is reasonably available.
2. For the purpose of a profession, trade or business carried on by, or the necessary household affairs of, the person on whose behalf the motor vehicle is being used, where the journey cannot otherwise be reasonably and conveniently accomplished, provided that the conveyance of a person

---

1. Set up under the aegis of the Mayor, Jonathan North, there was much deliberation at the time as to whether representatives of the Co-operative Society should be excluded as not being impartial. This seems to have been a national problem as the Government Food Controller, Lord Rhondda (who had succeeded Devonport), in late August advised that local authorities should include members of Co-operative Societies, irrespective of who else might be excluded.

for the whole or part of the distance between his residence and place of business shall not be deemed to be a journey undertaken for the purpose of his profession, trade or business, if a railway or other means of communication be reasonably available.

The Order allowed for the use of motor vehicles in the case of public duties (eg the fire brigade), ambulance purposes and where life and limb were at risk.

SATURDAY, SEPTEMBER 2, 1916

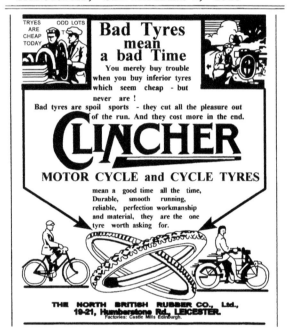

Whilst only a relatively small number of people in the town possessed or had access to a motor car, the legislation imposed severe constraints upon them. By virtue of Leicester being an urban town, everyone living in the borough was served by a tram route, which in its turn could easily deliver them to a railway station. Plus the fact that horse-drawn cabs and transport were also readily available. Therefore, other than for emergency purposes, such as fires, accidents requiring someone being taken to hospital or the transport of wounded from the convoy trains to hospital, vehicular activities in Leicester were returned to the pre-motor car era.[1]

Inextricably linked to the problems of shortages and the cost of living, wage disputes some of which

– as in the instances of women workers attempting to achieve parity with their male counterparts – had a basis in real need, contributed to making 1917 a singularly miserable year.

July was the high point for unrest, both in the public and private sectors. During this month, the 320 women cigar makers in the town came out on strike demanding that their weekly pay should be increased from 20s a week to the 25s which women in the boot and shoe industry were earning. At the same time 46 women employees at W. Evans and Son, Brunswick Street, were locked out in a dispute over pay and union membership. Women employed by the Tramways Department clashed with the Corporation over their demands that they receive the same rates of pay as the male employees. Dismayed Tramways Department officials pointed out that if, along with the payment of a 10s war bonus, this demand were to be acceded to, the women would be earning £2 0s 6d a week!

The midsummer crisis continued for the Corporation with the police and teachers asking for substantial pay increases (the latter were asking for a 25 per cent pay rise). The teachers were deflected with small interim payments, while the police were promised a comprehensive pay review after the war was ended.[2]

The largest strike in terms of a workforce downing tools was at the wholesale clothing company of Hart and Levy in Wimbledon Street when 1,000 workers went on strike over the levels of their war bonuses.

One of the ways in which the Corporation attempted to alleviate the harsh realities of 1917 was in the encouragement of local people to cultivate allotment gardens. Many years before the exhortation in a later war to 'Dig for Victory', the working classes of Leicester (and other towns throughout the country) were urged to take advantage of the offer by the local authority to acquire a piece of land upon which they themselves might grow the produce which was now in such short supply in the shops.

The first mention of the scheme comes at the very beginning of the year, in a small piece in the *Leicester Daily Mercury*. This refers to the acquisition

---

1. The Fire Brigade, who had been delivering tobacco and other items around the auxiliary hospitals to help out the War Hospitals Committee, were now forced to withdraw their assistance in order to comply with the law.

2. In January 1918 the Education Committee were given a Grant of £24,500 to increase teachers salaries. This resulted in Head Teachers receiving an increase of 25 per cent and Assistants 20 per cent.

by the Dulverton Road War Land Association of 3,000 square yards of land at the rear of Dulverton Road in Westcotes Drive for use by its ten members as allotments, along with an adjacent 500 square yards under cultivation by the 5th Leicester Scouts. This is obviously the result of a local government initiative, because on the same day, 3 January, the Town Council announced that the Government had given to local authorities the right to sequestrate any unoccupied land for the purposes of rent-free cultivation. To set the scene, the Corporation declared its intention to put up 260 acres of its own land to create 2,000 rent-free allotments. This announcement was followed the next day by the Board of Agriculture offering to supply seed potatoes to allotment societies in order to get them started. Under the title of The Food Production Scheme, the Corporation advised that '...the procedure to be adopted by would-be land cultivators is for them to spot a bit of land which is uncultivated and unrated, and to ascertain who is the owner, then to proceed to the Town Hall and find the necessary particulars when the requisite steps will be taken by the local authority...'

It should be pointed out that the practice of using ground as allotment gardens was a well-established part of life prior to the outbreak of the war and that this scheme merely sought to exploit existing skills. Within three months, the Corporation had under its new powers secured 90 acres of unoccupied land and 77½ acres of occupied ground which it parcelled up into 2,100 allotment plots. Not all the land was given up freely or with a willing mind. A deal of controversy accompanied the Corporation's decision to close the Western Park golf course in April 1917 and an eventual compromise resulted in the land being given over to mowing grass for animal feed. (As other stretches of parkland, specifically parts of Abbey Park, Victoria Park, Spinney Hill Park and the recreation ground at Aylestone Road, had been given over to growing potatoes, one can only speculate that the golfing fraternity in the town had some degree of influence when it came to civic matters.)

A spin-off of this cultivation project was that the question of pest control became quite relevant. In May, with the depredations of the late winter which had persisted past Easter into April, now behind them, the allotment holders became aware of a new difficulty. Hungry rats (which their activities had doubtless displaced) and scavenging birds were despoiling their agronomic efforts. Unemployed locals were made an offer – for a fixed scale of prices, they could assist in ridding the gardeners of their problem:

Rats' tails	½d per dozen
Heads of fully-fledged House Sparrows	
	3d per dozen
Heads of unfledged House Sparrows	
	2d per dozen
Eggs of House Sparrows	1d per dozen

The offer was accompanied by the stricture: 'Children cannot collect the money for rats' tails. Children can only collect for sparrows and eggs if killed under the supervision of a schoolmaster or mistress. House sparrows are not to be confused with hedge sparrows which are useful birds.'

The importance with which the success of the allotments scheme was viewed is illustrated by the case of Samuel Saunt, a labourer of no fixed address, who in September 1917 was sent to prison by the magistrates for one month with hard labour, having been found guilty of stealing 12lbs of potatoes, valued at 1s 6d from an allotment at Evington.

Overall, the allotment scheme was a resounding success. Being free of rental, those who would benefit most, the poorer inhabitants, had the opportunity to find some respite from the ever-increasing burdens of the cost of living. Many of the societies formed also undertook to manage the allotments of men who had to go away to war, thus ensuring that the man's family were still provided for. After the war, in April 1919, 1,500 acres of land within the borough remained under cultivation.

If it were needed, more immediate evidence of what was happening at the Front was being presented on a daily basis in the presence of the disabled men who, having received their discharges from the Forces, had returned home to be cared for by those for whom they had fought.

Rehabilitation of these men fell squarely upon the shoulders of the local authorities of the towns and cities to which they were returning. The Leicester War Pensions Committee, chaired by William Hincks and funded out of the Lord Mayor's Fund, reported in January of 1917 that there were approximately 700 disabled soldiers in the town. During the next three months this number had risen to 890. Having registered as disabled, a man was visited at his home by an assessor (usually this person would be a volunteer schoolteacher, resulting often in a sadly traumatic process, as those involved would very likely have had a recent relationship as teacher and pupil) who would present his findings to a panel of medical practitioners sitting twice a month alongside representatives of the Labour Exchange. Dependent upon the nature and severity of the disability, a suitable retraining course at the Technical and Art School could then be recommended. During the period February-March, 260 men visited the committee's offices at New Street to register as disabled.

With the military reversals being suffered in France, things were not going to improve. At its annual general meeting for the year August 1916 to June 1917, the War Pensions Committee were not optimistic. The Discharged Disabled Soldiers and Sailors Sub-Committee report showed that of the 1,207 men currently registered with them, less than half had been found employment. Some 598 were either under supervision or receiving specialist treatment, while a further 192 were unable, due to incapacity, to leave their homes.

Although many had received money from the Lord Mayor's Fund, compensation paid to them by the Government was negligible. Those who had lost two or more fingers on either hand received a Ministry of Pensions allowance of 5s 6d per week. Loss of two or more limbs qualified the recipient for the sum of 27s 6d a week. (The vexed question of disability pensions was to haunt this and later governments for years to come.)

Employers were, wherever possible, encouraged to re-employ the men in some position, or other. Police and Corporation found work as gatekeepers, cleaners and clerks for as many of the men as they could. Still there were many who had returned too badly injured to work.

Help was at hand for some of the men in the form of a proposed convalescent home, to be known as the Leicester Frith Recovery Home. Jonathan North had instigated a Lord Mayor's Fund with a view to helping with the war effort and funding needy causes. With a proposed target of £100,000, the fund was in the first instance intended to benefit men from the town and county, who had gone away to war, by supplementing local government funding. However, the County Council, despite a deal of

mediation by the High Sheriff, Hugh Goodacre, considered the fund to be unnecessary and declined to participate. No doubt this would have put a limitation upon the projections in relation to its target.

In July 1917 the Lord Mayor's Fund stood at £62,432 which sum North – impressed by the work being undertaken by two hospitals in London – wanted to utilise for the establishment of a home for men coming back suffering from shell shock. The location decided upon was at the Leicester Frith. Situated on the road out of Leicester towards the village of Groby, between Gilroes Cemetery and Anstey Pastures, an added attraction was that the land already belonged to the Corporation.

The existing premises were examined by Sir John Colley, the Director of the Institute for Neurasthenics, who considered that they would be suitable to care for about 90 patients. North went ahead and put in hand arrangements for the leasing by a Management Board, of the house and part of the grounds of Leicester Frith from the Estates Committee for the annual sum of £150. (Lease of the entire estate, which comprised between 90 and 100 acres, was not possible as part of it was already under lease to the Sanitary Committee.) Responsibility for the provision of a Medical Director and nursing staff was undertaken by the Leicester War Pensions Committee. Speaking to the newly-formed Management Committee (which comprised men such as Sir Samuel Faire, Colonel C. J. Bond and Colonel Astley Clarke, along with a host of other civic dignitaries who had formed the Lord Mayor's Fund Committee), the Mayor, obviously alluding to the County Council, remarked that he felt that '…they [the Town Council] should be magnanimous as far as the County [Council] were concerned and that everything in the shape of institutional treatment should be placed at the disposal of the men in the county just as the men in the town.' It was at this point that the name of the Lord Mayor's Fund was changed to the Disabled Warriors Fund (sometimes referred to as the Disabled Heroes Fund). The Medical Director was Colonel Astley Clarke, who with Louis K. Harrison had been instrumental in setting up the 5th Northern General Hospital. Having spent £8,000 in overhauling the house and annexe to give a bed capacity of 100 patients and with the workmen still on the premises converting outhouses into workshops, the first patient arrived on 1 February 1918.[1]

Meanwhile, not everyone in the borough was weighed down with despondency. As is needed in such times, there were those whose indomitable spirit continued to focus on the way forward. In August, Tom Crumbie set about raising yet another volunteer youth unit. Gazetted as captain with responsibility for administering the unit, which was to be the 2nd Battalion Leicestershire Volunteers, he set about recruiting any local youths of 17 who had not already been enlisted into the ranks of one or more of the existing organisations. With the assistance of 'volunteer stalwarts' such as Major Evan Barlow, Captain J. H. Corah and others, he enlisted about 100 members of the Junior Training Corps. The exact title of this battalion is not clear, as it is referred to differently at different times.[2] In January 1918, as the 2nd/1st Battalion Leicestershire Volunteer Regiment, under the leadership of Major Evan Barlow and the overall command of Colonel Sarson (who at this point was in excess of 70 years of age), its objectives seem to have shifted as it was now seeking to enrol men aged between 41 and 50. This move is more likely to have been an effort to prepare a Home Defence unit than to provide an overseas fighting battalion.

Politically, 1917 was probably the most important year of the war. Prior to this, Leicester, in common with many other towns, had been a single constituency which returned two Members of Parliament, namely Gordon Hewart and James Ramsay MacDonald. In August 1917 the Representation of the People (Redistribution of Seats) Bill altered this by creating three divisions and redefining the political boundaries of the borough to incorporate the districts of Belgrave, North Evington, New Found Pool and Knighton, along with their attendant voters. The new divisions were: North Eastern Division made up of Belgrave, Latimer, West Humberstone and Spinney Hill Wards; North Western Division with Abbey, Charnwood, Newton, Wycliffe and Wyggeston Wards; and finally Southern Division with Aylestone, Castle, de Montfort, Knighton, St Martin's and Westcotes Wards.

From an administration standpoint the implications of boundary alterations were daunting for the Town Clerk's office. Entire new lists of voters had to be compiled before any form of election could take place. (Previously the system of registration to vote, based upon rates books, had been relatively easy; now actual knowledge of occupancy changed the whole system, although the fact that there was a requirement for the individual to register their right to vote alleviated the situation to a degree.)

On a more personal basis, while a decision had been taken nationally within days of war being declared that in order to avoid political upheaval there would be no local elections for the duration of the war,[3] it was now time for the office of Mayor to rotate from Jonathan North to his successor. The heir apparent was Percy Litton Baker. Born the son of a tobacco factor at Stockport in 1863, Baker had moved to Leicester in 1889 at the age of 26. Having set up as a tobacco dealer in Belvoir Street, he then moved to Rutland Street and later set up a bonded warehouse. Standing as a Conservative, he was elected to the Town Council in 1908. Unfortunately, Baker, who had been ill for some time, died at his home in Stoughton Road in October 1917. This led to an unprecedented situation: North was due to stand down, but there was now no agreed successor. After a deal of discussion in the Council Chamber, Jonathan North was persuaded to continue his term in office through into the following year.

1. The official opening took place on Thursday, 25 July 1918.

2. This would indicate that the Junior Training Corps was now possibly being disbanded in favour of the new Volunteer Battalion.

3. Those members of local councils due to retire would remain in place provided that they were willing.

With shortages an ever-present fact of life, shopkeeper and customers debate the state of the war.

With impending food rationing and the closing down of pork butchers' shops imminent, food queues began to form in the borough during the early months of 1917. Seen here outside of Squires' butcher's shop in Welford Road at the corner of Mill Street, this crowd of men and women wait patiently for the shop to open.

Pictured outside of the bride's father's shop in Down Street, off Melton Road, on 17 June 1917, this wedding group provides a little light relief during the depressing days of 1917. The young couple who have just got married are Charlie Batt and Nellie Ball. A friendly pun at the time of the couple's names being 'bat and ball', sadly became misplaced when later Nellie Batt's young brother, Arthur, (seated at the front on the left), was killed by a cricket ball hitting him on the temple during a game on Victoria Park. Two noteworthy local figures also appear in the picture. At the back of the group, standing in the shop doorway, wearing a straw boater, is the groom's father, Inspector Batt of the Borough Police. In uniform, front left, leaning on his stick, is Staff Sergeant Lake of the Leicestershire Regiment, who after the war became a familiar face in the Belgrave area as licensee of the Balmoral Hotel on Belgrave Road.

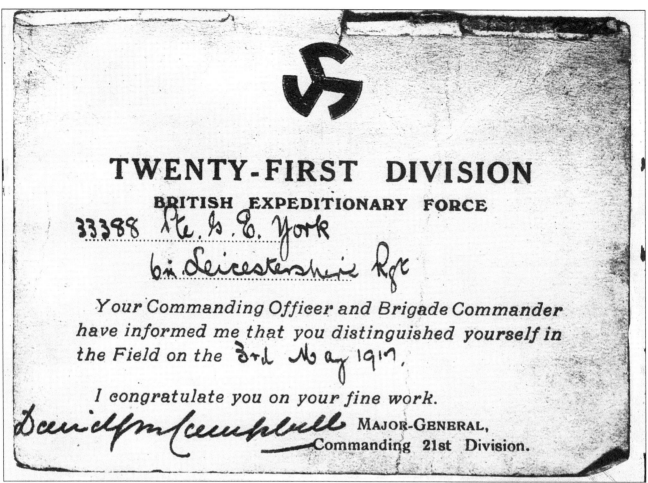

TWENTY-FIRST DIVISION

BRITISH EXPEDITIONARY FORCE

33388 Pte. G. E. York
6th Leicestershire Rgt

Your Commanding Officer and Brigade Commander have informed me that you distinguished yourself in the Field on the 3rd May 1917,

I congratulate you on your fine work.

David M Campbell MAJOR-GENERAL,
Commanding 21st Division.

This citation was awarded to Private 33388 G. E. York, 6th Battalion, Leicestershire Regiment for gallantry whilst serving with the BEF in France. Due to his commanding officer being killed in action before completing a full citation, Private York did not subsequently receive a decoration for his actions.

A view along Charles Street, taken soon after the end of the war. On the right at the corner of Rutland Street is the Queen's Head Hotel. On the opposite side can be seen the circular name and logo painted on the side of 45-49 Charles Street, declaring it to be the premises of Frank Johnson's Cigar Works. Going further back into the picture, behind where the group of people are standing is the corner of Halford Street, with the portmanteau manufacturer Arthur Halford & Co on the corner.

A favourite of the Leicester music halls, Vesta Tilley performing on stage.

During the closing years of the 19th century and into the first two decades of the 20th, Leicester was a centre of British cigar making. The *Leicester Trades Directory* for 1911 lists 14 cigar manufactures in the borough. Pictured *(bottom left)* Charles Theodore Harris, of the firm Goodman & Harris, Cigar Manufacturers, 89 Humbertsone Gate (at the corner of Vestry Street). The wages of female labour in this industry was to be one of the areas of dispute when in July 1917, 320 women cigar makers in the town went on strike.

It was from Sir John Fowkes Lancelot Rolleston *(bottom right)* that the Corporation purchased in July 1917 the ground in East Park Road to build a new converting plant in order to cope with the increased electricity demands being made by the tramways service.

A traditionally a woman's domain, laundresses working at the Leicester Royal Infirmary. The picture was probably taken just before the war, around 1912. The workloads would be vastly increased by the influx of wounded treated at the hospital during the next few years. Note the gas lighting and the heavy flat-iron being used by the woman second from the right.

The wholesale fruit and vegetable market in Halford Street, seen at the beginning of the war. Piles of baskets such as these belonging to A. Marks Ltd of 41 Halford Street had become a rarity by 1917. Marks also had premises in Queen's Street, incidentally.

Every Day

WHATEVER influences the war had upon the everyday lives of those living in the town, life and its problems carried on. To those living in Leicester, as in every other town in the land, the process of earning a living, keeping a home and coping with the everyday crises which come along, continued – sometimes as of old, more often weaving its way through the ever-present difficulties presented by a wartime existence.

By a sad turn of fate, the war was ushered both in and out by the death of a child. Five weeks after the declaration of hostilities, on 7 September 1914, Cecil Spence, aged five, who lived at 54 Newmarket Street on the borders of Clarendon Park and Knighton, was killed when he fell under the wheels of a horse-drawn wagon at the nearby Home Farm. On the afternoon of 11 November 1918, five hours after the last shots were fired, seven-year-old Cyril Godsall was run over and killed by a laundry van near to his home at the corner of Arbour Road and Melton Road. The youth driving the van, 15-year-old Archie Woollat – who himself lived in Arbour Road – was standing on the shafts of the rig due to his driving seat being taken up by a large parcel, and as a consequence could neither control the horse to avoid the toddler, nor reach the brake to halt the wagon. Recording the incident as 'accidental death', the Coroner, E. G. B. Fowler, with what can only be described as a degree of understatement, commented that 'you cannot put an old head on young shoulders'.

During the Great War, Leicester saw many famous visitors, and many of those living in the town became, for a short time at least, well known themselves.

In March 1915, the Chief Scout and the hero of Mafeking, Sir Robert Baden-Powell, inspected 2,000 Boy Scouts on the County Cricket Ground. In April, Sir Arthur Conan Doyle, the creator of Sherlock Holmes, addressed an audience at the De Montfort Hall to explain British strategy.

Vesta Tilley, probably the most famous music hall personality of the day, gave concerts at the Palace Theatre, and at the Base Hospital in 1915 and again in 1917.

On a cold wet day in October 1916, the Leicestershire Volunteer Regiment was inspected by Field-Marshal Sir John Denton Pinkstone French, who having been replaced by Douglas Haig as the commander of the British Expeditionary Force at the end of 1915, was now Commander-in-Chief of the army in Great Britain. His visit was followed a week later, on 8 November, by Richard Burdon, Lord Haldane, the man responsible for re-organising the British Army during the pre-war years, who spoke at the De Montfort Hall on the subject of 'Education and Industry after the War'.

There were also a great many local men and women who, however reluctantly, came to notice. There was Colonel Louis Kenneth Harrison, who throughout the four years of war managed both the Base Hospital and the North Evington War Hospitals. Private Buckingham and Captain Robert Gee were both awarded the Victoria Cross.[1] Lieutenant William Spurrett Fielding Johnson, who was with Major Martin when he was killed commanding the Leicestershire Yeomanry at Ypres in 1915, was awarded the Military Cross for his part in the action. Lieutenant-Colonel H. Stoney Smith DSO was killed in October 1915 commanding the 5th Leicesters. Lieutenant Jack Wakerley, the son of Arthur Wakerley, the architect who planned and built North Evington, was killed in action in June 1917.

---

1. A third local man who had moved away from the district prior to the war was also awarded the VC. Sgt Wm. Edward Butler, Northamptonshire Regt., a Wigston man, who had moved to live in Kettering, was awarded the medal in 1916 during the battle of the Somme for attacking and destroying single handed a machine-gun emplacement which was pinning down his unit.

The list of people who could be mentioned is as long as the researcher has the time to pursue the subject and the space to write about them. If it were possible to examine the letters which many of the men wrote home, they would illustrate happenings which those at home at the time would have found incomprehensible.

From 1901 until 1935, the position of Borough Medical Officer of Health was held by Dr Charles Killick Millard who, for what was, even by the standards of the day, a relatively low retainer – in 1918 he was earning £800 a year – laboured to ensure the continued good health of the town, coped with and orchestrated the management of epidemics and prepared lists of statistics relating to his work for the benefit of the town fathers.

Throughout the war the age-old maladies continued to afflict the town's population. The bed occupancy of consumptives at the Isolation Hospital rarely dropped below 100 and more commonly ran at between 160 and 170 cases at any one time. Among notifiable diseases, measles, scarlet fever and diphtheria remained the most prevalent.

During the last quarter before the outbreak of the war, April to June 1914, the death rate in the borough was 14.5 per 1,000 head of population while the birth rate was 23.2. For the same quarter of the following year (1915) the death rate was 12.3 per 1,000 and the birth rate 20.3 per 1,000. By 1916 the death rate had fallen to 9.7 per 1,000 and the birth rate had risen slightly to 21.4.

These figures do not vary significantly from year to year and it is also difficult to accurately assess their significance in relation to the population remaining in Leicester. On one hand it can be argued that a vital factor, the presence of a large proportion of the active male population, is missing. On the other hand it can be said that this is a reflection of those remaining. One fundamental in the equation is that the percentages are based upon Dr Killick Millard's computation of the population of the borough by taking the last known figure and deducting from it the number of men absent at the war. At the best, although performed with the highest of motives, this must be a tenuous proposition upon which to base percentages.

The extract opposite is taken from Dr Killick Millard's Annual Report for 1916-17, published in the *Leicester Journal* on Friday, 10 August 1917.

Report of Borough Medical Officer of Health for 1916-17

Population of town, other than soldiers and sailors is roughly, 225,907

Rates of births and deaths are inevitably not exactly accurate due to census difficulties.

Births

1914	5,144
1915	4,851
1916	4,684 (illegitimate 262)

Deaths

1915	2,793
1916	3,093 (males: 1,562/females: 1,531)

General death rate for the year 13.69 per 1,000.

Deaths of infants under 1 year – 491 equivalent to a rate of 104.8 per 1,000 which is the lowest on record.

Deaths from zymotic disease – 227 (Measles, diarrhoea, whooping cough).

Phthisis and diarrhoea rate for the year is a little lower than for 1915.

Cancer rate is also below average.

The worst figure for the year is in relation to measles deaths which occurred in the first quarter of the year.

At the beginning of the year measles became a notifiable disease.

In relation to child welfare, additional health visitors have been employed to do home visits.

Borough Hospital and Isolation Hospital:
Matron is Miss E. A. Davies
During the year 2,000 patients have been treated, of which 826 were soldiers. These were sick, wounded, convalescent and infectious cases.

Infectious diseases
Other than 1 imported case, there has been no smallpox reported in the borough since 1906 and no deaths from same since 1904. This follows a general trend nationally.

Marriages

1914	1,949
1915	2,808
1916	2,670

There is good statistical evidence to indicate that despite the hardships imposed by poor diet and shortages, nationally health improved and life expectancy increased.[1] Certainly, the subject of public health is a study on its own and was beyond the remit of this work.

Information as to the progress of the war was restricted almost entirely to newspaper coverage. This, in turn, was usually retrospective and based upon releases by the War Office. A few documentary films found their way on to the screen. During the second week of October 1914, the Picture House in Granby Street advertised that it was showing, 'for a few days only', *Antwerp Under Shot And Shell* which promised 'British Marines in the firing line. Thrilling scenes of the actual bombardment of Antwerp – British Marines arriving in Antwerp – Fighting in the trenches. – Armoured train defending the town.'

These were very much in the minority and in order to satisfy the public's interest film makers soon got busy producing fictional films for general consumption. During the run-up to Christmas 1914 the Coliseum on Melton Road was showing *By the Kaiser's Orders*, 'a three-part drama about the invasion of England'. This was followed by such dramas as *Defenders of Our Empire*, 'a film showing how raiders on our coast will be dealt with', and *A Belgian Girl's Honour*, which was described as 'a short story of German brutality, acted by a Belgian family – the show will be accompanied by an expert lecturer'.

The Watch Committee notes for 15 December 1914 give a list of cinemas in the town applying for the annual renewal of their licence to operate: (This is not a definitive list of cinemas operating in the borough):

The Palace Theatre	Belgrave Gate
The Floral Hall	Belgrave Gate
The Pavilion	Belgrave Gate
The Picture House	Granby Street
The Coliseum	Melton Road
The Olympia	Narborough Road
The Lyric	Clarendon Park Road
The Tudor Cinema	Vaughan Street
The Belgrave Cinema	Belgrave Road

The Shaftesbury	Uppingham Road
The Imperial Picture House	Green Lane Road
The Star Picture House	Belgrave Road
The Picture Drome	Mere Road
The Grand Electric Palace	Silver Street
The Empire	Wharf Street
The Boulevard	Western Boulevard

As in other areas of commerce, the question of unpatriotic involvement soon raised its head.[2] In December 1914, the licence for the High Street Electric Theatre (in later years to become the Cameo, although the original name was left in place over the doors) was suspended while the Town Clerk made enquiries as to whether or not the management of the company owning it, along with some London-based cinemas and theatres, was funded by German money.

The roles of cinemas and theatres on occasion became a little blurred. As all the films at this time were silent, it was necessary for any cinema to at least have a pianist and, in some instances, as at the Silver Street Cinema, what passed for an orchestra.

1. *Blighty British Society in the Era of the Great War*, Gerard J. DeGroot.

2. The firm of G. D. Caffin, Opticians, 6 Granby Street, advertised themselves as 'The only British Opticians in Leicester!'

The Picture House proudly boasted orchestral music along with, 'solo violin performances by Mr Zacharewitsch'. In December 1916 a Cinematograph Licence was granted to the Opera House in Silver Street for one month, while in July 1917, a charity concert of symphony music was performed by an orchestra at the Picture House in aid of the Royal Infirmary. Throughout the war, cinemas and theatres were used as venues for recruiting speeches and war effort appeals. One such occasion was in March 1917, when, with the nation was at its lowest ebb, a letter was circulated by the National Service Department at Westminster asking all local authorities to grant licences for local cinemas to open on 1 April (Sunday), in order that propaganda films advertising National Service might be shown, followed by speeches given by representatives of the Local National Service Committee.

The hours which cinemas were allowed to open were strictly controlled by the Watch Committee acting under the Cinematograph Act 1909. No cinema was allowed to be open before 2pm or after 11pm on any day. Opening on Sunday, Christmas Day, Public Holidays or Good Friday required the consent of the Watch Committee. The Act laid upon the management a host of requirements, for instance that all male attendants should wear uniform (females to be 'distinctively dressed'); that all gas taps in passages and on staircases be suitably guarded; that 'no improper character, reputed thief, or other notoriously disorderly person shall knowingly be admitted or allowed to remain on the premises'. It also made the slightly odd provision that cinemas could open (subject to the consent of the local authority) after 3pm on Christmas Day, provided employees were paid at double rate and given another day off. An evening's entertainment usually comprised a series of six or seven short films, including the main feature. The prices of seats, which were fixed by the cinema owners, usually cost 2d, 4d and 6d with soldiers in uniform being admitted at half price. Unfortunately, in a competitive business, if two cinemas were showing the same film at the same time, it was not unheard of for one of them to change the title in order to appear to be showing a different film.

The possible perception of a later age, that to regulate entertainment on a Sunday was a rather restrictive practice, was certainly not prevalent during the second decade of the 20th century. The granting by the Corporation of permission for picture theatres in Leicester to be open between 7.45pm and 9.45pm on Sunday, 18 February 1917 in order that collections could be taken for the Kitchener Memorial Fund resulted in a letter of protest signed by the incumbents of 20 churches in the town decrying the blasphemy of such a practice.

With female labour entering into so many walks of life, it was not unexpected that as the men who were managing cinemas and theatres were called up for military service, so women would replace them. Whilst being a fact of life, those in authority did not necessarily like it.

William Hincks, as chairman of the Watch Committee, commented in the minutes in May 1917 that '…while the Committee was generally against women managing cinemas, it was not inflexible, and would grant a temporary transfer of the licence of the High Street Playhouse, for one month, to the "wife of the manager" during his absence away at war'.

At this time even before the age of talking pictures, film making was a burgeoning industry and perceptive businessmen were building cinemas wherever a suitable site could be found and purchased. The Star in Belgrave Gate was opened in July 1914, only six months after the plans had been submitted. In October of the same year, the Shaftesbury on Overton Road showed its first films. Not everyone was quite so receptive to the idea of having a new cinema on their doorstep. On 21 March 1916 a petition, signed by I. H. Stevens, W. B. Pearson, G. A. Hewitt and several others, was presented to the Watch Committee, 'against a Cinematograph Licence being granted for premises proposed to be erected on East Park Road'. That the petition was unsuccessful is evidenced by the fact that what for the time was a large cinema (the Evington), seating some 900 people, was approved and opened in 1916. That it was deemed to be a high-class cinema theatre can be judged by the existence of a café which opened daily, and by the fact that a seat in the balcony cost 9d.

During this period the cinema was in the process of supplanting the music hall as the average person's primary source of entertainment. This should not, however, lead one to assume that the live theatre was dead. Among those establishments still listed during the war years and after were: the Royal Opera House, 26-28 Silver Street and 17 Cank Street; the

Theatre Royal, Horsefair Street; Palace Theatre of Varieties, Belgrave Gate; the Pavilion Theatre of Varieties (formerly the Tivoli), 153 Belgrave Gate; New Empire Music Hall, 27 Wharf Street. Of these, the first two were to survive both world wars before finally closing their doors.

While still viable enterprises, it is obvious from the inspections carried out by the licensing authorities prior to renewing the annual licences that many of these establishments were less than pristine. The following letter from the Borough Surveyor provides a good example.

BOROUGH SURVEYOR'S OFFICE,
TOWN HALL,
LEICESTER.
Dec.18 1916

H. A. Pritchard Esquire,
Town Clerk.

My Dear Sir,
    Theatre Royal. Royal Opera House.
    Pavilion and Palace Concert Halls

<u>Theatre Royal.</u>
    I found this Theatre generally in good condition. The gas has been replaced by electric lighting as proposed last year which enhances the cleanliness of the different parts of the house. The manager promises that the dressing rooms and lavatories generally shall be cleaned, lime and colour washed etc., as usual immediately after Christmas.

<u>Royal Opera House.</u>
    I found that the cleanliness and sanitary condition of the dressing rooms, lavatories and other parts of the house have been satisfactorily maintained. This work is usually done about July during the summer vacation. A great improvement has been effected by the provision of electric light in place of gas in those places.

<u>Pavilion and Concert Hall.</u>
    I found that the dressing rooms, lavatories and other parts which are usually cleansed, lime and colour washed etc., after Christmas has already been done this year; also that the condition of the basement, under the stage – about which complaints had, a few months ago, to be made – is now greatly improved; and generally speaking, everything is now satisfactory.

<u>Palace Concert Hall and Floral Hall.</u>
    I found that the improvement I recommended last year with regard to the drainage of the floor in one of the lavatories at the Palace Theatre, and also as to the renewal of the plaster in one of the lavatories in the Floral Hall, have been attended to and that, generally the cleanliness and good sanitary condition of these houses has been satisfactorily maintained. Small repairs to the plaster of the walls in the Ladies' lavatory at the Floral Hall are necessary. These and the usual cleaning, lime whiting, painting etc., are to be put in hand immediately after Christmas.

Yours faithfully,
E. George Mawbey,
Borough Surveyor

Despite the occasional foray into the world of cinema – a cinematograph licence for one month was granted to the Opera House in December 1916 – they could not compete with the film industry. While people were flocking to the new cinemas which were being built at every available location and showing brand new – albeit silent – films, the theatre was being left behind as a mainstream entertainment. The Opera House had opened in 1877, the Theatre Royal was restored in 1873, and the Pavilion in Belgrave Gate (originally costing £10,000) had been open since 1890.

The Pavilion Theatre of Varieties at 153 Belgrave Gate. This picture dates to between 1914 and 1920. In 1914 the premises next door at no 159 belonged to James Hawes, a confectioner. Some time before 1920 they had been taken over by the Royal Liver Friendly Society.

Soldiers from one of the town's war hospitals queuing for the next performance at the Pavilion Theatre of Varieties. The multiplicity of units served by the 5th Northern General and the Evington War Hospitals can be seen by the men's differing cap badges. (Although required to wear a standard hospital uniform, men retained their regimental headgear). Among those seen in the crowd is the Tam O'Shanter of a Scottish regiment and the bush hat of an ANZAC. Situated at the corner of Belgrave Gate and Wilton Street, under the proprietorship of Frank MacNaughten, the Pavilion was one of the most popular music halls in Leicester.

The Palace Theatre in Belgrave Gate. Visited by such performers as Vesta Tilley, during 1916 it was also the scene of a police and army raid calculated to round up conscription dodgers. During the war years the stage of the Palace was given over on several occasions by its owner Oswald Stoll to fund raising concerts. It was from the front balcony that the Mayor, Walter Lovell, made one of his Armistice Day speeches to crowds gathered in Belgrave Gate.

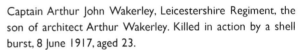

Captain Arthur John Wakerley, Leicestershire Regiment, the son of architect Arthur Wakerley. Killed in action by a shell burst, 8 June 1917, aged 23.

Pictured at a farm near Cassel in France during April 1916, this is 16 Company, No 2 Section of the Machine Gun Corps, Leicestershire Regiment. It is worth noting that the men wear not the usual 'Tigers' insignia, but a cap badge depicting crossed machine guns surmounted by a crown, The Sergeant standing sixth from the right on the back row is Ernest E. Neale, who joined the Leicesters in December 1912 and went to France with the initial units of the British Expeditionary Force in 1914. Apart from the 1914 Star, Sergeant Neale was mentioned in despatches four times, awarded the Cross of St George (Russian), 4th Class for gallantry in September 1915, and the Military Medal in 1916. Surviving the war, Ernest Neale left the army after the Armistice.

A group of officers and NCOs of the Leicesters seen here taking their leave before catching a train from the Midland Railway Station to return to the Front.

Courtesy of the De Montfort Association, this group of men from the 5th Northern General Hospital have their photograph taken a short distance from the hospital, outside of the studio of Harvey Earnshaw, a local photographer of 68 New Walk.

Out for an excursion, this group of recuperating soldiers is pictured in the town centre.

1918

A DEPRESSING year, 1917 ended with violence at home as well as abroad. Thomas and Elizabeth Taylor had been married for nine years when, after a period of domestic upheavals, he killed her on Boxing Day 1917. Taylor, aged 35, had been a regular soldier in the Dublin Fusiliers, and had seen service during the Boer War in South Africa. In 1911 the couple emigrated to Canada and it was there, in September 1914, that he enlisted in the Canadian Expeditionary Force. With Taylor posted to England for training, the couple returned to live in Leicester. Involved in an accident when some billets caught fire on Salisbury Plain during a training exercise, Thomas Taylor sustained severe burns to his back and arms. Although in June 1915 he went France with his unit, he was sent back in March 1916 to England for hospitalisation and then returned to Canada to be medically discharged from the army.

Elizabeth refused to join Taylor in Canada, so he returned to England, where he found that during his absence, she had begun an affair with a foreman at the factory where she was working. The marriage in tatters, the couple separated and she went to live at Beeston in Nottinghamshire, taking with her their five-year-old daughter, Frances Edna. Their elder daughter, Edith Jesse (seven), remained with her father, who was now working as a dyer's labourer, in his lodgings at 28 Raglan Street.

Elizabeth Taylor spent Christmas 1917 in Leicester with her sister at 139 Sheridan Street. During that time, her husband made approaches to her to return home and resume the marriage. On Boxing Day, Thomas Taylor took Jessie to the house to be with her mother for the day. Returning for the child about half past six that evening, Taylor took his wife out into the back yard of the house to discuss their situation. At his trial Thomas Taylor gave evidence that he had again asked Elizabeth to return to him with the children, to which she replied that

'she would think about it' and that she '…could get a ******* man anytime she wanted'. At this point, Taylor pulled a cut-throat razor from his pocket and slashed her throat, fatally injuring her. While his sister-in-law and others were occupied with the woman in the house (she died within minutes in a chair in the front room), Taylor quietly took his daughter back to their lodgings where he was later arrested.

Tried at Leicester Assizes before Mr Justice Horridge, Thomas Taylor was found guilty of the murder of his wife, with a strong recommendation for mercy. Taylor's situation evoked a great deal of public sympathy and on 12 February 1918, as the result of a 12,000-signature petition, his sentence was commuted to penal servitude for life.

Meanwhile, the town was in the grip of a measles epidemic. The outbreak had started before Christmas and during the three months from November 1917 to January 1918, 2,785 cases had been reported. With 50 to 60 new patients being reported each day, the very worried Borough Medical Officer of Health, C. Killick Millard, reported in March, before the epidemic had burnt itself out, that there had been 2,000 reported cases with 60 deaths. What was not known by Millard, or anyone else at the time, was that this was a forerunner to one of the greatest epidemics of the 20th century – a particularly virulent influenza which would wipe out huge numbers of people in the civilised world, including Leicester, later that year.

In previous years, while the emphasis in the cost of living increases had focussed upon food and fuel prices, food had been the prime concern of the average citizen. Now the cost of domestic fuel was escalating alarmingly and there was some reason for concern over gas supplies. At the beginning of the 1917-18 winter, the retail price of coal varied (dependent upon quality) between 28s 6d and 35s a ton (a figure which in October 1918 had reached 42s), which in some cases was equivalent to one week's wages going into a household. At the end of the winter Hubert Pooley, the manager of the Gas Department, expressed to the Corporation concern over the budgets available to him. In 1909 his department paid out £99,367 for the coal, coke and oil required to supply the borough's gas needs. His estimated budget for the same supplies during the forthcoming year was £197,500.[1] In 1909 wages to his department's employees totalled £89,361 – the 1918 wages estimate was £142,000. Nationally the gas industry was asking for an increase of 12 per cent in wages, in addition to any war bonus. If this were granted in Leicester it would add another £18,000 to the year's estimates. (There is a small irony here, in that, while lamenting the costs involved in a 12 per cent rise for the workers, Mr Pooley had, in January, negotiated for himself a 25 per cent rise, taking his salary from £1,000 per year to £1,250.)

In the early months of 1918, the fact that this was actually the last year of the war was not apparent to either the Government or to the man and woman in the street. Formal rationing was now being enforced in some areas of supply, while local rationing by Food Control Committees throughout the country amounted to the same thing. Lloyd George and his advisers, both military and civil, were preparing for the war and all its consequences to extend past 1918 into 1919. That continued fighting was imminent appeared to be confirmed by the successful German Spring Offensive launched in March 1918 which threatened to erode any gains which the Allies might have made in France. That the Spring Offensive would collapse in ruins was not at this point apparent.

In Leicester the local Food Control Committee, based at 83 Granby Street, began butter rationing in the town on Monday, 7 January. Every person was allowed four ounces per week of butter or margarine – but not both. Five weeks later, on 13 February, the pork butchers in Leicester took a decision *en masse* to close down in order to reduce food queues. All their products, such as pork, sausages and pies, were sold by the town's beef butchers, while commodities such as bacon and lard were retailed by grocers.[2] In order to prevent hoarding of food, it was agreed in February that tinned meat could only be sold at the rate of one pound per person after the tin had been opened in the shop. Following the example set by the Home Counties, the Food Control Committee elected to ration all meat products, including bacon. By March, forms were being prepared in readiness for full rationing.

The *Leicester Daily Mercury*, abandoning its well-known broadsheet format and appearing for the first time in tabloid in April, announced that 'meat rationing comes into force on Sunday, 7 April…' The procedure in relation to ration cards was explained to the townspeople.

> Coupons are dated for the week during which they are valid. (The week is actually extended to an 11-day period.) When a purchase is made, the seller will detach the relevant coupons from the purchaser's card. Each coupon on an adult's card permits the purchase of 5d worth of meat.
>
> Beef and mutton may only be purchased at the butcher with whom the person is registered. Pork and offal can be purchased anywhere. (Each coupon valid for 5d worth of tongue, kidney or skirt, or 10d worth of edible offal other than tongue, kidney or skirt.)
>
> Until 5th May, bacon and ham may be bought at any shop – an adult coupon entitling the holder to 5oz of uncooked bacon or ham on the bone.
>
> Coupons may be used anywhere for the purchase of poultry, game, rabbit, tinned or cooked meat.
>
> In restaurants or eating houses, meat dishes can only be sold in exchange for the customer's relevant meat coupons.
>
> Children are on half an adult ration.

Later in the year, for the purposes of formal food rationing Leicester was incorporated into the North Midland Division along with Nottingham, Derby, Northampton, Rutland and the Soke of Peter-borough.

---

1. In July 1918, there were in the town 55,600 gas cookers and 9,000 gas fires.

2. It is not clear what the pork butchers then did for a living. One presumption may be that they continued to supply those who were retailing the goods. This move would explain why the premises of Henry Walker (pork butchers), in Oxford Street were available in March 1918 to be used as a food kitchen.

In May 1916 the Summertime Daylight Saving Act had come into force, requiring people throughout the country to alter their clocks by one hour. (Because the Act represented a completely new concept, the Government went to considerable trouble to explain to the populace that town clocks must be altered, licensees would have to close an hour earlier and 'housewives should be made aware that they must put the dinner on an hour early'.) In an effort to conserve fuel, in April 1918 an Order under the Lighting Regulations directed that no hot meals were to be cooked or served in any inn, hotel or restaurant between 9.30pm and 5am. Likewise, no lectures or entertainment were to be given between 10pm and 1pm the following day. Except for cleaning purposes no lights were to be exhibited between 10pm and 5am, nor any gas or electric current to be consumed between those hours.

Apparently oblivious to the straitened circumstances of the nation, the Government in January launched a National Appeal for subscriptions to a stock flotation to be known as the 'Tank Bank'. The concept of the tank was still something new and wonderful. The first tanks had seen action, albeit on a small, scale, in France during the latter part of the Somme Offensive during Sep - tember 1916; thereafter they were used with varying degrees of success for the remainder of the war. Few members of the public, however, had set eyes upon, let alone had the opportunity to inspect one of these masterpieces of technology.[1]

A league table quickly developed between different towns and cities as to how much money each could amass. (This was vigorously exploited by the Press, especially in those towns where most money was collected.) Eventual figures for this, one of the final great efforts to squeeze contributions from the country, were quite impressive. Glasgow was one of the top cities with £3.25 million, followed by Edinburgh with £2.086 million. Figures ran right back down the scale to Cardiff which managed only £18,127. North, taking a middle line, proposed that Leicester, in conjunction with the county (who had agreed to make the appeal a joint venture), should target a contribution of £1.5 million. An initial promise, of £350,000 came from businesses in the town[2] and a tank was duly despatched to Leicester by the War Office.

Given the name 'Old Bill' (after Billy Merson, a music hall turn of the day), the machine arrived accompanied by a procession of discharged soldiers, Boy Scouts, mounted police and the Leicester Military Band, on Sunday, 13 January. To the delight of the assembled crowds, gathered in the freezing cold, the event was recorded on cinematograph by the Gaumont Company. The tank's presence in Town Hall Square during the following week provided a fascinated public with the greatest spectacle since the *Leicester* aeroplane had taken off from Western Park in the summer of 1916. Children were allowed to clamber on to the monster, while parents chatted with the tank commander, Lieutenant Brocklehurst, and his three crew members.

Despite the inclement wintery conditions – eight inches of snow had fallen by Wednesday – the week was a resounding success. Each day saw some form of entertainment in the Square, including on Thursday evening a display of aircraft flying low over the town firing Very lights and dropping cardboard discs promoting the Tank Week. The culmination of the seven days was a torchlight tattoo on the final Saturday night, arranged by the Leicester Discharged Soldiers' and Sailors' Association, prior to 'Old Bill' moving off to the Midland Railway Station whence it travelled to the neighbouring county of Nottinghamshire. The eventual total for the week's activities amounted to an investment by the people of the town and county of £2.045 million.

The position of many of the women whose husbands were away in the army was becoming desperate. Tied into the home environment by virtue of having to care for a family, they were among those unable to share the wages boom in the town, and had to 'make do' on the army allowances and such other monies as were available from associations such as the War Pensions Committee. That organisation was now becoming swamped with applications for aid from both the wives and from disabled men being discharged.

At the end of January, the War Pensions

---

1. Whilst still at the development stage, the original test model, in an attempt to keep the project a secret, was described as a 'water tank for Mesopotamia'. Thereafter the vehicle was referred to as the 'tank'.

2. Leicester Corporation undertook to purchase £21,000 worth of Tank Bank Stock, while the Leicester Permanent Building Society and the British United Shoe Machinery Company pledged £250,000 between them.

Committee was registering on average 180 men per week. (In April the total of registered disabled men in the borough had reached 3,117.) Training was being found, where practicable, for men as tailors, crayon makers and hosiery workers. Where possible jobs were found in munitions factories, although this was difficult as all those men still in the munitions industry had already been given low medical categories, and as such were by now permanent fixtures. Financially, the best that could be offered to the trainees was an allowance which, according to circumstances, could be as low as 27s 6d a week.

Supplementary Separation Allowances were being paid to 190 wives who were in dire financial need. Additionally, cash advances were paid out to 223 women whose Army Allowance Papers had been delayed or lost either by the War Office or the Post Office.

The example below, based upon the circumstances of a woman with two children living in Leicester in June 1918, puts into perspective how difficult things had become for some of the servicemen's wives.

Army Separation Allowance for wife with two dependent children = 24s 6d per week

Outgoings:		
	Rent	6s 9d
	Coal	3s 4d
	Milk	2s 4d
	Bread	2s 11d
	Meat	8s 0d
	Groceries	4s 0d
	Bacon	1s 0d
	Gas	1s 4d
	Total	29s 8d

In November 1914, the allowance due to this woman would have been 17s 6d. The fact that in June 1918 she received 24s 8d constituted a 40 per cent increase in the allowance. During that same period, the cost of living had risen by 107 per cent. It did not take an accountant to realise that the sums did not add up.

In June, William Hincks, who had worked tirelessly throughout the war, resigned as chairman of the War Pensions Committee to take a job with the Ministry of Pensions. He was replaced by Councillor Sherriff. In October of 1918, with the end of the war in sight, Hincks was presented by the township with a £1,000 War Bond in recognition of his efforts in relation to his work with this and the Prince of Wales's Fund.

As winter progressed into spring, a slightly bizarre and somewhat belated example of patriotism mixed with war-weary frustration came in the form of a petition to the Town Council to be rid of those streets in the borough which carried German names. The move originated with the residents of Saxe-Coburg, Mecklenberg, Gotha, and Hanover Streets, in the Highfields district, who petitioned to have these names expunged and for the streets to be renamed more suitably. After due process (which continued to within two weeks of the Armistice), Hanover Street became Andover Street, Mecklenberg Street was made into an extension of Severn Street, Gotha Street changed to Gotham Street and Saxe-Coburg Street was renamed Saxby Street. The final erasing of the Germanic titles came in February 1919 when Bismarck Street became Beaconsfield Road.

The final annual Labour Party May Day meeting of the war, held in the open air as usual, on Sunday, 5 May, was to be the scene of the most serious public disorders witnessed in Leicester for many years. The event polarised many of the mixed feelings and political divisions running strongly through the town.

The main speaker at the meeting was, as in previous years, James Ramsay MacDonald, with the inevitable keynote speech being on an anti-war theme. MacDonald's presence in itself was anathema to those who had lost husbands and sons in the war and to the ever-growing ranks of the wounded and disabled.[1] Large crowds gathered in the Market Place from early morning and the organisers of the meeting were disturbed to discover that a conflicting meeting was to held by the local branch of the War Aims Committee.

Between 6,000 and 7,000 people thronged the Market Place by the time MacDonald, accompanied by Alderman George Banton and his wife, along with Amos Mann who was chairman of the Leicester Co-operative Society, Councillor Hand who was

---

1. The other MP for Leicester, Gordon Hewart (who was a Liberal), was never subjected to this disparagement by those opposed to him. Much of this was due to the fact that irrespective of any personal feelings (his son, a young subaltern had been killed in August 1915 in the Dardanelles), he had continued to represent the borough on the basis that the war must be won.

chairman of the Leicester Labour Party and several other local politicians (some of whom were accompanied by young children), took their places – doubtless with some trepidation – on the makeshift platform.

Their supporters then filled the space in front of the group in order to listen to the proceedings, leaving the rear of the platform exposed. The War Aims Committee, which had assembled near to the Fish Market, soon established itself in a strong position, covering the vulnerable points left by MacDonald's supporters. A third contingent in the form of Leicester Borough Police officers, some mounted, others on foot, now appeared on the scene and attempted to position themselves between the opposing factions.

MacDonald, obviously unwell and speaking with some difficulty, attempted for a short while to address the crowd. This was rendered impossible by the opposition shouting, heckling and singing *God Save The King*. After a short time, MacDonald was forced to give up and his place was taken by George Banton. Banton, obviously incensed by what he saw as deliberate sabotage, launched a personal attack on the character of Jonathan North, whom he declared had engineered the whole thing as a political ploy to discredit the Labour Movement. (In this he may or may not have been correct; however, later on, in the cold light of the Council Chamber and due to his total lack of evidence to substantiate his outburst, he was obliged to publicly apologise to North.)

MacDonald, in turn, was obliged to beat a retreat when a band of soldiers in uniform, some wounded from the 5th Northern General Hospital and others recently discharged, carrying a Union Flag, cut a swathe through his supporters and attacked the platform party. (As can be imagined the success of such an action carried out by men recently returned from the trenches was never in any doubt.) General fist fighting broke out immediately and the platform, which comprised two drays pushed together, was in danger of being overturned. Two police inspectors and a dozen constables formed a guard around the speakers, while the remainder of the police reserves attempted to quell the mob. After some considerable time, order was restored and several people were arrested and taken to the police cells. George Banton hastily thanked the police for their efforts, and the meeting was abandoned.

Eleven weeks later, on 21 July, Ramsay MacDonald, who by now was a spent force so far as Leicester was concerned, made one further attempt to address a crowd in the Market Place. Convened by a joint group of Labour and Trades Councils representatives, the meeting was to lobby for an increase in Army Separation Allowances. Mac - Donald, still in poor health, had declined to speak until the end of the proceedings. As soon as he started to address the meeting, an opposition group of about 40 men attempted to take the platform by force. After some limited fighting between those present and police, the meeting was discontinued. Ramsay MacDonald's policy of peace at any cost was by now wearing thin even with the staunchest Labour supporters in the town.

In August, soon after the July fiasco, Alderman Jabez Chaplin, a founder member of the Independent Labour Party, wrote from his home at 114 Harrow Road resigning from the party. Born the son of a shoemaker in 1860 at Hinckley, Chaplin had been taken out of school at the age of eight and put into a factory as a winder. At 13 he left home and walked to Leicester to find work in the hosiery trade. Appointed secretary of the Amalgamated Hosiery Union in 1892, he was a founder member of the ILP, being elected to Leicester Town Council in 1898. The loss of his support was a further severe blow to MacDonald's dwindling prestige locally.

A more welcome visitor to the town during July was Captain Robert Gee, VC, MC. As in the earlier case of Private Buckingham VC, Gee was an ex-Countesthorpe Cottage Homes boy. Having left Countesthorpe, he joined the Royal Fusiliers in 1892 and rose through the ranks to become an officer. He was awarded the Victoria Cross in April 1918, when having led two companies of infantry in a clearing operation near to a small village in France, he was wounded attacking a machine-gun post. Enjoying better fortune than Buckingham (who, having survived to receive his decoration, was later killed in action), Robert Gee was sent back home to take part in a drive to recruit officer candidates from public schools. It was during this whistle-stop tour that he and his wife arrived in Leicester. Provided with a guard of honour by members of the Cadet Battalion, the couple were met by Walter Carver, the chairman of the Board of Guardians, and given a civic reception by the Corporation. Prior to their departure, Captain Gee was presented by the Mayor with a gold watch and chain, while Mrs Gee received a gold brooch.

Throughout the summer of 1918, work continued apace to train young men in readiness to send them away to the army as soon as they were of age. In May the trustees of the Junior Training Hall on Aylestone Road negotiated the purchase of the Empress Skating Rink. Two new trustees – Major Rolleston and Lieutenant-Colonel North – were drafted in during October and they announced that, due to the present lack of accommodation, the two buildings would be amalgamated into one for training purposes. The termination of the war shortly after effectively put an end to any need for training and the building, known to future generations as the Granby Halls, was turned over to become a venue for exhibitions, roller skating and other functions.

Without a doubt, other than the Great War itself, the most devastating occurrence of recent years to hit Leicester was the 1918 influenza epidemic. Probably originating among the troops in France late in 1918, the 'flu virus spread with alarming rapidity to become a worldwide epidemic which lasted through into 1919. Overall the death toll was estimated at 20 million.

The first indications of a problem in Leicester came during June and July. In the middle of summer, people young and old began to go down with the virus at an alarming rate. The first fatality was Evelyn Fearn, a 19-year-old wool spinner. Starting with what appeared to be a cold on the morning of Friday, 28 June, by 11pm the same night she had died. Soon Leicester factories were reporting up to ten per cent of their workforces being absent. On 11 July the Education Committee stated that of 37,000 elementary school pupils on its books, 7,000 were away ill with the 'flu. All places of entertainment in the town were declared off-limits to soldiers in an effort to limit the spread of the virus. By the end of July the infection seemed to have run its course.

However, October and November saw a violent resurgence of the illness. As in almost every other part of the civilised world, doctors were helpless to do anything other than attempt to alleviate the symptoms; a cure was just not available. Figures for the period 12 October to 23 November 1918 show that the number of deaths in Leicester from the

sickness were 747. The epidemic peaked during the three weeks from 19 October to 9 November when 603 patients died,[1] 207 of these being children under the age of 15.

One of the first places to feel the impact of the ailment was the Workhouse in Swain Street. The inmates, already on the most basic of diets, were among those most quickly afflicted. During the third week of October, 11 inmates died in the Poor Law Infirmary. To a great extent sharing the inmates' living conditions, the staff at the Workhouse also quickly succumbed. The weekly return for Saturday, 19 October showed that 28 nurses at the Poor Law Hospital were sick, one of whom had already died. By the end of October, all Leicester's elementary schools were closed.

The absence due to sickness of 70 of the tramways staff severely affected the Corporation's capability to provide public transport. The visiting of patients at the Royal Infirmary was suspended and posters were put up all around the town requesting people to stay away from places of public entertainment. While theatres and cinemas agreed to close their doors in the public interest, the incumbents of the town's churches and chapels steadfastly refused to shut their portals to parishioners seeking help and guidance. The Medical Officer of Health, Dr Millard, adopting a pragmatic view, advised the Corporation that there was little point in closing down places of public resort when people gathered together in the workplace. Managers of cinemas and theatres, glad of the reprieve, willingly agreed to close their premises between performances in order to allow them to be fumigated.

At the height of the outbreak, the Borough Surveyor's and the Tramways Departments had to assist local undertakers who could not cope with the volume of work thrust upon them. Boy Scouts worked as messengers, running between hospitals and surgeries. The District Nursing Association helped out the overburdened medical services, while Voluntary Aid Detachments supplemented the fire brigade's limited ambulance service.

During late November a distinct tailing-off of reported instances signified that for the second time the epidemic had nearly run its course. Again, the respite was not destined to last for long, however.

In the second week of February 1919, Leicester, along with the rest of the nation, was in the grip of

1. Deaths recorded = w/e 26 October, 194; w/e 2nd November, 262; w/e 9 November 147.

what was to be the final wave of infection. For some reason the Midlands, along with the mining districts of Northumberland, South Durham and North Yorkshire, were particularly hard hit. This last phase started in Leicester with a series of soldiers being received at the 5th Northern General Military Hospital. Of 238 admissions, 84 died. The situation was soon reflected in the town. The borough saw 12 deaths in the second week of February and the toll continued to mount. The highest number of deaths in any one day was 51 on Friday, 7 March.

The figures below show the deaths in Leicester from influenza and related illnesses, pneumonia, bronchitis etc, up to the middle of March when locally the severity of the epidemic waned.

Week-ending	Influenza	Associated illnesses	Total
8 February	2	72	74
15 February	12	84	96
22 February	61	119	180
Sat 1 March	90	97	187
Sat 8 March	50	128	178
Sat 15 March	41	68	109

Other towns fared no better. The figures in the table below are intended to give a broad impression of the situation nationally and are by no means exhaustive, as a study of the actual epidemic is a research project on its own. Unless otherwise stated the figure shown is for death from influenza itself.

Town/City	**Week Ending**		
	15 February	22 February	1 March
Birmingham	29	84	159
Bradford	50	152	129
Glasgow	* * *	* * *	580*
	(*inc. associated illnesses)		
Greater London	* * *	974	* * *
Leeds	29	82	130
Leicester	12	61	90
Liverpool	148	188	196
Manchester	44	130	196
Middlesbrough	* * *	36	56*
	(*inc. associated illnesses)		
Newcastle upon Tyne	* * *	163	* * *
Nottingham	7	37	47
Sheffield	18	53	64
Stoke-on-Trent	* * *	60	* * *
Sunderland	* * *	36	58

Despite all the precautions which were taken by the authorities and the medical profession (again in the February-March outbreak, schools had been closed and everything possible was done to prevent the spread of infection), the mortality rate was extremely high. An estimated total of the deaths attributable to influenza and its associated illnesses in Leicester during the three outbreaks, between June 1918 and March 1919 is 1,600 adults and children.[1]

The 28 December saw the demobilisation in Germany of Sgt 7826 W. Birch, the first soldier of the 1st Battalion Leicestershire Regiment on active duty abroad to be released. The overall plans for the demobilisation of men were complex and initially ill-conceived. At an early stage it was realised that schemes intended to make the first releases men who could recreate industrial stability, or who had jobs to go to, would not work and the unrest generated within the ranks in some places came near to mutiny. The Government quickly reverted to a plan based upon length of service. On leaving the army each man was offered a package consisting of a railway warrant to his home town, four weeks' paid leave, a set of civilian clothes which soon became known as a 'demob suit' (in addition he was allowed to keep his uniform and tin hat), a ration book and a short-term unemployment insurance policy.[2]

On 19 May 1919 a Cadre of the 1st Battalion of the Leicesters, comprising six officers and 35 other ranks, plus 41 NCOs and men of the Band and Drums, arrived back at the Regimental Depot in South Wigston from Wesseling, near Cologne. The event is best described by the *Leicester Mail* on 20 May.

'The Cadre, commanded by Colonel Latham DSO, arrived at the Midland Station about a quarter past two. The men formed up on the station platform and their officers were greeted by the Mayor of Leicester, Councillor J. Lovell, who was accompanied by the Mayoress, Miss Winnie Lovell and Mrs W. H. Lovell. Amongst those present were the Revd W. Williamson, CF (Presbyterian Chaplain for No 3 Area), Captain Simpson and many interested spectators. Among the officers who arrived with the party were Major Bacchus (in command Glen Parva), Major Greasley (quartermaster of the battalion), and Captain Davis, (adjutant).

1. *Leicester Past and Present*, Jack Simmon.
2. Officers did not receive the unemployment insurance. This was based historically upon a premise held by the army that officers were by default gentlemen of private means. This concept had during the recent war been overturned by the promotion of men through the ranks due to severe battle losses, and caused much hardship to individuals who returned to a working or middle-class environment.

'After a brief delay the men commenced their march to the Municipal Buildings. The Cadre was headed by the band of the 1st Leicestershire, discoursing lively music, and in the midst of the party the Battalion Colours, uncased and borne by 2/Lt. Stewart and 2/Lt. Burns, waved their silken folds, resplendent in colour with their embroidered gold thread glittering in the sunlight. In the station yard were assembled a large number of wounded men now at local hospitals who greeted their comrades with the restrained warmth of those who have "been through it". Outside, no restraint and the progress down Granby Street was a veritable triumphal procession. The men cheered, the women waved handkerchiefs and shouted shrill greetings and every window en route was alive with faces. Many were the recognitions of old comrades, especially among the demobilised men, who had assembled in good force to witness the official return of their old unit. The soldiers were pelted with confetti and good wishes and the police on duty had hard work to keep the road clear for the procession through the dense crowd which extended as far as Horsefair Street.

'At the Municipal Buildings the men formed up in front of the main entrance, where Major Sergeantson, OBE (secretary of the Leicestershire Territorial Association), the Territorial veteran Colonel Sarson, and Major Evan Barlow, awaited the civic party.

'The Mayor in his address of welcome said: "Officers, non-commissioned officers and men of the Tigers, I am exceedingly pleased to be in this position, and to have the opportunity of welcoming back from the fields of war, this Cadre of the Leicestershire Regiment. I do so most heartily. The Leicestershire Regiment has always had a proud record. You have worthily maintained that record and the deeds you have performed, when we read them in the Press, have filled us with wonder and admiration. The gratitude of the Leicester people – of all English people – is due to the Leicesters for the way in which they have conducted themselves. We in the good old town of Leicester have done our best to back you up. Not only have we subscribed towards carrying on this war to a successful end in which you have participated, but we have attended to your wounded who were sent home, and thousands of people have given their charitable efforts in the relief of suffering. We have had a quiet time industrially. No man has raised his voice or by action sought to hinder the work you have done so nobly and so well. Therefore it gives us great pleasure to welcome you. We know you are reduced in numbers but your spirit has remained firm. There are many who went out with you who, alas, will never return. We mourn for them. Only last week I took part in a large joint meeting of the town and county at which a resolution was passed that a fitting memorial to those men should be raised.[1] That is as it should be. I am sure the whole of Leicester will support that effort. I thank you on behalf of the town whose name you so nobly bear for the services you have so gallantly rendered."

'Colonel Latham responded to the Mayor on behalf of the regiment.

'The officers and men were then entertained to tea at the Town Hall. The officers sat down to a cold collation in the ante-room of the Council Chamber and afterwards were conducted over the Town Hall by their host and hostess. The non-commissioned officers' tea party was in another part of the building. All present wore one or more decorations and all with the exception of one had been through the entire campaign. The men sat down to a good spread in the Police Muster Room.

'Afterwards the Cadre marched to Glen Parva amid renewed scenes of enthusiasm. The Mayor and Mayoress headed the procession along Aylestone Road in their motor car.'

In fact the Cadre was not to remain long at Glen Parva. On 3 August 1919 it was amalgamated with the remnants of the 1st Battalion and sent to Liverpool to intervene in the disorders resulting from the police strike of 1919. Within months the battalion was posted to Athlone in Ireland where it remained until December 1921.

1. During the inter-war years a memorial designed by Sir Edwin Lutyens was erected on Victoria Park.

Used in action for the first time on 15 September 1916 during the Battle of the Somme, and later the following year in greater numbers in November 1917 at Cambrai, the tank was to the average citizen an amazing invention. Brought to Leicester in January 1918 as part of National Tank Week, this huge machine, known as 'Old Bill', (after a popular music hall turn, Billy Merson), stood in Town Hall Square for a week, before departing by rail for Nottingham.

Viewed from the steps of the Town Hall, the bearded figure standing on 'Old Bill' is Colonel R. Dalgliesh. Working with his equipment in the background can be seen the cameraman from the Gaumont Company recording the day's events.

Tank Week, January 1918. Music hall star Vesta Tilley stands on 'Old Bill' in Town Hall Square, encouraging the citizens of Leicester to invest in the war effort.

11 November 1918. Standing on a dray in front of the Town Hall beneath the flags of the Triple Alliance of France, Britain and America, the Mayor of Leicester, Walter Lovell, declares to the assembled crowd that 'the war is over!' At the other end of the dray, with his hands resting on the makeshift platform, is Jonathan North. Having guided the town through the trials and tribulations of the previous four years, North, who had only been succeeded as mayor two days previously, must have felt keenly the anticlimax of being a bystander at this historic moment.

Distributing flags for the Armistice celebrations in the town.

Celebrating the end of the war, the Borough Fire Brigade festoon the fire station in Rutland Street with decorations including a figure of Britannia flanked by two lions. The banner over the arches reads: 'Peace After Victory'.

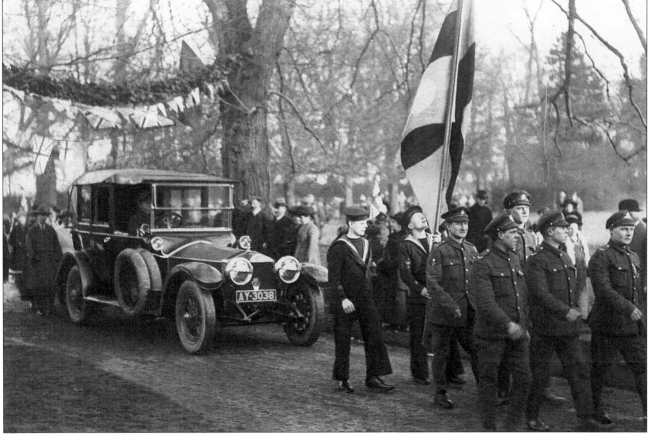

With the war over, men and leaders began to return home. Given a hero's welcome, Admiral Beatty returns in a chauffeured car to Brooksby Hall on 12 February 1919.

Pictured centre among friends and locals, Admiral Sir David Beatty on his arrival at Brooksby Hall. His habit of wearing both uniform and civilian hats tipped slightly to one side and forward – which became known in the Royal Navy as 'the Beatty Angle' – makes him easily distinguishable in a crowd.

The influenza epidemic of 1918 saw hospitals such as the Leicester Royal Infirmary taxed to their limits.

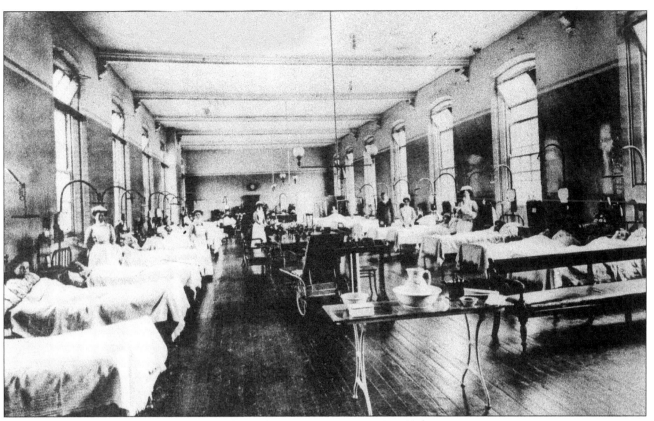

Pictured in 1917 just prior to the 'flu epidemic, St Luke's Ward at the Leicester Royal Infirmary.

William Edwin Hincks, seen here after the war during his term of office as Lord Mayor of the City of Leicester in 1929. (The term 'Lord Mayor' was not taken into use until 1927.) As chairman of the Watch Committee and administrator of the War Relief Fund along with a host of other activities throughout the four years of the war, Hincks, along with a handful of others, formed a nucleus of people working determinedly to ensure the well-being of the families of men away at the Front. In October 1918, in recognition of his efforts, he was presented with a £1,000 War Bond.

Electioneering 1918 style. The Liberal Party poster carries the legend: 'We mobilised for war – let us mobilise for prosperity!'

Implacable political enemies throughout the war years, Sir Jonathan North and George Banton are seen here at an Armistice Service on the steps of the Town Hall in 1925 during Banton's period of office as Mayor of Leicester. The bearded figure of North, who was knighted by King George V in 1919, is standing at the rear of Mr and Mrs Banton.

Final Days

APRIL 1917 was a pivotal point in the war for both sides. For the Central Powers, the Russian Revolution was of immense significance. If the Bolsheviks succeeded in taking Russia out of the war, then the Kaiser's divisions on the Eastern Front could be rushed across Europe to bolster his beleaguered troops on the Western Front. For the Allies, the entry of America into the war in April 1917 was to provide the desperately needed injection of manpower required to move from the defensive to the offensive.

In early 1918, fully aware of how close run the timings would be, as to who managed to achieve their objectives first, General Erich Ludendorff, by now virtual dictator of Germany, hastened to plan a massive attack against the Allied trenches. Codenamed 'St Michael', the plan proposed a mammoth strike along the British-held part of the trenches between Arras, St Quentin and La Fère. Under no illusions, Ludendorff knew that should this offensive fail, he had insufficient troops to mount a second attack.

The opening barrage began at 5am on the morning of Thursday, 21 March. Fighting all along the Front continued for several days until on 29 March, German soldiers, pushing the Allies back towards the coast, reached the village of Albert. In this small hamlet, physically worn out, their numbers depleted by heavy casualties and critically short of supplies, they began to loot. At this point, with discipline lost, the advance ground to a halt.

Mustering his faltering divisions, General Ludendorff attempted a further strike down through Champagne country, reaching to within 50 miles of Paris. To the dismay of the High Command, yet again fatigued and disillusioned men found their way into the wine cellars of the towns and villages through which they passed and the offensive failed.

As a counterpoint to the German loss of impetus,

American soldiers, fresh from the United States, under Generals Pershing and Bliss, now began to take an effective role in the Allied defence. On 18 July, under the overall command of General Foch, the British, French and American armies began a counter-offensive which brought a rapid conclusion to the war.

The failure of the German Spring Offensive of 1918 signalled loud and clear to soldiers and politicians alike that the Great War was drawing to a close.

With the signing of the Armistice, the Great War was ended on Monday, 11 November 1918. An official announcement was made by the new Mayor of Leicester, Councillor Walter Lovell[1], from a platform erected on a dray in Town Hall Square, to a tumultuous gathering of several thousand people. Among those forming an official party accompanying Lovell on the dray was Jonathan North, whose tenure as Mayor had ended two days previously on Saturday, 9 November. Celebrations on a grand scale followed the announcement. Buildings throughout the town were decked out with Union Flags. Great crowds of men and women, all in their best clothes, filled the streets. Soldiers from the Base Hospital were mobbed and kissed by women and factory girls while children, singing *Rule Britannia* and the *Marseillaise*, paraded through the town carrying effigies of the Kaiser with a drooping moustache, decorated in red white and blue bunting. Church bells were rung out at two o'clock and factory whistles were sounded at three o'clock. (The first time for four years that they had not signified an impending air-raid.) One ringer, the verger at St Leonard's in Clarendon Park for the past 45 years, Mr Cooper, had in his youth rung the bells to signify the end of the Crimean War in 1856.

An impromptu public holiday was declared while

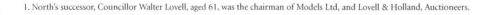

1. North's successor, Councillor Walter Lovell, aged 61, was the chairman of Models Ltd, and Lovell & Holland, Auctioneers.

preparations continued to mark the event. During the afternoon, aircraft displayed over the town and Boy Scout bands played patriotic tunes.

Next day, Tuesday, 12 November, as the early winter darkness began to fall, bonfires were lighted in the thoroughfares in lieu of the darkened street lights, which for so long had been painted out to give only the faintest illumination. (Prior to the war the town had been lit at night by an estimated 5,000 gas lamps. Due to the exigencies of war this number had over the years reduced to 350, all of which were currently blacked out. Once cleaned off, along with another 350 which were brought back into service, they constituted, due to a lack of fuel, the total street lighting during the forthcoming winter.) As the early winter evening drew in, all the lamps in Town Hall Square were restored to service and lit. Along with a torchlight procession organised by Tom Crumbie and Councillor Joseph Sturge Collier, these provided a focal point for the revelries.

Following a Service of Thanksgiving at St Martin's Cathedral, Walter Lovell went on to the stage of the Palace Theatre between houses to thank the citizens of Leicester for all their efforts during the previous four years. After the second house he appeared on the balcony of the theatre overlooking Belgrave Gate and again later on the Clock Tower where he made similar speeches.

The party atmosphere continued throughout the next day and night with church services during the day and torchlight processions after dark. Huge bonfires were lit in Welford Place, St George Street and Northampton Square, and public houses did a record trade. While individual celebrations continued for some days, the main events culminated that night with a parade by firemen in full regalia on decorated fire appliances, and a huge celebration on Victoria Park.

One of the first opportunities to celebrate a return to normality was at Christmas. For the first time in living memory, the holiday was generally extended to a week. The boot and shoe trade announced a closure of factories at 12 noon on Tuesday, 24 December until the following Monday[1], shops in the town put up their shutters from Christmas Eve until Saturday 28. The week prior to the holiday was as festive as in pre-war days. Shops and stores once again had illuminated displays, even if goods were not as yet back in plentiful supply.

With Christmas cakes on sale at 2s 6d a pound and turkeys at 2s 4d (pork remained on ration until 31 December), grocers, confectioners and butchers did a roaring trade. The insistent posters, affixed to prominent places throughout the town by the Gas Department proclaiming: 'Consumers must cut back on the consumption of gas during the winter due to lack of fuel,' were, after nearly four years of restrictive practices, totally ignored.

The new Mayor, Walter Lovell, paid a visit to the Base Hospital, spending some time among the men and distributing cigars to those in the officers' wards. Although 700 men had been allowed to return to their homes on leave, approximately 1,000 patients still remained in the hospital during the holiday period.

A particularly poignant event for the families concerned was the return home on Christmas night of a convoy of 200 prisoners-of-war from Cologne.

In December, following close on the heels of the Armistice, came the long-awaited General Election of 1918. After four years of war, during which there had not even been any local government elections, it was appropriate that the nation should have the opportunity to elect a new Government.

Polling stations were crowded with vast numbers of people eager to cast their votes in the new era after the 'war to end all future wars'. Because demobilisation proper had not yet begun, services personnel were granted a postal vote from their units, which had to be registered by the 27th of the month. The result, both nationally and locally, was predictable. In an overall show of confidence, David Lloyd George's Coalition were elected with a majority of 248 seats.

The three new divisions of Leicester Town each returned a Coalition candidate with huge majorities. In the Eastern Division, Gordon (by now Sir Gordon) Hewart, standing as a Coalition candidate, polled 18,024 votes against Alderman George Banton, for Labour, who drew 6,697 – a majority of 11,327. In the Southern Division, Councillor Frederick Fox Riley scored only 5,463 votes against the Coalition candidate, T. A. Blane who, securing 18,498 votes, won the division by a majority of 13,035. As was expected, the biggest loser was Ramsay MacDonald who polled only 6,347 votes as the candidate for the Western Division, standing against another Coalition nominee, J. F. Green, who

---

1. It was not until a much later date that New Year came to be formally recognised as a Bank Holiday.

with a poll of 20,570 went to Westminster with a majority of 14,223. Similarly, Coalition candidates also swept the board across the county.

Lloyd George's appointments, published early in January, contained (with the hindsight of history) some most auspicious names. Counted among his team were one previous Premier and three future Prime Ministers. Sir Gordon Hewart was rewarded for his services with the post of Attorney General. The discordant note which sounds out is that of the 67-year-old Field Marshall Viscount French of Ypres, in the post of Lord Lieutenant of Ireland. An inveterate and choleric cavalry officer who has been described as 'being less renowned for mental ability than irritability'[1], he was hardly the candidate to take the political mantle of a province recently in rebellion and currently in turmoil.

With the return to a peacetime existence, the people of the town, not unnaturally found that the necessary adjustments were not always easy. Housing, already identified by the Corporation as being a potential problem, along with the re-employment of demobilised men, became a priority. Crime, which in recent years had not been a prominent issue, now became more apparent. Men freshly returned from an environment where violence was the everyday norm were inclined to be volatile when challenged. When in early December, Constable Stretton attempted to eject David Bunney, a newly-returned soldier, from a public house in the Haymarket, he first had to relieve him of a loaded revolver. A spate of street robberies in January 1919 resulted in the arrest of four deserters who were attacking passers-by after dark in the area of Evington footpath.

In March 1919 the newly-created 'Discharged and Demobilised Soldiers' and Sailors' Club and Institute' opened its doors in New Bond Street. (The premises had previously been the Unionist Working Men's Club.) The need, which was born out by the club's initial membership of 1,000 men, for some form of recreational institute for returning service-men had been recognised in the summer of 1918. Again the usual figures stepped up to undertake the management and running of the establishment. The trustees were Alderman North, Charles Bennion, Sir Samuel Faire, Percy Gee and Evan Barlow. A committee was formed from among the ranks of discharged men with Admiral Sir David Beatty

standing as first president of the club. The property along with the adjacent premises (to be used as the association's offices) were acquired for £2,257 (from local donations) and a further £1,148 was spent on repairs and the equipping of a bar, concert room, billiard room and, in the basement, a skittle alley. The legal costs involved were born by Evan Barlow.

Regrettably, the townspeople of Leicester now turned their attentions and a deal of ill-will towards the refugees living in the borough. With the prevalent shortage of housing and work, a general perception grew in the town that it was time for the foreigners, mainly Belgians, living in Leicester to return to their own countries. On Thursday, 27 February 1919 some 300 Belgian nationals, men women and children, left the Midland Railway Station to begin their journey back to the Continent. Although the Mayor, along with other local dignitaries, was present at the station to witness the departure, there was no farewell ceremony. Leicester Borough Police officers carefully examined each person's documents against the Register of Aliens living in the town before ensuring that they boarded the train. Stopping at Barrow-on-Soar and Loughborough to pick up other refugees who had been living in the county, the train then continued on to the port of Hull from where, on the SS Quilpue, just under 600 exiles, recently living in Leicester and Leicestershire, along with a further 200 from Derbyshire, were returned across the Channel to Antwerp.

The question of housing had begun to be addressed during the spring of 1918 when a proposal was made by the Corporation to purchase from Lieutenant Tailby of Skeffington for the sum of £15,000, 71 acres of land next to the Borough Asylum at Humberstone to facilitate the building of a housing estate. In January 1919, based on a pro-jection that 1,250 houses would be required to accommodate post-war needs, the matter again came under discussion. The scheme envisaged around 420 houses in the Uppingham Road area near to the asylum, with 15 acres of ground set aside for recreational purposes. On the Coleman Road site a further 480 houses would be built, after leaving some ground to be used as allotment gardens, the balance to be utilised for industrial purposes.

In 1919 Leicester Corporation had to address the financial legacy left behind by four years of war,

1. August 1914, Barbara Tuchman.

during which costs of materials and wages in every sector had spiralled.

The overall cost of maintaining the basic services of the borough had increased since 1913 by approximately £500,000 a year. Councillor Amos Sherriff made the point: 'Overall costs have risen by a total of half a million pounds a year since 1913. Where is the money to come from? For 300 years the costs have been born from the rates. When the rating system was introduced there was no machinery as we know today. The tram service, while feeding some robs others, [presumably a reference to shoppers using the town to the detriment of local corner shops], it is increasing the value of property in the centre of town and this is where a re-valuation of property should be made – some people take more money on a Saturday in the Market than they do all week in a shop. Machinery in factories should be rated – a boiler providing heat and power for the running of machinery should be rated – this is what happens in other towns. Most of the Corporation can remember when Highfields, Westcotes, North Evington and West Humberstone were green fields. If all that land belonged to the Corporation 40 years ago, there would be no problems financially now.'

In many ways Sherriff was correct. An inevitable corollary of recent events was that the generation of income had to be a prime objective. This was evident by the immediate budgets proposed by the various Corporation departments. During the year 1918-19, departmental spending (irrespective of independently generated income) had amounted to £507,385. For the year 1919-20 a sum of £632,177 was projected, an increase of £124,792. A commitment had been made to install electric lighting on the main thoroughfares starting, as soon as they were electrified, with the tram routes. At the beginning of the winter of 1915-16 the Gas Department had been working '…to complete the installation of gas lights on the principle main roads in the borough after complaints about the dark streets… [when completed] they will have to be switched off at 10pm'.

The Watch Committee were heavily committed to unknown wage increases with a police force on the verge of a national strike over pay. New schemes to provide housing and to train and relocate men coming back into the employment sector were all going to cost money. The Corporation was in discussion with the County Council over the viability of establishing a university and moves were afoot to change the status of Leicester to that of a city. Inevitably, the result was a rise in the rates. Due to the hardships imposed during the war years, a substantial increase in rateable values had been avoided. Now, as a consequence, the rise was to be a difficult one. The rate in the pound for 1918-19 was 7s 9d; for the subsequent year it had to be increased by almost a third to 10s 2d.

In the aftermath of the war, there was a strong feeling among those with influence that some long-term legacy was now due to the citizens of Leicester.

For some considerable time there had been a desire by many for the town to be restored to its medieval status of a city. This aspiration was further enhanced by those who wished it to become a university city.

It was shortly after the Corporation's deliberations over the state of its finances that it examined the possibility of purchasing the site of the 5th Northern General Hospital which was winding down its activities (the last patient was discharged in September of 1919) for the purpose of establishing a university.

While the matter was being debated, Thomas Fielding Johnson, a local businessman, took a hand. Born in 1828 at Langwith in the Dukeries, Fielding Johnson had come to Leicester early in his life to work at the worsted manufacturing firm owned by his grandfather. Now at the age of 91, Thomas Fielding Johnson, having served as a town councillor, a trustee of the Wyggeston Charity and a Justice of the Peace, was a wealthy man. It was his decision to buy the site and donate it to the town. For reasons best known to himself, the old gentleman wished to keep the proposed gift a secret until it was completed. However, his hand was forced when he became aware that Dr Astley Clarke, one of the university's strongest proponents, was about to speak publicly about the project. In a private conversation with Clarke, Fielding Johnson disclosed to him that he had been in contact with Sir Thomas Cope, the chairman of the County Council, and was in the process of completing the purchase of the land, a matter that he would make public as soon as the transaction had been completed.

It was thus that, on 4 April 1919, Fielding Johnson sent a letter to Walter Lovell making the offer of the site to the town.

Brookfield,
April 4th 1919

Dear Mr Mayor,

I have been reading with much interest the report of the meeting for the consideration of the proposed University Scheme of which you were the chairman.

As the proposition somewhat forces my hand, it may perhaps be well for me to state my wishes and intentions in the matter. I have long felt that the beautiful site of the old Asylum must be secured for the benefit of the borough of Leicester. War Office requirements prevented my taking any steps for a time, but on the Armistice being signed the position changed, and I ventured to negotiate, with the kind assistance of the chairman of the County Council, for the purchase of the whole property – not as a speculation but in the interest of the Borough of Leicester.

I am happy to say terms have been agreed upon and only await for the convenience of the military authorities for completion when I shall be ready to submit my scheme, which will embrace, firstly a site for the two Wyggeston Schools (boys and girls), in which I have been interested for many years, and also for the proposed University College, now under consideration.

This land which adjoins Victoria Park from the north to the south, will provide ample space for all the requirements of the three institutions, which, in conjunction might form an effective architectural group, and a Peace Memorial worthy of our ancient borough.

I am faithfully yours,
T. FIELDING JOHNSON

Thomas Fielding Johnson bought the site of the old Asylum from the County Council for the sum of £40,000. Once the gift had been made, a fund was set up and others contributed heavily. Some of the most notable contributions came from the following: H. Simpson Gee (£20,000); Freeman Hardy and Willis (£10,000); Jonathan North (£5,000); Sir Samuel Faire (£5,000.) With an eventual balance of £100,000, the project was secure and Leicester University took its first students in 1921.

The granting to Leicester of city status was combined with a Royal Visit by HM King George V and Queen Mary in the summer of 1919.[1] This was without doubt the most prestigious event in the history of the town, and has not been surpassed since. Taking place at a time when the popularity of royalty among the common people was at its peak, the arrangements were lavish and enthusiasm was without parallel. The streets of the town were bedecked with shields and banners which were hung from every lamp and tram standard. Union Flags hung from first-floor windows and mock arches were built along the route for the procession to pass through. On Victoria Park, a Royal Pavilion was erected from which the King could review the march past of troops brought in from all points of the region.

The morning of Tuesday, 10 June dawned fine with a light breeze to cool the crowds of onlookers who began to line the route, gathering behind the newly-erected barricades in much the same manner as they had done four years previously to cheer the lines of soldiers who were marching off to war. People began to assemble several hours before the arrival of the Royal Train at 11.15am. One hundred men of the Leicester Borough Fire Brigade, parading in dress uniform, lined the road from the Midland Station to Halford Street while 1,500 ex-servicemen gathered in Bond Street near to the Discharged Soldiers' and Sailors' Club which the Royal Party would pass on its way to visit Corah's premises at St Margaret's Works. Four hundred Boy Scouts assembled in Churchgate and St Margaret Street while 300 members of the Church Lads' Brigade stood along Canning Street, Harcourt Street and Orchard Street. Belgrave Gate was thronged with over 200 Junior Volunteers, while 800 VAD members and nurses spread from Horsefair Street to Hastings Street. Managing the crowds throughout the day were 200 men of Leicester Borough Police assisted by a further 680 police officers drafted in from surrounding forces.

The arrival of the King was signalled by a 21-gun salute, fired by an anti-aircraft battery positioned on Welford Road Recreation Ground as the Royal Train passed on its way to pull into the railway station. The Royal Party alighted from the train and were greeted by a reception party which included the Mayor, the Lord Lieutenant of the County, the Duke

1. The visit had originally been scheduled during November 1918 but was cancelled due to the signing of the Armistice.

of Rutland, Sir Samuel Faire and the Town Clerk. In the main courtyard of the Midland Station, paraded in two files for inspection, were 100 demobilised soldiers, each wearing the 1914 Star. Outside at the front of the crowds was a small contingent of Crimean War and Indian Mutiny veterans, who had been brought into Leicester from Lady Boot's Home at Wilford in Nottingham. Dressed in scarlet, they matched the regalia of the royal outriders manning the carriages which, along with their horses had arrived from London the day before. Processing through the cheering crowds along Granby Street and past the Clock Tower, the King and Queen stopped at the headquarters of the Discharged Soldiers' and Sailors' Association in Bond Street where the King went in to inspect the premises and, upon spotting a portrait of Sir David Beatty, commented on how fortunate the club was in its choice of president. Outside in Bond Street were the remaining nine members of the Nottingham and Nottinghamshire Crimean and Indian Mutiny Veterans Association. Along with those at the railway station this made a total of 16, one of whom had been at the Relief of Lucknow.

The second stop was a visit to Corah and Sons' nearby factory at St Margaret's Works. From there, returning along Belgrave Gate and Gallowtree Gate, along Horsefair Street, the procession made its way to Victoria Park and the main events of the day.

At the De Montfort Hall, after inspecting a guard of honour mounted by the regular soldiers of the 2nd Leicestershire Regiment, the King was presented by the Mayor of Leicester with a Loyal Address, after which, having knighted the borough's former Mayor, Jonathan North, he conducted an investiture of those local men from the town and county who were still awaiting the gallantry decorations which they had been awarded.

After a civic lunch, the party adjourned to the Royal Pavilion on Victoria Park to take the salute at the greatest march past in Leicester's history. On either side of the pavilion, designated areas had been set aside for those of the public deemed to have first claim to the prime places, both to see the afternoon's events and to be near the Royal Party. On one side of the pavilion was a platform for 300 of those wounded men, still hospitalised, who could not stand. On the other side were some 300 invited guests of the Mayor and Corporation. At the rear

were places for 900 wounded men, 300 VAD members and nurses, 300 discharged [disabled] men, and 1,400 widows and orphans of men who had died during the conflict.

Opposite the saluting point were the massed bands of the Leicestershire and Lincolnshire Regiments, who were to play the military parade through, flanked on either side by 1,500 school-children. The approaches to and from the saluting point were lined by members of the cadet battalions.

Having spent days preparing equipment and rehearsing for the great event, an early morning start meant that for those participating in the march past it had been a long day. Split into four separated 'forces'[1] the participants began to form up at lunchtime.

Force 'A', the men of the Regular Army regiments who had travelled in from all over the region, assembled at the Leicester rugby football ground and the Junior Training Hall, from where they marched via Welford Road and Victoria Park to the starting point on London Road.

Force 'B', men who had been demobilised from local units, having assembled at the Welford Road Recreation Ground fell in behind the regulars as they passed by along Welford Road.

Force 'C', which was made up of demobilised men and men from a miscellany of other units, who formed up in the Magazine and marched along Oxford Street into Infirmary Square to take up position at the rear of Force 'B'.

Finally, the Volunteer Units making up Force 'D' marched from the Technical School in the Newarkes to Infirmary Square to join up with Force 'C'.

The scale of the contingents involved can be judged by the Regular Army's presence alone which involved units from nine different regiments, some of whom had more than one unit marching. Not including the bands at the saluting point, the parade was accompanied by seven separate bands.

Starting at 3pm, the parade took three quarters of an hour to pass by the King at the Royal Pavilion.

On leaving the park just before 4pm, the King and Queen paid one final visit of the day to the premises of Taylor, Taylor and Hobson on Stoughton Street, which throughout the preceding four years had supplied the war effort with optical goods.

As its arrival had been signalled by an artillery

---

1. A full list of the participating units is given in the Appendices.

salute, so the departure of the Royal Train was punctuated by an aerial salute. The successor of the original *Leicester* aeroplane, flown by Major D. M. Maclaren, a much-decorated war ace, flew in escort to King George V as his party travelled back to London.

After the hardships and adventure of four years of war, the new City of Leicester was born.

Senior NCOs of the 7th Battalion, Leicestershire Regiment. Although this photograph is not dated, it is likely to be during the early or middle years of the war as Colour Sergeant Cave is shown on a later photograph with the rank of Regimental Quarter Master Sergeant. Most of the men are named. Back row, left to right: Colour Sergeant Hemmings, Sergeant Ladford, Company Sergeant Major Geary, Colour Sergeant Cave, (the sergeant at the end is not identified). Front row, left to right: Regimental Sergeant Major Thorburn, Regimental Quarter Master Sergeant Horner.

Seen outside of their battalion HQ at the end of the war, officers and men of the 7th Battalion, Leicestershire Regiment. Centre is the commanding officer, Lt Colonel Challenor. Seated to his right is Regimental Quarter Master Sergeant Cave.

Midsummer 1919 and these residents of Clarendon Park have their own peace celebration.

Among the military units an open carriage precedes one of the marching bands in the procession along London Road, en route to the De Montfort Hall for the visit of the King and Queen on 10 June 1919. The police officer seated next to the army officer is probably Herbert Allen, Chief Constable of the Borough Force.

The Borough Fire Brigade, led by an appliance with a turntable ladder, moves past the packed crowds on London Road.

The Royal Navy contingent marches past the Leicester Dye Works in London Road on 10 June 1919.

Massed regiments parading past the royal podium on Victoria Park on 10 June 1919.

Inspecting his troops, King George V passes along the lines of soldiers gathered on Victoria Park prior to the ceremonies inside the De Montfort Hall.

King George and Queen Mary returning across Swain Street Bridge to London Road Railway Station after their visit to Taylor, Taylor and Hobson in Stoughton Street, 10 June 1919.

Appendix I

**Boot and shoe, and allied trades in Leicester as shown in
the *Leicester & Districts Trade Directory 1911***

Trade	Businesses in Borough
Boot Makers	186
Boot and Shoe Manufacturers	162
Boot and Shoe Factors	36
Boot and Shoe Machinery and Tool Manufacturers	7
Boot Heel Manufacturers	6
Boot Upper Manufacturers	5
Boot and Shoe Knife Manufacturers	3
Boot Lace Manufacturers	3
Boot Polish Manufacturers	3
Boot and Shoe Machinists	1
Boot and Shoe Tip Manufacturers	1
Boot Sewers (Machine)	1
TOTAL	414

Appendix II

Auxiliary Units administered by the 5 Northern General Hospital

Hospital	Opened	Closed	Accommodation	Total Admissions
Base Hospital	5/ 8/14	9/ 9/19	1,750	51,406
North Evington	6/ 4/15	30/ 5/19	1,010	20,456
Gilroes Hospital	31/10/14	20/ 9/19	144	4,260
Leicester Royal Infirmary	29/10/14	15/ 2/19	184	2,790
Desford Hall	5/11/14	30/ 4/19	66	1,901
Wicklow Lodge (Melton)	2/ 1/15	19/ 4/19	50	1,484
Glen Parva Depot Hospital	10/10/14	30/ 9/19	36	1,271
Charnwood Forest VAD	2/12/14	28/ 2/19	36	*977-1,059
Lutterworth VAD	29/ 4/15	9/12/18	20	539
Ullesthorpe Court	28/ 6/15	16/12/18	20	489
Wistow Hall	15/11/14	1/ 9/19	30	459
Swain Street Auxiliary Hospital	21/7/18	11/12/18	200	378
Dalby Hall	14/11/14	17/ 9/15		118
Brooksby Hall	25/ 9/15	18/ 9/16	20	93

The figures above in relation to the Base Hospital and the North Evington War Hospital are actual admissions. In fact the overall number of people dealt with by the two hospital sites during their period of activity was 74,625.

Brooksby Hall remained a naval hospital until after the Armistice and continued to be supplied with duty-free items.

* Different sources give conflicting figures

Appendix III

Auxiliary hospitals affiliated to the 5th Northern General Hospital

Hospital	No. of patients dealt with
Arnott Hall VAD (Notts)	34
Ashbourne VAD	477
Ashby de la Zouch Cottage Hospital	369
Bayley Hospital (Notts)	20
Belper RCH	2,461
Belvoir Castle (Duchess of Rutland)	28
Billesdon Workhouse	91
Brooksby Hall (Lady Beatty)	93
Burghley House (Marchioness of Exeter)	14
Burley on the Hill (Hon Mrs Guest)	32
Burton Infirmary (Burton upon Trent)	739
Burton VAD (Burton upon Trent)	2,834
Burton Hall VAD (Lady Ernest St Maur)	13
Buxton VAD	1,696
Charnwood Forest VAD	# 977-1,059
Coalville VAD	1,059
Dalby Hall (Mrs Burns Hartopp)	118
Darley Dale VAD	2,112
Derbyshire Royal Infirmary	3,945
Desford Hall VAD	1,901
Duffield VAD	715
Eastwood VAD	906
Egginton Hall VAD	1,888
Foremark Hall (Lady Ida Burdett)	105
Gilroes Hospital	4,260
Glen Parva Military Hospital	1,271
Hambleton Hall (Mrs Coper)	698
Haye Leigh VAD (Derbys)	534
Ilkeston VAD	644
Ilkeston Cottage Hospital	241
Kedleston Hall VAD (Lady Blanche Curzon)	22
Knighton House VAD	877
Leicester Royal Infirmary	2,790
Long Eaton VAD	1,454
Loughborough General Hospital	1,585
Lutterworth VAD	539
Manton Grange (Mrs Blackett)	104
Market Harborough VAD	693
Morley Manor (Mrs Lister Kaye)	41
Nottingham General Hospital	****
Ockbrook VAD	684
Osmaston Manor RCH (Lady Walker)	34
Pailton House (Rugby) (Mrs Morris)	905
Shardlow VAD	1,516
Smalley Hall (Derby) (Mrs Swingler)	*****

South Wingfield VAD	459
Spondon VAD	1,005
Stamford Infirmary	709
Stapleford Park (Hon Mrs G. Gretton)	390
Swain Street, Leicester	378
Temple House (Derby)	*****
Tettenhall VAD (Wolverhampton)	712
Trent Bridge VAD (Notts)	63
Ullesthorpe Court VAD	489
Uppingham VAD	3,829
Wicklow Lodge Hospital, Melton Mowbray	1,484
Wistow Hall	459
Wothorpe Hospital Stamford (Lady Wrightson)	80
Wolverhampton Eye Infirmary	184
Wolverhampton General Hospital	1,450

Different sources give conflicting figures

Appendix IV

Items supplied by the Leicester & Leicestershire War Hospitals Committee to local hospitals Aug 1914 – Sept 1919

Cigarettes:	11,788,340
Tobacco:	12,345lbs
Stationary & Envelopes:	500,000
Gramophone needles:	350,000
Visitors passes:	300,000
Matches:	73,000 boxes
Magazines & Periodicals:	36,700
Picture postcards:	28,000
Books:	6,200
Records:	5,070
Ash trays:	2,700
Indoor games:	2,000
Packs of playing cards:	1,400
Writing pads:	1,000
Evening papers (max each day):	332
Morning papers (max each day):	290
Vases for flowers:	168
Outdoor games:	90
Gramophones:	66
Billiard Tables (by purchase £105):	23
Spinal carriages:	9
Pianos (loaned):	8
Bagatelle boards (gifted):	5
Self propelled ward chairs:	3

For Christmas festivities at the hospitals cash grants to the value £136 10s 0d.

Collected for the Wounded Soldiers Rest Rooms at Leicester railway station: 160lbs of tobacco and cigarettes.

Appendix V

Total Clearances, Bonded Warehouse, Leicester
April 1915-Sept 1919

To Leicester. Hospitals
Cigarettes:	11,788,340
Tobacco:	12,354lbs

To 52 hospitals in the Midlands and East Midlands
Cigarettes:	10,552,618
Cigars:	12,300
Tobacco:	6,824 lbs
Coffee for VAD Hospitals	28 lbs

To POWs Fund
Cigarettes:	4,050,000
Tobacco:	1,642lbs
Chocolate:	1,422lbs
Tea:	12 tons. 8 cwts. 30lbs
Sugar:	20 tons. 9.cwts. 104lbs
Cocoa:	1 ton.

Appendix VI

Leicestershire Territorial Force in August 1914

Leicestershire (Prince of Wales' Own) Yeomanry and the 'B' Squadron of the Leicestershire Royal Horse Artillery and the North Midland Mounted Brigade Transport and Supply Column.
(These units form part of the North Midland Mounted Brigade.)

4th and 5th Battalions Leicestershire Regiment.

Lincoln and Leicester Brigade Co Divisional Transport and Supply Column, Army Service Corps.

2nd North Midland Divisional Field Ambulance. Royal Army Medical Corps.

North Midland Divisional Signal Company.

5th Northern General Hospital.

Appendix VII

1st Cadet Battalion Leicestershire Regiment

'A' Company
Wyggeston Grammar School	190 members

'B' Company
Loughborough Grammar School	80 members
Ratcliffe College	50 members
Quorn Grammar School	40 members

Barrow on Soar Grammar School	40 members
Total	210 members

'C' Company

Ashby de la Zouch Grammar School	80 members
Coalville Grammar School	45 members
Market Bosworth Grammar School	40 members
Hinckley Grammar School	35 members
Total	200 members

'D' Company

Lutterworth Grammar School	30 members
Melton Mowbray grammar School	63 members
Market Harborough Grammar School	53 members
Alderman Newton's School	43 members
Newarke Secondary School	61 members
Total	250 members
Overall Total	850 cadets

*The above figures indicate the initial numbers of those joining. Membership varied at different stages of the war.

Appendix VIII

Members and Officers of the Borough of Leicester Corporation 1914

Locally Appointed Officers

Town Clerk	Herbert Arthur Pritchard
Coroner	Edward G. B. Fowler
Medical Officer of Health	Charles Killick Millard MD
Borough Surveyor	Enoch George Mawbey
Borough Treasurer	William Penn-Lewis
Police Surgeon	Neville Ivens Spriggs MD

Members of Town Council

Aldermen

George Banton	Jonathan North
Jabez Chaplin	Samuel Patey
George Chitham	Thomas Squire
George Clifton	Samuel Squire
George Collins	Arthur Tollington
Albert Edwin Sawday	Sir William Wilkins Vincent
Samuel Flint	Thomas Windley
Charles Lakin	Edwin John Yearby

Councillors

Thomas Adnitt	Harry Carver	Thomas Luther Geary
Percy Litton Baker	Charles Crossley	Sydney Ansell Gimson
Walter Bates	Robert Curtis	William Gunby
Arthur Ireland Baum	George Folwell	Herbert William Hallam
Joseph Sturge Collier	John Russell Frears	Harry Hand

Arthur Hawkes
Jas Wedgewood Heath
Alfred Hill
George Edward Hilton
William Edwin Hincks
John Holmes
John Mantle Hubbard
Samuel Hudson
John Hurley
John Johnson
James King Kelly

George Albert Kenney
John Loseby
Walter John Lovell
James McCall
George Arthur Mitchell
John William Murby
John Parsons
Nathaniel Charles Perkins
Arthur Herbert Reynolds
Frederick Fox Riley
John Stanton Salt

Frederick Charles Shardlow
Amos Sherriff
Herbert Simpson
Joseph William Smith
Harry Cyprian Snow
Charles Squire
Frederick Sutton
James Thomas
Alfred Thomas Underwood
Thomas Watson Walker
Walter Wilford

Appendix IX

Extract from the official returns of casualties sustained in air attacks and coastal bombardments during the war years.
(Published in the *Leicester Daily Mercury,* Monday, 13 January 1919.)

There have been 108 air-raids and 12 bombardments from the sea.

The raids were begun by the famous 'tip and run' bombardment from the sea off Hartlepool, Scarborough and Whitby on 6 December 1914. The final raid was by aircraft on 13 April 1918.
There were no raids by aircraft on the Midlands. Zeppelins reached the Midlands on five occasions in 1916 and once in 1917.

Viz: 1916

3 Jan-1 Feb	West Suffolk and Midland Counties 70 killed (29 men, 26 women, 15 children) 113 injured (44 men – including one soldier, 50 women, 19 children)
5/6 March	Hull, East Riding, Lincs, Leics, Rutland, Kent 18 killed (9 men, 4 women, 5 children) 52 injured (22 men, 22 women, 8 children)
2/3 Sept	East Riding, Lincs, Notts, Norfolk, Suffolk, Cambs., Huntingdonshire, Essex, Beds, Kent, London 4 killed (1 man, 2 women, 1 child) 12 injured (6 men, 5 women, 1 child)
23/24 Sept	Lincs, Notts, Norfolk, Kent, London 40 killed (24 men, 12 women, 4 children) 130 injured (61 men – including 4 soldiers, 44 women, 25 children)
1/2 Oct	Lincs, Norfolk, Cambs., Northants, Herts, London 1 killed – soldier 1 injured (Woman)

<u>1917</u>

19/20 Oct	Midlands, Eastern Counties, London
	36 killed (8 soldiers, 12 women, 16 children)
Total of:	51 Airship Raids
	57 Aircraft Raids
	12 Naval Bombardments

<u>Overall casualties</u>

Airship Raids

	Killed	Injured	
Men	217	587	
Women	171	431	
Children	110	218	
Soldiers	<u>58</u>	<u>121</u>	
Total	556	1357	= 1,913 overall casualties

Aircraft Raids

	Killed	Injured	
Men	282	741	
Women	195	585	
Children	142	324	
Soldiers	<u>238</u>	<u>400</u>	
Total	857	2050	= 2,907 overall casualties

Bombardments

	Killed	Injured	
Men	55	180	
Women	45	194	
Children	43	230	
Soldiers/Sailors	<u>14</u>	<u>30</u>	
Total	157	634	= 791 overall casualties

Appendix X

Order of March of the Military Parade
Royal Visit HM King George V and Queen Mary on 10 June 1919

Overall CO:	Colonel C. B. West Macott ADC
	Commanding No. 6 District

Regular Army Units

2nd Batt.	Royal Warwickshire Regt	(Capt. N. B. F. Collins in command)
2nd Batt.	Lincolnshire Regt	(Lieutenant-Colonel C. Toogod DSO in command)
2nd Batt.	Leicestershire Regt	(Lieutenant-Colonel B. C. Dent CMG, DSO in command)
1st Batt.	South Staffordshire Regt	(Lieutenant-Colonel W. R. English Murphy MC in command)
2nd Batt.	Sherwood Foresters	
	(Nottingham and Derbyshire Regt)	(Capt. G. S. Dobbie MC in command)

2nd Batt.	Prince of Wales	
	(North Staffordshire Regt)	(Capt. P. Bradbury MC in command)
3rd Batt.	Bedfordshire Regt	(Major C. Clutton in command)
3rd batt.	Royal Irish Regt	(Lieutenant-Colonel Lloyd DSO in command)
Depot.	Leicestershire Regt	(Major R. S. Dyer-Bennet in command)
Depot.	South Staffordshire Regt	(Lieut. G. W. R. Hearn in command)
Depot.	Sherwood Foresters	
	(Nottingham and Derbyshire Regt)	(Capt. J. Sheldon DSO, MC in command)
Depot.	Prince of Wales	
	(North Staffordshire Regt)	(Capt. C. B. Startin in command)
	Royal Army Medical Corps	(Colonel L. K. Harrison in command)

Demobilised Men of Local Units

Band of the Royal Irish Regt	
Royal Navy	(Lieut-Commander C.G.Pearse RNVR)
Leicestershire Yeomanry (Prince Albert's Own)	(Lieutenant-Colonel W. Byron in command)
Royal Regt. of Artillery	(Major S. V. Hodgkins MC in command)
4th Batt. Leicestershire Regt	(Lieutenant-Colonel T. P. Fielding Johnson in command)
5th Batt. Leicestershire Regt	(Lieutenant-Colonel S. Toller DSO in command)
Service Batts. Leicestershire Regt	(Lieutenant-Colonel C. Turner DSO in command)
Royal Army Service Corps	(Capt. R. T. Cooper in command)
Royal Army Medical Corps	(Colonel Astley Clarke in command)
Royal Air Force	(Capt. R. G. Tyler in command)

Volunteer Regiments

| Composite Batt. Leicestershire Regt | (Major W. G. S. Rollestone in command) |

Demobilised Men of Volunteer Regiments

| Leicestershire Regt | (Colonel C. F. Oliver in command) |

Guard of Honour

| 2nd Batt. | Leicestershire Regt. | (Capt. J. G. Herring Cooper in command) |

Accompanied by Regimental Band and Colours.

Bibliography

August 1914, Barbara Tuchman (Constable, 1962).

Book of Leicester (The), Richard Gill (Barracuda Books Ltd, 1985).

Blighty, British Society in the Era of the Great War, Gerard J. de Groot (Longman, 1996).

Changing Face of Leicester (The), Paul & Yolande Courtney, Stroud Gloucs (Alan Sutton Publishing, 1995).

Cinema in Leicester 1896-1931, David R. Williams (Heart of Albion Press, 1993).

Dictionary of World War I, Hutchinson (Helicon Publishing, 1994).

Fifth Leicestershire (The), Capt. J. D. Hills (Echo Press Loughborough, 1919).

First Day on the Somme (The), Martin Middlebrook (Penguin Books Ltd, 1971).

Grave Matters, A Walk Through Welford Road Cemetery, Leicester, Max Wade-Matthews.

History of the First World War, A. J. P. Taylor (MacDonald & Co Ltd, 1988).

History of the First World War, Monthly/Various Contributors (Purnell for BPC Publishing, London).

History in Leicester, Colin Ellis (Recreational & Cultural Services Dept. Leicester City Council).

History of the Leicestershire Regiment, Colonel H. C. Wylly (Gale & Polden Ltd).

New University, Jack Simmons (Leicester University Press, 1958).

Leicester As It Was, A. Broadfield (Hendon Publishing Co, 1972).

Leicester General Hospital 1905-1976, D. R. Cairns (Leicester General Hospital, 1976).

Leicester Royal Infirmary (The) 1771-1971, Ernest R. Frizelle & Janet D. Martin (Leicester No1 Hospital Management Committee).

Leicester in the Twentieth Century, David Nash & David Reeder (Alan Sutton Publishing & Leicester City Council).

Leicester Past and Present, Jack Simmons (Eyre Methuen London, 1974).

Leicester's Battle Against Fire, Malcolm Tovey (Anderson Publications, 1982).

Leicestershire's Lunatics – The Institutional Care of

Leicestershire's Lunatics during the 19th century, Henry Gilbert Orme & William H. Brock (Leicestershire Museums Publication No87, 1987).

Light Amid the Shadows, Derek Seaton (Royal Leicestershire, Rutland & Wycliffe Society for the Blind, 1994).

Men of Gallipoli, Peter Liddle (David & Charles, 1976).

Modern Military Techniques, Ian V. Hogg (Dragon Hardbacks, 1984, Granada Publishing, London).

My Escape from Donington Hall, Günther Plüschow (Bodley Head).

On the Breadline, Alan Evans (Batsford, 1994).

Prisoners (The) 1914-18, Robert Jackson (London: Routledge, 1989).

Tigers (The) – A short history of the Royal Leicestershire Regt., Major Gen. J. M. K. Spurling (Leicester Museums, 1969).

Tiger's Tale (The) Official History of Leicester Football Club 1880-1993, Stuart Farmer & David Hands (ACL & Polar Publishing UK Ltd).

Quality of Leicester (The), Michael Taylor & George Wilson (Leicester City Council, 1993).

Tramways Remembered, Leslie Oppitz (Countryside Books, 3 Catherine Road, Newbury Berks).

University of Leicester (The) A History 1921-1996, Brian Birch, OBE (Leicester University, 1996).

Victorian Leicester, Malcolm Elliott (Phillimore & Co, 1979).

Who's Buried Where in Leicester, Joyce Lee (Leicestershire County Council, 1991).

Daily Post, 1914-18.

History of the 5th Northern General Hospital, Leicester, Colonel L. K. *Harrison RAMC(T)* (Unpublished).

Leicester Daily Mercury, 1914-18.

Leicester Journal, 1914-18.

Leicester Trades Directory, 1911.

Plan of 5th Northern General Hospital prepared by Pick Everard and Keay, Architects, 1919 (Leicestershire Record Office).

Watch Committee Minutes, 1913-1919.

War Hospital Reports, 1915-1919.

Annual Reports.

Wright's Directory, 1914.

Index

ND - #0360 - 270225 - C0 - 297/210/12 - PB - 9781780910635 - Gloss Lamination